To Claire
with lots of love
from Shaman Schkhut x

Shmel The Rat

(The Yiddisher Pimp)

Sharman Schiffer
True-Life Story

authorHOUSE™

1663 LIBERTY DRIVE, SUITE 200
BLOOMINGTON, INDIANA 47403
(800) 839-8640
WWW.AUTHORHOUSE.COM

Some names have been changed to protect family members and friends.

First published by AuthorHouse 01/03/06

ISBN: 1-4208-9339-4 (e)
ISBN: 1-4208-8038-1 (sc)

Printed in the United States of America
Bloomington, Indiana

This book is printed on acid-free paper.

DEDICATION

~ ~ ~

This book is dedicated to my Mum, Darren, and Shireen,
my two brothers, Larry and Michael
and all the good friends who supported
me through my 16 years of heartache, and not forgetting Benson.

I would also like to thank Joan Vine FSSA my ghost writer and
say how lucky I was to have met her and her wonderful family.
A special thank you must go to
Andy Vine
for his amusing, cartoon artwork.

~ ~ ~

Table of Contents

1988

Chapter 1 – In the Beginning.

It All Started When... I thought my dreams were being answered at long last. He was a fifty-year-old married man looking for some extra fun and I was a thirty-six year-old mother of two young children, an ex-model and air hostess who had fallen on bad times.

My first marriage had broken down around four years earlier and I had been left without a home. I had two young children to support and nowhere to live, so, I was more than grateful to my two older brothers, Larry and Michael when they suggested that between them they would be able to set me and the children up in a small, two-bedroom apartment in a purpose built block. Both my brothers were and still are successful stockbrokers and as neither of them lacked a few quid I eagerly jumped at the chance of being able to get settled and on my feet again.

After looking around for a while we found a beautiful, conveniently located apartment and my brothers not only helped me to move in, they also assisted me in selecting all the furniture and fixtures which they were generous enough to pay for. Being used to a well managed home from an early age, I soon sorted out the apartment and made it as comfortable as I could. In fact, by the time I had finished it looked like a show place. My brothers made sure I had more or less everything I wanted, including the most fashionable, latest style, dual purpose headboard which housed a TV and radio for my bedroom. We had the place carpeted throughout in royal blue and the lounge looked plush with its cream, leather sofa and armchairs. I managed to get a tasteful dining room suite and the whole apartment was set off with two beautiful crystal chandeliers that graced the lounge.

The children and I soon settled into our new home and were all very happy for a couple of years. However, as time went on, I began to get rather depressed feeling that my life was going nowhere and had become somewhat dull. With two small children to care for, I wasn't able to get out very much and having been without a man for around four years I was at my most vulnerable when a friend of one of my brothers suggested that he could introduce me to someone who had plenty of money and was looking for some fun…

Although I was wary at first, I threw caution to the wind and convinced myself that I had nothing much to lose and perhaps, everything to gain. I gave my brother the go-ahead and said that his friend could give this man my telephone number; after all, on a bad day I could always ignore the telephone, while on a good day… Well, who knows? I must admit that I didn't really expect to have this strange man contact me, so I was quite surprised one afternoon when the phone rang and I said, hello. The reply came back…

"Hi, is that Sharman? I was given your telephone number…"

Oh my God! It was this man, my blind date! I took a big deep breath and tried to speak as casually as possible. "Oh, hi, I'm glad you called."

My morale shot up at least ten notches when I realised I was actually talking to a real man, a man who was not only interested enough to call my number but might have money to spend on me as well. Although I often spoke to my brothers, I hadn't had a real man-woman conversation in ages, so I leaned against the wall and made the most of each and every word he uttered. We chit-chatted for a while, you know the type of idle chatter that two strangers have when they first converse… I found his voice rich and pleasing; he was well spoken and most charming. I was extremely impressed. After a short conversation he suggested that perhaps we could meet. I couldn't see any reason why not, so when I agreed to see him, he promptly suggested that I go over to *his* place.

Alarm bells rang very loudly, so I declined the offer to go to his apartment, after all, I wasn't that much of a push-over, I assured myself. Sadly, I must have deflated his ego somewhat as after my refusal our conversation quickly petered out so, left with little more to talk about, we ended up saying goodbye, although, he did assure me that he would call again soon.

Three days later, true to his word, he rang. "Hi, it's me, Shmel!"

I was absolutely delighted. The fact that he had not been put off altogether meant that he was greeted with an excited, "Hello! It's lovely to hear from you again."

The pleasure must have oozed through my voice, the kind of sounds that he picked up on so easily. My delight and my need for love and a sexual relationship meant that he was able to manipulate me like the gullible fool I was! He was very easy to talk to so we chatted happily for a while until he again suggested that we meet, but this time he said that he would come round to my apartment, if that was alright with me. The alarm bells didn't ring at all this time so I agreed, saying I would be pleased to meet him. After all, I would be on my own ground, so what did I have to lose? If he did have plenty of money, as my brother's friend assured me he had, I could indulge in some much needed fun and if I played my cards right, well… I might even be able to secure myself and my two children a bright and comfortable future.

The ill-fated day of his intended visit arrived.

Ding Dong… I was so excited at the prospect of having been set up with such a promising catch, that I couldn't believe we were actually going to meet. Owing to my senses being so heightened that afternoon, when my date rang, the chime of my door-bell seemed to echo unbelievably around the apartment. I ran to the bedroom window and peeked out from behind the curtain, and there on the driveway was a machine that spelled 'SEX ON WHEELS', A 500 SEC Mercedes – pale metallic green, WOW! My imagination ran away with me. I wondered just what sort of a man could own and drive a car like this. What a hunk he must be I thought, my mind instantly visualised nothing less than a tall, handsome, sex machine to match. I ran to the front door, but hesitated for a couple of moments to check my hair yet again and to make sure my make-up was just so. My mirror never lied and today I especially wanted to make sure everything was perfect. My mirror assured me I was okay, so I proceeded to the door full of hope and anticipation. I looked eagerly through the spy-hole that was centred in my front door and was immediately taken aback as I couldn't see the tall, handsome hunk I was expecting. Thinking it to be a little strange, I went up on tip-toe and took a more intense look and to my surprise all I could see was a balding, bearded man who only stood around 5' 4" at most. My excitement quickly melted away as I slowly opened the door to this greying, middle-aged man. He on the other hand, leaned forward and in his eagerness to greet me, who stands around 5' 8", stepped directly into my boobs. I was instantly disappointed and my hopes were dashed, whereas he seemed absolutely thrilled to bits and I was to learn later that he was a 'boob' man to the core! Looking back, I suppose, the disappointment that showed on my face when I opened the door proved to be a challenge he couldn't resist so, with his natural self-assurance and charisma turned up to full throttle he quickly made up for his lack of good looks with charm and appeal. He shook my hand warmly and said how pleased he was to meet me.

"Me too," I said flatly, stepping back inside the hall…"Come in," a few simple words, so easily spoken, yet words that spelled misery, for it was at this very point that my sixteen years of anguish and heartache began.

I led the way through the hall and into the lounge and showed him to a comfortable armchair, I settled myself on the nearby sofa and we talked for a while. After about fifteen minutes I offered him a coffee, to which he said, "No thank you," and suggested instead, that he take me out. I still didn't feel too sure about this man but when I thought about the flash Mercedes, standing all lonesome on the driveway below I thought, well – what the hell, why not?

I quickly popped next door to ask my neighbour if she would be kind enough to collect my children from school that afternoon and she agreed, saying she would keep them with her until I came back. Knowing my children would be in safe hands and with my new man waiting, I hurriedly put on my coat, gathered up my bag and set off.

Once out on the driveway, I walked slowly round to the passenger side of the supersonic, top of the range, Mercedes that he drove, I just couldn't wait to get in. The interior of the car was as sumptuous as one would expect. The seats were of beige leather with a smooth virgin-carpet that perfectly matched the upholstery. The dashboard was of polished walnut with a dazzling array of silver instruments. Definitely built to impress! I settled myself in the passenger seat while he casually jumped into the car beside me, turned on the ignition, went into drive and pulled smoothly away. I smiled contentedly to myself as the car carried me away from the apartment and my old world, into an opulent and exciting world I was yet to sample.

Foaming Coffee... Shmel seemed to know his way around the area and he wasn't driving too long before he turned into the parking area of our local, smart, coffee shop. We wandered in and found a table by a window. A waitress came over and Shmel ordered us each a drink, while I draped my coat over the back of the chair and made myself comfortable. It was a place I knew and liked as I had been to this particular coffee shop on a couple of occasions with a girlfriend. I so enjoyed sitting among the quaint little tables with their dainty white tablecloths and petite vases of flowers. I especially enjoyed the delightful aroma of coffee that filled the air. The shop was quite busy considering it was a little late in the afternoon, but it wasn't too long before the waitress came back and put a frothy cappuccino down in front of me and placed a cup of tea down for Shmel. I crossed my legs, leaned forward and waited for him to settle. There were masses of things I wanted to know about this man and we talked quietly as we occasionally sipped our drinks. He told me briefly about himself while I listened closely. He said that he owned six video shops that kept him very busy indeed, unless he was abroad and even then there was always something or the other that needed his attention.

I didn't have anything like as exciting to tell him, but as I am seldom lost for words, I found him easy to respond to. A couple of times while I was speaking, I noticed Shmel glance away and although I took no notice of it at first, gradually it made me feel a little on edge. So after looking away yet again I asked him what the matter was and he replied saying that, "Nothing was the matter." So the very next time he looked away, I followed his line of vision and saw an attractive blonde sitting a few tables away from us. Now I could easily see what was making my date appear so fidgety and why he hadn't been paying as much attention to me as I would have expected, after all, being so pre-occupied with this other woman how could he concentrate? I asked him quietly what the hell he thought he was up to and he quickly replied saying that he wasn't up to anything, why, what was my problem? This made me even more annoyed, the fact that he had thrown the ball back into my court, so I decided it was time for us to go. Getting up from the table, and leaving half my cappuccino still sitting there; I pulled my coat from the back of the chair, snatched up my bag and turned quickly on my heel. Shmel jumped up behind me and, knowing him the way I do now, I suspect he gave this blonde one more glance before following me out to the car.

He opened the car door quickly for me and far from slithering into the plush seat I threw myself in and fastened the seatbelt abruptly, I was furious and dumping my bag on my lap I crossed my arms protectively in front of me. He jumped into the driving seat, and cast me a quick look.

"Take me home!" I said sharply.

We stayed silent throughout the short journey back to my place. I just couldn't believe the arrogance of this man, the man I was supposed to be out on a first date with, having the audacity to eye-up some other woman and in front of me too!

When we pulled up outside my apartment, I got out of the car. Shmel leaned across my empty seat and looked up at me rather sheepishly.

I couldn't resist rebuking this guy and said angrily. "How could you do that? How could you keep looking at this, this blonde woman when you were supposed to be out with me?"

"I, I," he stammered. But I wasn't really interested in any excuses he might want to give me.

"How could you?" I butt in, throwing up my hand even more agitated.

"I thought I knew her that's all!"

"Rubbish," I replied. "If you had known her you would have gone over and said hello, but you didn't."

"I *was* going to speak to her." He said as he got out of the car and walked towards me. But I turned away saying. "How could you tell me such lies, you weren't."

"Look," He said very matter-of-factly, "I thought I knew her from somewhere, that's all, I'm sorry if I have upset you, I didn't mean anything by it."

My annoyance was cooling a little now. Was I being unreasonable? Was I making a mountain out of that old molehill? I didn't know! All I knew was that I was very upset with this man after all, it had been the first date I had been on in years and I felt that he had been ignoring me. How could I not be cross? How could I not have remarked on this man's overtures to some unknown blonde in a coffee shop, especially when he was sitting with me? It was embarrassing to say the least! I walked off towards the entrance to my apartment and ran up the stairs, while he quickly followed up behind me. When I got to my front door he took hold of my arm and turned me around to face him.

"Look!" He said. Please don't be so upset, I really didn't mean to hurt your feelings, it was harmless, I just thought I knew the lady and was trying to catch her eye so that I could say hello!"

I looked away,

"Please listen," he pleaded, his voice lowering to a more soothing tone. "Please forgive me. I'm sorry, please give me another chance."

I relaxed down and sighed! I didn't know what to do, but eventually I turned back to the door, turned the key and walked into the safety of my apartment, leaving him standing there alone on the doorstep. I closed the door behind me and shut him out of my life.

During the week that followed, Shmel inundated me with telephone calls, speaking always in a thoughtful, kind and attentive manner. He talked of many things. He was interesting and made me laugh, but in actual fact he was playing with my feelings and emotions, him being the charmer and I the snake. It seems that I was destined to be a helpless marionette while he manipulated the strings. Unfortunately and against my better judgement I eventually gave in to him, mainly to shut him up and to stop him from wearing out my telephone connection. Somehow, he managed to captivate me with his words and calm me with his soothing voice. He twisted me around his little finger and I foolishly fell for his enchanting manner.

We were dating for about a month before we finally became a real couple. He made it quite clear that he had wanted me right from the start but being a little old fashioned I felt the need to be courted awhile first. Our lovemaking was spectacular to say the least; he certainly knew how to please a woman and he created sensations within me that I had never experienced before, despite the fact that I had been married and had two children. There was definitely something different and exciting about this man that made me thrill at the thought of him. We became very close and he tried to visit me as often as he could. My children didn't appear to take to him very well, but on the whole, he was good to them and attentive to their needs. Now and again he would come over on a Sunday afternoon and take us all out to lunch and although I was reasonably happy, his visits were not frequent enough for me. At the time, he was still married and living in the same house as his wife and although he assured me that the marriage was over in all but name he would, more often than not, go back to the marital home at the week-ends to see his three grown up children. Although he appeared to be making a real effort to see me at least a couple of times during the week, due to the demands made on him by his businesses, he spent what little time he had left to himself either at a West End bridge club, or at the London-based, hotel bed-sit that he had occupied for many years.

During those early months, it was great getting used to having a man in my life, for he was not only showing me a good time, he was giving me love, comfort and above all sex, something I was in dire need of at the time. He became someone with whom I could confide in and lean upon as well as love. About a year prior to meeting Shmel my father had passed away and deep down I was still grieving for him. My dear dad had been seriously ill for many months and the trauma of his illness and his eventual demise had all taken its toll on me. I now believe that all the emotional feelings I had locked away inside my heart during my father's long illness, pushed me into seeking solace and relief in the arms of this older man.

The Brighton Lanes… I cannot tell you how delighted I would be when from time to time, Shmel would ring me up during the week and suggest taking me out for the evening, or occasionally he would propose that we go away on holiday for a few days. I hardly ever said no if at all possible, as I knew full well what it was like to spend days, even weeks alone, and as I was a person who loved life and couldn't get enough of it, I was only too eager and willing to oblige. Therefore, a few months after our first meeting he suggested we go away for a few days to Brighton and as my mother lived there I thought it was a great idea as I would be able to pay a long overdue visit to her.

At the time my children were safely tucked away at a school summer camp for the week so it was a good opportunity for us to get away together. My mother was eager to see me and meet my new boyfriend and was very pleased to get my telephone call to say that we would be coming to visit her the following Tuesday. The ninety minute journey to Brighton was pleasant but uneventful and we eventually arrived at mother's apartment around 11:00am. Mum was at the door to meet us as we arrived and I introduced Shmel to her, I think she must have been a bit surprised when she first saw him, as she would have known immediately that he wasn't the kind of man I would have normally been attracted to. But he was as charming as ever and greeted her with his usual air of quiet confidence. Mum, of course, was delighted to see me and remarked on how well and happy I looked. She invited us in and we sat in her comfortable, cosy lounge for a while catching up with all the family news.

Shmel had arranged to take us out to lunch, so it wasn't long before he glanced down at his watch and suggested we start making our way to the restaurant. He was vaguely familiar with the area as he had been there a couple of times before and he knew that if we didn't start out in plenty of time we would never get around to eating. He was well aware of the shopping habits of women, especially when they window-shopped around the quaint, but expensive shops that graced the old part of Brighton. I, on the other hand, couldn't wait to show off Shmel's flash car so I encouraged mum to get her jacket, saying that it really was time for us to go. She looked delightful as usual; wearing a lovely, pale lavender outfit, just perfect for a summer's day. I thought she was beautiful and so discreetly made up for a lady of her years, Shmel remarked, saying how lovely he thought she looked, which pleased her. It hadn't taken him long to win her over; just as it hadn't taken him long to do the same with me.

Sedately and quietly moving through the thick traffic, the sleek Mercedes provoked many an envious stare from the, would-be, self-made men and the young girls who were looking for a good time. I ignored them of course and watched mum through the rear view mirror as she lounged in the back seat of the car surveying the interior, while occasionally running her hands over the smooth, leather arm rests. Yes! I could tell she was very impressed both with the car and with my new partner. I settled back in my seat and smiled contentedly to myself.

After parking as close as we could to the restaurant, we made our way through the holiday crowds and walked down through the busy, bustling lanes, picking our way along the narrow maze of streets that were packed with holiday makers. The tiny, old-fashioned shops, some having stood there for a century or more, were ablaze with lights and full to the brim with jewellery, clothes, paintings and gifts of all descriptions that were being displayed in the shop windows. We eventually came upon the restaurant which sits snugly in a plaza, central to the tangle of narrow streets. We chose a table outside and settled ourselves under a huge umbrella, happy and ready to enjoy a welcome drink and a meal.

I looked around happily at my mother and then at Shmel, who was sitting the other side of me and instead of gazing into his attentive eyes he had his head turned fully away from me. I shifted my gaze past his head into the same direction and there, in my line of vision was a young girl, bending over shuffling around for something in her bag. She was standing quite a few tables away from us but still near enough for him to be getting a good eyeful, as her mini skirt was so miniscule it left little to the imagination. I rolled my eyes up and turned back to look in my mother's direction. Shmel was very astute and would take any opportunity to check out the local talent, so I wasn't that surprised to catch him having a good look. I was becoming ever more used to my man's roving eye and, after all I thought, if I allowed myself to take offence every time he looked at another woman, I would be in one long state of umbrage!

My mental deliberation on the mini-skirted girl was interrupted by a small voice coming from behind. It was a pert little waitress with pad and pencil to hand, ready to take our order.

"Can I get you a drink?"

Shmel shifted his gaze from the mini-skirted girl and looked attentively up into the downcast eyes of the young waitress as she wrote down the order. I could see that his eyes were already stuck like glue to the girl, as he watched her closely. She handed us a couple of menus and Shmel thanked her as she walked away. He watched her for a moment or two more before turning back to me, "She's a sweet little thing." He remarked casually, looking down at the plastic coated menu. I sighed a little resentfully, clenched my jaw and opened the menu.

After a few minutes the young waitress arrived with the drinks on a round tray and carefully set them on the table. She couldn't have been more than sixteen, a mere schoolgirl, I recall thinking.

"You're beautiful." He said to her, in a velvety, smooth voice.

She broke into a broad smile and looked down. She quickly produced her pad and pencil again and, still smiling from the compliment, shyly asked him if he was ready to order…Little did she know he was *always* ready to order…

He told her what lunches we had decided on and then let her go with yet a further, flattering compliment, which enabled her to walk off full of confidence after having received such a bevy of unwarranted praise.

Feeling rather uncomfortable at Shmel's attempts to overwhelm this poor young girl, I instinctively turned my chair away from him. The little waitress, who unfortunately, bore a very large and unsightly, brown birthmark down one side of her face, made several unnecessary trips to our table, eager to pick up as many compliments as possible I suppose, and of course, she wasn't to be disappointed as he commented, yet again, on her beauty. I sighed and looked towards my mother who gave me one of her 'furrowed brow' looks, which silently said; Good heavens, whatever is the matter with the man?

The whole episode was quite bizarre. I had been so looking forward to taking mother out to lunch so that she could meet Shmel and get to know him a little, but all I can recollect is feeling rather embarrassed by his antics with this young girl. We argued about it later once we were home, the way we would argue constantly throughout our relationship. I never ceased to feel awkward and uneasy by the attention he paid to other women in front of my own family, my mum especially. During the many rows we were to have, I would frequently bring up incidents involving his womanising, the kind of incidents that caused me so much discomfort and disquiet. Even though he would always assure me that… "He spoke to everybody, whether man or woman."

Bed Mates… I often questioned my own motives for putting up with this man or, indeed, why I was ever attracted to him in the first place. But, as different as we were, when we were happy we shared many a good laugh together, such as the time I bought myself two new plump pillows, a thicker duvet and some new stylish bed linen. It wasn't that long after meeting Shmel when I decided to treat myself to some new bedding in order to enhance the look of my bedroom and make it appear more romantic, attractive and alluring. During the day I had worked hard giving my bedroom an extra bit of sparkle and had given the bed a thorough makeover by adorning it with all its new covers and pillow cases. All in all, when finished, my bedroom looked rather, Wow! Shmel came over to see me that evening and I told him about my new purchases and after having a peek at my bed he decided to stay overnight in order to help me christen it and, as he seldom chose to stay over I was very pleased and happy.

At this particular time of the year the weather had turned somewhat cold outside, making it feel chilly indoors as well. So with little more than that as an excuse we decided to retire to bed a little earlier than usual. We showered before making our way to the posh boudoir then we eagerly slid between the new covers and snuggled up close for warmth as best we could, taking into consideration the difference in our height. Not that four inches is much, I thought, but it can make a great deal of difference, ask any man? Nevertheless, after a few giggles and some tender moments we eventually settled down and drifted off to sleep.

I couldn't have been asleep for very long when suddenly I was awakened by the loudest snores you could ever imagine. I tossed and turned for a while trying to get back off to sleep, but with Shmel making enough noise to wake the dead and knowing that if I didn't get a decent nights sleep I wouldn't be able to function properly the next day, I decided to take some decisive action. I got up and surveyed the situation from all angles and I noticed that he had part of the duvet tucked under him so I thought that if I gave it a bit of a tug he would roll over, which hopefully, would stop him snoring. I steadied myself at the side of the bed and taking hold of the duvet with both hands I gave it a pull, but nothing happened so, bracing myself this time, I gave the duvet another tug but this time I pulled sharply with all my might. Unfortunately, I must have overdone it a bit as, before I knew what had happened, my snoring man shot straight off the side of the bed and landed with a hefty thump on the floor.

I was so surprised when his legs went up in the air and his body disappeared over the side of the bed that I stood quite still with my eyes wide, my mouth open and with the duvet still grasped firmly in my hands. Suddenly, a little red face appeared over the side of the bed, dozy but grinning. We both collapsed into hysterical laughter, before he eventually fell asleep again all snuggled up in my romantic bedroom, while I took refuge under a thick blanket on the settee in the lounge.

-:: *Bed Mates* ::-

Regrets... During this early part of our relationship, I was to experience the first real heartache of our ill-fated partnership. One night while lying close together in our bed, he whispered to me saying how much he would love me to have his baby. He told me that I was so beautiful, that any child born to us would indeed be lovely and a joy to behold. I smiled to myself with happiness in the darkness of the night, yet realised full well that when morning came I would have to face reality. The reality was - that owing to my first disastrous marriage and already having had two children and afraid of becoming pregnant again I had been sterilised. Not wanting to disappoint Shmel I said nothing at the time but kept all this in my heart and resolved to try anything in order to fulfil his wishes.

As soon as possible I sought the expertise of my doctor, saying how much I regretted having been sterilised as I now wanted to have a child with my new partner... The doctor was very understanding and quite hopeful, saying that he was sure that my operation could be reversed if that was what I wanted. I jumped at the opportunity and went home full to the brim with happiness. All I had to do was to start taking my temperature every morning and at a given point I was to telephone the surgery and they would make arrangements to have me admitted to hospital immediately for the reversal operation. Unfortunately, a couple of weeks into my morning temperature checks Shmel and I rowed over something quite trivial and he walked out on me. If he had returned after a couple of hours, or even the next morning, I could have continued the checks, but as the days went by with no word from him, I abandoned my resolve, hoping that if he came back to me and our relationship settled down I could resume my quest for an operation that would enable us to have a child, but the way things were panning out I could not risk having a new baby at this moment in time.

I would often lay awake when alone at night, weeping for the child I never had and for a love that Shmel did not value enough to hold on to. I am sure he never knew that at the time, I would have done anything, absolutely anything possible to please him and cement our relationship...

The Killing... When things were good between us I loved talking to Shmel and whenever we were alone with no distractions we would, like any other couple, reminisce about past events. On one such occasion, as we were driving through Streatham on our way back from visiting my mother. Seeing familiar streets and landmarks must have jogged Shmel's memory as he suddenly started to tell me about someone he knew, who had been murdered here during a robbery many years before.

"Why, how strange that is," I cut in, "I also know of someone who was murdered around here."

Before Shmel was able to get another word in, I went on to say, that it was in fact, my auntie's husband. I told him how shocked and devastated my mum's sister, as well as all the family had been when this poor man had been so brutally killed.

Shmel listened but made no further comments and once I had finished telling my story we continued driving in silence for a few minutes when his in-car phone suddenly started to ring. It was a large, ugly and cumbersome looking phone, not a bit like today's smart jobs, but, at the time, I would venture to say that it was the real McCoy, and Shmel used it all the time to keep in touch with his business associates and staff, as he always wanted to be informed promptly if any problems arose at his video shops.

On this occasion the person contacting him was a friend; in fact, I later learned that it was the guy who had been best man at Shmel's wedding to his second wife, Anne. He chatted away to his friend for a while and as they were on the open speaker I could hear everything that was being said. I smiled lovingly and happily at Shmel when he told his friend that he was just passing through Streatham on his way back from Brighton, after spending a great week-end with his girlfriend.

"I'm dating a really lovely young lady." He turned and smiled back at me.

Shmel continued talking to his friend for a while longer but as they started to discuss business matters I just lay back in my seat, closed my eyes and let their words drift over my head. After a short while they signed off and we continued our journey home.

The Yiddisher Boy... A few weeks after the conversation about the murder, one of my brothers who lived in a beautiful London apartment, organized a family get-together that he laid on especially for mum. She must have mentioned that she hadn't seen many of her family members in a while, so he invited us all over one Sunday. We had a lovely, tasty, lunch and then spent the rest of the afternoon chatting. I so loved meeting all my aunts and uncles and we mingled and laughed as we caught up on all the ins and outs of family matters. Much later that afternoon, while nattering away to a couple of my uncles, I suddenly remembered I had a date with Shmel. I looked down at my watch and on seeing the time; I said that as it was getting late, I was going to have to leave shortly; as I had a date with a very nice Jewish man that I had been seeing for some months now. Both my uncles raised their eyebrows and nodded and winked at each other.

"So, who is this fine *Yiddisher* boy you're going out with then?" laughed one of them.

"Oh! No one you would know."

"Well, come on, try me," said the other.

With just a little hesitation I said, okay and that his name was Shmel!

My uncles looked at each other inquiringly and then Uncle Sol said, jokingly. "It's not Shmel, the schmuck with the roving eye, is it?"

"Mmm! Well, Strangely enough, he does have a bit of a reputation as a woman's man and a rover." I replied, and when I told him Shmel's surname my uncle Sol said, with some amount of shock and surprise, "Good heavens! I have been friends with him for years; in fact, I was best man at his wedding to Anne." He faltered slightly and then said, "You *did* know he was married, didn't you?"

It immediately became apparent that the conversation Shmel had in the car a couple of weeks earlier with a 'friend' was indeed, my own Uncle Sol and that the man who we had spoken of as having been murdered had, in fact, been one and the same person. How strange was that?

Owing to all these revelations, my relationship with this man caused quite a stir within the family, especially when we remarked on how small the world was and how, in a roundabout way, we must have all known each other. After a while and not being able to resist the temptation Uncle Sol urged me to get Shmel on the phone, saying, "Ring your boyfriend, just to see if it really *is* the same person we are all talking about."

I was wary at first for I knew Shmel would, without doubt, be in the bridge club. But I eventually gave way to the pressure imposed on me by my uncles and so bringing up his number on my mobile I hit the call button. The phone started to ring and as Shmel picked up, Uncle Sol grabbed the phone off me and as soon as he recognised Shmel's voice he part jokingly, yet part seriously said. "Hey! What the hell are you doing, dating my niece?"

There must have been an equal amount of amazement at Shmel's end of the phone on hearing my uncle's voice, as people and events we had often discussed began to fall swiftly into place and I would like to bet that the game of bridge my boyfriend was involved in at the time was completely ruined.

After a few exchanged words between Shmel and Uncle Sol, my uncle then handed the phone back to me and, on hearing Shmel's voice for myself I realised that there had been no mistaking the identity of my new man.

The very fact that my uncle had known Shmel for years and that I was in a serious relationship with him created an unusual amount of tension and speculation and in fact, my affair with Shmel turned out to be the family's main talking point for many days. Everyone close to me became very concerned about my affair and I was to be warned often about my boyfriend's reputation with women.

Regardless of my family's warning, our relationship continued to flourish. I would often try to convince myself that somewhere in the great scheme of things Shmel and I had been destined to meet, a happening that was out of my hands and of which I had no control over.

The Toy Store... The fact that we were destined to meet became even more apparent when reminiscing one day, for it transpired that, when I was about eighteen or so, I took a job modelling for a toy company that Shmel was once connected with.

I made him laugh one afternoon, telling him how I was instructed to dress up like a bunny girl for a convention at the Metropole Hotel in Brighton.

"Well, that's strange," he said. "I did some advertising for a toy company there at one time."

Being intrigued by this story I wasn't satisfied until we were able to compare notes and dates etc., only to discover that we had indeed, both been employed by the same company; we even had the same boss, yet, at that time, our paths never once crossed.

Today: I suppose it would have been better all round for both my family and I, if our life-paths could have remained parallel without ever crossing, but unfortunately, destiny dictated that they did. An occurrence I would live to regret.

About six months or so into our affair, we gradually began to adopt the pattern that our relationship was destined to follow until the end. That was, for us to have great times together and then, because of his womanising, or something equally annoying we would argue and he would storm off leaving me alone for days, sometimes weeks at a time before calling me or coming around to make the peace and to pick up were we had left off.

Late Night Video Showdown... It was during one of our frequent partings that he rang me up, out of the blue one Saturday evening. Having been on my own for what felt like an eternity, I was bored and lonely so had decided to have an early night. I hadn't been in bed for very long and was just drifting off to sleep when the telephone rang. In my 'twilight' state, I sleepily picked up the receiver from my bedside cabinet and dozily said, "Hello," and to my surprise it was him!

"Hi! Shar, how are you?"

On hearing his voice I immediately awoke properly and smiled to myself thinking that this was one of his usual, 'time to come back' calls. I must admit that it was pleasing to hear his voice again, and after a couple of weeks without him I was missing him like mad.

I threw back the covers, eased my legs out of bed and just sat quietly, listening to his soothing voice. We talked softly for a while and all the time I was eagerly waiting for him to ask if he could come around to see me, but I grew impatient when this didn't happen. After a while I became curious as to why, exactly, he *had* phoned me, so at the first opportunity I asked him where he was. To my question he had the audacity to say that he was in one of his video shops, the one that was relatively local to me and that he was with a friend and his wife Anne. He then told me that when they closed up the shop for the night he intended to take her out to dinner.

Instantly I became absolutely furious with him. My mood changed immediately from one of expectation to one of provocation. I just couldn't believe that this man would ring me up at this time of night, wake me up out of my twilight sleep, only to tell me that he was taking his *wife* out to dinner. I slammed the telephone down; I didn't want to hear any more. I just couldn't understand him at all, there he was telling me, constantly, that his marriage was on the rocks and that he loved *me* and there was I, in bed alone, while he was preparing to take his wife out to dinner. My God... He made me so mad!

It would be totally useless trying to go back to sleep now; I was wide awake and fuming. I grabbed my dressing gown and threw it around my shoulders and paced up and down the bedroom, but after a few minutes decided it was no good, I would have to get dressed and go and sort this man out. My children were away with mum in Brighton for the week-end so I had no need to worry about them, thankfully.

I dragged on a pair of jeans and a tee-shirt, grabbed my mobile and contacted his pager saying that I was on my way to the video shop. I ran downstairs from my apartment and jumped into the car, turned the ignition key and paged him again, saying that I was in the car and wouldn't be long. I drove like fury, paging him every time I was obliged to stop at traffic lights on the way, informing him of my progress.

Little did I know that Shmel had lent his pager to his youngest son for the night and that he had no idea whatsoever, that I *was* on my way? *Likewise*, I had no idea *he* didn't know. And of course, his youngest son must have thought I was completely off my trolley, for having paged him so many times.

I drew up outside the video shop about fifteen minutes before it was due to close, got out of the car, walked up to the shop-front and peered inside. The dazzling spotlights inside the shop meant that the people inside could not see out of the windows or me approaching. I must admit to being a bit surprised when I saw them all just standing around, casually chatting. Shmel looked so calm, so relaxed as he leaned on the counter passing the time of day with his friend and wife Anne, none of whom showed any signs of apprehension at my expected appearance. It seemed as though they had no idea that I was about to walk in and that there was trouble brewing.

As I had not yet been introduced to his wife or his friend, I thought I would casually walk into the video shop and up to the counter and ask if I could become a member, so I did just that. Shmel's wife turned smiling towards the new 'customer' while my boyfriend, on seeing me, had a silent panic attack.

Call it woman's intuition if you like, but Anne, immediately turned and looked at Shmel and from the dumb look of shock on his face and the fact that he had suddenly become rooted to the spot, she guessed that I was the 'other woman'. She then whispered quietly and calmly to her shocked husband, "That's her, isn't it?"

To which he took a deep breath and reluctantly said, "Yes!"

Anne immediately brought all her womanly wiles into play, by launching into a 'loving relationship' talk to Shmel about the fantastic holiday they were looking forward to in Hong Kong. She desperately tried to imply that she had a very solid relationship with her husband and then went on to talk about the outfits she was intending to purchase from Harrods during the coming week. Obviously she was saying these things in order to make me feel jealous, and even angrier than I already was.

Finally, Shmel found his feet again and quickly walked over to me asking if I would please go. His friend, having picked up the ever increasing tense atmosphere, and realising I must be one of Shmel's 'women' and not a potential customer after all, quickly came over to me and very gently backed up what Shmel was saying, as he guessed the pot could so easily boil over.

"Please go Shar." Shmel said again, in a somewhat pleading tone.

I turned on my heel and headed towards the door accompanied by the friend. Once outside, the friend continued to advise me to 'go home' trying to assure me that it wasn't worth all the aggravation. Shmel's pal jumped into his car hoping, I suppose, that I would follow suit and get into mine, but I wasn't having any of it; I decided to hang around outside the shop just to see what would happen. Eventually, Shmel had no option but to close up. His friend reluctantly got out of his car and helped Shmel shut up shop for the night and once the last shutter had been fastened and the last lock secured, the four of us stood outside the darkened shop-front glaring at each other.

I cannot quite remember all that was said, it was one of those confrontations where everyone tried to speak at once or momentarily, nothing was said at all. Naturally, Shmel and his friend tried desperately hard to keep the situation from getting out of hand, but all came to an abrupt end when Anne, in desperation, decided to inform me that the relationship she had with her husband was solid and wonderful, other than the fact that she hadn't slept with him for years in case he had contracted AIDS!

That was it! I was shocked and horrified at her statement and filled with fear of what might lay ahead for *me* and my children if Shmel *did* have Aids. I burst into tears and ran to my car, followed by Shmel's friend. As I opened my car door and got in, the friend tried to reassure me by telling me that everything was all right and not to worry, and that if I went home everything would be okay. I couldn't handle this new and worrying implication; I was overwrought, tired and very angry.

My sudden flight to the car brought on a mass exodus of cars from the video shop, and as I drove off, I noticed that Shmel's friend followed up quickly behind me. He in turn was followed by 'the wife' and hot on her heels was Shmel, hoping, I suppose, to make sure we all finished up going our own separate ways home, and of course, it would mean that he could make a quick getaway if the situation suddenly changed for the worst. Naturally, I was filled with worry as I tearfully made my way home. I was confused and unsure. But I later consoled myself with the thought that a woman will say anything, do anything, if her security is threatened and this time, Anne had won the fight.

Today: Shmel did NOT have AIDS, neither was he to become a victim of this dreadful disease or anything relating to it during our relationship.

1989

Chapter 2 – A Brush with the Loo.

The Video Convention... Shortly after the video showdown, Shmel and I got together again and he suggested that I go with him to The Las Vegas International Annual Video Convention. I was thrilled to bits, it was to be our first real holiday-come-business venture abroad and I was so terribly excited. I had of course been to the States many times before in my air hostess days, but never as a holiday maker and I certainly hadn't been to Las Vegas, so as you can imagine, I felt like a young girl about to go out on her very first, important date.

The days before the holiday were hectic indeed as I had to do lots of shopping in order to buy clothes, shoes, eveningwear and everything else I thought necessary. Shmel came with me on some of my shopping sprees and would calmly wait around while I tried on garment after garment, either nodding his approval or shaking his head. Not that he disapproved of very much I chose, as I was always considered to have excellent taste with a flair for style in outfits as well as accessories that suited me.

Finally the day came for our holiday to begin. We had planned to meet up with a crowd of other people who were attending the video convention, most of which were men involved in some aspect or other with the video business. Apart from Shmel and one other guy, the rest of the men were due to travel alone as this was not really a couples trip. In fact, I was made to feel quite special, being only one of two women in the party.

Shmel and I made our way to Heathrow Airport together, where we met up with all the others in the party and eventually boarded a British Airways scheduled flight to the States. It was a long-haul trip, which included a short stop in order to switch planes, so we had to be prepared for many hours travelling. Armed with a book and a couple of magazines I settled down happily and very excitedly next to Shmel. All the men attending the video convention were in the business, or at least had a vested interest in it, so once the seat-belt sign had been turned off one or other of the guys would occasionally come over and converse with Shmel about this or that video or film, or perhaps something to do with the business. I found most of their conversation rather dull and boring, but sitting by the window I was able to concentrate on my book or magazine without appearing rude although, I always made sure to respond with a smile and an appropriate comment if someone spoke specifically to me.

Throughout the many tedious hours on the flight, Shmel would occasionally go missing. I tried to ignore his absences by reading, watching the in-flight entertainment or trying to catch up on some sleep, but at one stage I gradually became aware of an extra long time away. He seemed to have been on the missing list for so long that I took to glancing around to see if I could locate his whereabouts although, I desperately tried not to do this as it inevitably ended up with me being annoyed or upset. I knew I shouldn't have looked for him, as I eventually spotted him chatting up an attractive air-hostess. He had managed to get himself positioned as near as possible to the business-class section of the aeroplane from where he was able to corner and captivate this poor lady with his smooth chat-up line.

He must have accosted this poor girl for a good quarter of an hour at least, before she was finally able to free herself from him and, being an ex-air hostess, I noticed that once she got away, she tried to make up her squandered time by hurrying through her duties. I, on the other hand, closed my eyes and settled down, telling myself that I was not going to let Shmel's fascination with other women ruin the holiday I had been so looking forward to. We were due to arrive at the airport late in the evening and as we descended ever nearer to Las Vegas the cabin lights were dimmed so we could take in the amazing spectacle of one of Americas most famous landmarks, that of the 'strip'.

The city of Las Vegas is known as the entertainment capital of the world, a 24-hour - 7-day a week town where no one sleeps as there is always so much to do. It is a paradise for those who are looking for fun with a capital F. Las Vegas is a fantasy town, aimed at the rich, famous and anyone else with money to burn. Each hotel is casino based, ablaze with light, heat and colour, a place where fortunes can be won or lost on the turn of a wheel or throw of the dice. There was everything to see and do and I wanted to see and do it all. Known as Sin City, looking through the window of the plane I couldn't wait to get there, even though I felt exhausted and tired after the long journey.

When we eventually arrived at the McCarran International Airport in Las Vegas the heat was overwhelming, but we were quickly transported by limousine to the air-conditioned hotel. The Treasure Island Hotel itself was absolutely fabulous; a huge casino fronted and underpinned the hotel, creating for me an atmosphere full of excitement and energy. I didn't know where or what to look at first.

After checking into the hotel we were given the keys and shown to our room, which was way up on the seventeenth floor. It was a beautiful, spacious room, with a large, ornate double bed and plenty of cupboard space in which to hang our clothes. We quickly unpacked a few necessary items and after freshening up we went for a short walk around the town before taking to our bed around two-thirty am.

Twangoed... I was up bright and early the next morning, ready and raring to take on the day. There was a remarkable view from the huge windows overlooking Las Vegas. Standing there, far above the bustling crowds, I felt cool and relaxed. I showered, while Shmel was still sleeping but he was up and about when I came back into the room. While he was showering, I unpacked the rest of my stuff, being careful to hang up all my wonderful new designer gear neatly. Then, rather than waste one minute more of my holiday, I hung up my bathrobe, put on one of my new swimsuits and made my way down to the welcoming pool, leaving Shmel to follow when he was ready.

Each day when the guys were not attending the video convention everyone would take the opportunity to laze around the pool to relax and let the world go by. There was a great atmosphere in and around the hotel and although large, it was very friendly. There would often be a small group of musicians playing all the latest music over by the pool-bar, and as an added extra, to delight the guests and supply refreshments there was usually a scantily clad bar-girl strolling around with a tray of chilled Cokes, Tangos, juices and beers, serving anyone who was too tired or just too plain lazy to get up from their lounger and go over to the bar.

One afternoon, a crowd of us were all soaking up the scorching sunshine when, as usual, the bar-girl came over offering us some ice-cold drinks. Most people were glad of the offer as it gave them a brief opportunity to cool down although; on this occasion I didn't even bother to open my eyes as I was okay with my bottle of water. Shmel, on the other hand, must have been in one of his chat-up moods for, as the girl approached his sun bed, he sat up quickly to survey what was on offer. I turned and opened one eye discreetly, to see what had stirred my man into action and there standing over him was this young, curvy girl silhouetted against the sun, carrying her tray of drinks. She was wearing a figure hugging bikini top with the briefest of shorts which showed off her shapely figure to the full. She looked quite young and when she smiled I noticed that she had a metal brace across her uneven teeth. I quickly closed my one eye again and sighed within myself and thought... Oh, no, don't tell me he fancies her! The small group of resident musicians had just launched into playing one of the popular pop tunes of the moment and I cringed when I heard the sound of Shmel's metal sun lounger give way to his movements. He stood up and leaned forward towards the 'braced' girl, and asked her if she wanted to dance. Oh, my God, how embarrassing, I thought. The young

American girl spoke with a real, Western cowboy accent, put on especially for the tourists I assumed. I think she must have been momentarily taken by his attention as she gave him a coy giggle and responded to him saying something along the lines of… "Well, I'll have to ask your wife first!"

I turned my head and opened my one eye again, carefully shielding it with my hand against the sun, I could see she was looking in my direction so I lifted my head off the sun-bed a little and said, "Darling, you can have him any day, he is not *my* husband."

She looked a little put out by my scornful remark and the smile quickly disappeared from her face. But then she probably wasn't all that interested in Shmel anyway, so it presented a good opportunity for her to turn her back on him without another word and go over to the next roasting-hot customer, to ask if *he* wanted an ice-cold drink instead, leaving Shmel all fired up and ready for a dance.

I closed my eyes again and lay quite still on my sun lounger. I could still hear the sound of music wafting over the air although; it now seemed to be somewhat quieter. In fact, everything seemed to go a little bit quiet for a few minutes, even the people splashing around in the pool sounded away off in the distance. Shmel had been refused, he had been denied and he had been left standing there with egg on his face. His associates must have seen and heard what happened; and I would like to bet he felt the rejection fully. A few seconds passed and I was almost on the point of having a pang of guilt well up inside me when I heard the sound of Shmel's vacant sun lounger take up his weight. The sun lounger carried on twanging and tweaking for a few moments longer while he settled himself. It wasn't until the lounger went completely quiet that the sounds of people splashing around in the pool and the pleasant strains of music began to sound normal again.

The Breakfast Meeting… We were only booked into this amazing hotel for just one week, and I wanted to see as much of it as possible. It was absolutely huge. So large, in fact, that it supported a number of different theme restaurants. The following morning I had awoken extra early and, after showering, I chose one of my smartest designer outfits to wear. It was a beautiful garment, bought from Liberty's of London where the assistant had assured me it was an exclusive design.

Shmel was still sleeping so I walked around the huge bed and glanced at myself in the long mirror that was set into the wall next to the floor-to-ceiling windows. The sun streamed in and the long, cream, gossamer-curtains billowed in the soft breeze created by the cooling, air-conditioning unit. The early morning sunshine combined with the fresh stream of air that circulated the room made me feel good all over. I ran my hands down each side of my hips, smoothing the silk skirt over my thighs; I opened an extra button at my cleavage and pulled the neck apart, turning this way, then that. Yes! I thought I looked great. I certainly felt confident that morning, so decided to leave my man sleeping in a little longer while I took the opportunity to venture out and have a good look around this amazing hotel.

I must have been looking even better than I had imagined, as I got quite a few admiring glances from people, women as well as men, as I strolled around. This of course not only made me feel good, but positive and happy too. I must have been walking around the different hotel areas for some time when eventually the strong aroma of breakfast food cooking made me feel a little hungry. I stopped at the next theme restaurant I came to and wandered in. Everything looked superb; it was spotless clean and the food looked absolutely delicious, attractively arranged on large silver platters and tucked away in huge silver tureens.

I turned and walked out of the restaurant and made my way over to a bank of telephones that were situated along one wall of the hotel foyer. I picked up an in-house telephone and dialled my room number. Shmel, answered almost instantaneously.

"Oh, hi, it's me, Shar, I am downstairs outside the Steak and Pancake restaurant and it looks really nice. Perhaps we can have our breakfast there?"

"Sure! Just give me five minutes to finish getting dressed and I'll join you. Ground floor isn't it?"

"Yes, see you there in a few minutes."

I hung the phone back on its cradle and strolled back into the restaurant. The smell of fresh steak sizzling on the griddle was wonderful. An attentive waiter walked over and asked if I was alone.

"No, I'm waiting for someone to join me." I smiled.

"Come this way, ma'am." He said in a Southern accent, and turned away.

I obediently followed him over to a small round table in a quiet corner. I walked around the table and seated myself down; I smoothed the crisp, white table cloth and slightly rearranged the cutlery. I felt comfortable sitting here. The table was in a kind of alcove, well lit without being stark, yes; I felt most relaxed as I picked up the menu and glanced through the cuisine of the day.

I fingered my shiny knife as I waited patiently for Shmel. Although it was still quite early, there was already a good smattering of people in this area of the restaurant. A few young couples sat cooing closely together, satisfied still I suspected, from their night before. There was a small group of older American couples sitting across from me, talking quietly, I expect they were deciding what to do that day, or perhaps they were looking forward to a pre-arranged trip out somewhere. Dotted here and there were, what I thought looked to be wealthy, middle-aged men, mainly on business trips. You can always recognise a rich business man, as they are almost always alone at breakfast and they usually have their noses in the financial section of the newspaper, watching the rise and fall of currency on the world's stock markets.

I looked over towards the entrance area just in time to see Shmel saunter in. He looked quite dapper with his crisp, opened-necked grey and white striped shirt, glowing so fresh against his tanned chest. Although he was short in stature, he was sturdy looking and strong. He supported a beautifully trimmed moustache and beard, and although he was balding, still had a small amount of well-groomed hair around the sides and back. I don't think I would have considered him handsome, but he did look distinguished. He was short, but held himself tall and although he was broad, he looked muscular, confident and very self-assured.

A smile swept across his face as he spotted me sitting in the alcove, I smiled back and raised my hand in greeting. He came across and looked down at me; he took hold of my hand as we kissed briefly across the table.

"Did you have a good night, darling?" Shmel inquired as he sat down opposite me.

I smiled and looked away. Well, *I* might not have had a fantastic night, but I had given him a great night, for sure. I looked back at him, inclined my head and smiled sweetly. He released my hand and took up the menu. I hadn't ordered any food of course as I had been waiting for Shmel, but I noticed that our attentive waiter was already on his way over.

During the wait for our breakfast to be served I happened to notice a couple of men who were sitting together at a table nearby. They both looked typical business men who were there in Las Vegas for no other reason but to make money. My attention was drawn to them specifically because, compared to Shmel, they both looked rather old and bloated as they each supported a large paunch. I certainly knew who I would rather be seated with and I smiled lovingly at Shmel. I cannot recall how long we spent over breakfast that morning, but we certainly didn't rush the pleasure.

From time to time I looked up from my breakfast plate and noted the two men looking across at me, I of course, ignored them as I wasn't at all interested in other men's stares. But, just as we were completing our meal the two portly gentlemen leisurely came across to our table and we both looked up at them as they approached. They introduced themselves, shaking hands first with Shmel and then me. They then proceeded to hand me a business card each, saying that they were film producers and were interested in inviting me to Los Angeles for a screen test.

I was quite taken by surprise, but instantly thrilled at the suggestion and I looked at Shmel for a reaction but unfortunately, there was hardly any. He didn't seem one little bit interested in the proposal at all; unlike me, who was immediately delighted. I could only assume that they had been looking across for a while and had discussed the possibility of me performing well during a screen test otherwise they wouldn't have taken the trouble to come over to leave their contact numbers.

I thanked them very much for their cards and said that I would consider their proposal and get back to them. They wished us a pleasant day and left us sitting there. I smiled broadly as I looked down at the two business cards in my hand and at the thought of being asked to go for a screen test. I couldn't believe it, and excitedly, I asked Shmel what he thought about it all. He said, rather flatly, that it was up to me what I did and then quickly shifted the conversation away and onto something quite different.

Shmel's lack of interest left me feeling very empty and all the good feelings I had that morning started to fade away fast. I would have loved him to have looked pleased for me and feel as excited as I felt, it would have been wonderful if he had offered me just a little bit of encouragement, but he didn't, he was just indifferent.

By the time we got back to our room I was feeling quite depressed and dismal so, trying to cheer me up, I suppose, Shmel suggested we go down to the pool for a spot of relaxation. I took off the designer outfit I had so happily put on that morning and after hanging it carefully in the wardrobe I pulled on a swimsuit and we wandered down to the pool hardly saying a word. Once there, he took up his usual pose that of lying flopped out on a sun lounger while I, instead of taking a lounger for myself, just sat on a chair beside him and thought deeply about the relationship we had.

The indifference he had shown towards me that morning was very worrying and I began to think that, rather than encouraging me to go for a screen test it would have been better if he had become jealous or infuriated, threatening perhaps, to punch the film-guys on the nose if they didn't clear off. But the fact that he didn't care one way or the other about what I did was disheartening and demoralizing to say the least.

Today: Stupidly, I didn't take up the film producers' offer and I have always had cause to wonder what might have happened if I had? I could have easily related some very funny situations and stories to them about some of the antics Shmel got up to in order to turn the head of a woman, such as a day or so later when he made a complete fool of himself in the hotel elevator. I thought this one would have made a great comedy sketch for a film or even a play.

Who's the Big Boy then?... Shmel was very generous when the mood took him and before we came on this video convention he bought me some very expensive designer wear. Naturally, I loved dressing up in all my fancy gear but he was no where near as fashion conscious as I was.

One late afternoon, after spending a good amount of our time by the swimming pool, I suggested to Shmel that as I was hot and had had enough sunbathing for one day, perhaps we could go upstairs, freshen up, get changed and go out for a leisurely stroll. He was up for that, as he too had taken enough sunshine for the day so I picked up my book and tanning lotion and together we made our way back into the hotel foyer and headed for the main elevator. I had to smile to myself as I passed some long mirrors on the way, for there was I looking very much like a film star, dressed in my flash designer swimwear draped with a matching sarong, wearing a pair of very smart Gucci sunglasses worth over three-hundred pounds, while Shmel padded along behind me in his flip-flops and long boxer shorts. The little bit of hair he supported had been pushed back behind his ears and he had a thick, barrier sun-block plastered around his mouth. I can assure you he wasn't a pretty sight.

When we arrived at the elevator there were quite a few people already waiting to be taken up to their relevant floors. Eventually the elevator arrived and when the doors opened, leaning against the back wall was a tall, willowy showgirl, still dressed in her brief, snazzy, stage outfit. Well, at the sight of her, Shmel's eyes nearly popped out of his head. We all made our way into the elevator and most of us turned to stand facing the doors, but Shmel turned the other way around so that he was standing and facing the girl. I realised immediately what he was thinking of and when the lift-gates closed I couldn't wait to see what he would do.

Most of us were heading for the higher floors so Shmel had plenty of time in which to perform one or two of his well-worn tricks in order to attract the attention of someone of the opposite sex. One of his scams was to plunge both fists at once into his trouser pockets and push them together in front of him in order to make himself look even more endowed than he already was. But unfortunately for him, on this particular day, he didn't have hip pockets in his new boxer shorts, so when he thrust his hands down into his non-existent pockets he had to pull up smartly and try again. He must have had about three or four goes, in quick succession, in order to locate the 'pockets' but unfortunately, he was to be thwarted. This rapid bobbing up and down action did nothing for his masculine prowess, in fact, it made him look remarkably stupid and of course, the object of his attention barely cast him a glance.

The seventeenth floor couldn't come quick enough for me and as we neared it I turned and patted him on top of his head saying, "Come on sonny, we are home at last."

When the elevator stopped and the doors opened we both got out, I first, then Shmel, who padded along miserably behind me. As the lift doors began to close I heard sniggers and giggles from the people left inside, then, with the doors having closed tight on the fun-lift it moved up and away, leaving us to walk off along the corridor, down towards our room.

Shmel was absolutely furious with me for having shown him up, but he hadn't taken into account the embarrassment he had caused me by making such a fool of himself in front of all those people. I felt especially uneasy about the show-girl, who had probably been performing in one of the hotel's classy shows for most of the afternoon. He hadn't stopped to consider, that she was probably tired and weary and couldn't have given a toss about some little man's foolish advances anyway. That was of course, if she had noticed them at all.

The last couple of days seemed to evaporate into thin air as eventually the video convention drew to a close and the subsequent meetings finished, soon it would be time for us to return home. Like the outward journey, the flight and eventual drive back to my home in London was quite uneventful, apart from the usual aggravations I had with Shmel. You would have thought that with all the adverse tell-tale signs I was gathering I would have got out of this relationship while the going was good, but unfortunately for me, I didn't.

Looking back, I suppose I must have enjoyed the holiday overall, but his continual attention to other women drove me to distraction and the fact that he spent most of the flight home chatting up every woman he laid eyes on didn't leave a good, lasting impression. In fact, I arrived home thoroughly fed up and annoyed, especially as he had dumped me with all the cases at the airport in Las Vegas while he went off ogling anything he could find in a skirt.

Because I was cross with him and we had argued, I didn't see Shmel for some weeks after this holiday come business venture, for what had started out as being the holiday of a lifetime for me, turned out to be quite disappointing. What with not having been on holiday for such a long time and having been so excited, I suppose it was doomed to fall a bit flat. I'm not saying it was all Shmel's fault in fact, looking back I would say that on the whole he was *reasonably* well behaved and as usual, he was overly generous. He spent a good deal of money on me before the holiday started, buying swimwear, clothes, shoes and handbags, anything I wanted in fact and the holiday itself didn't cost me a penny so in the main, I suppose I should have been satisfied and ignored his roving eye, but I couldn't.

Eventually, after leaving me alone for a couple of weeks, he called around and made it obvious that he was ready to pick up the threads of our life again and get back to normal. Normal for us, when we were on speaking terms, meant him spending the week-ends at his wife's house and a couple of weekdays with me... The only difference being, believe it or not, I had somehow grown to love him despite his faults.

Today: When he was being attentive he made me feel wanted, worthy and very special. He could be considerate and loving and he would spoil me by giving me anything to make me happy. But just as I would begin to feel safe, his eyes would start to wander resulting in me becoming angry and humiliated. I never did learn to cope with his constant interest in other women; it always made me feel cheap and degraded. These awful feelings would bug me and I would not be able to act normally towards him, which would result in us arguing and then having to spend several weeks apart while I got over it. I now believe that this was the only thing that kept our 'destined to fail' relationship going for as long as it did.

My Apartment... During the good times we spent together, Shmel would often remark on my apartment and say that he thought I ought to sell up and move into a house, a place with a bit more room. He seemed to like having a lot of space and as I had two children and there was plenty of money rolling in via Shmel, I must admit I was very tempted, so after one of our many rows and subsequent reunions I decided to take the bull by the horns, and put my apartment up for sale. With Shmel willing to pay the rent on a house, I decided that it would at least relieve my brothers of their burden, the heavy burden, of helping me out financially. Shmel suggested we look at properties in and around Redbridge, which he said would be suitable for both of us.

Anne's Last Holiday... Around about this time Shmel took Anne on what was to be their last holiday together as husband and wife and their destination was to be, Hong Kong. It was one of his special, 'no expense spared' holidays and, having been married to him for so many years she must have known for sure that this was indeed the swan-song or swan-holiday for them as a couple – Shmel and Anne's marriage was well and truly over.

Shmel constantly telephoned me while they were away, which must have incensed or at least, bored his wife beyond belief and upon their return to England she filed for divorce. She had known for a long time that he was seeing somebody else and although he had been involved in affairs before, with many other women, she must have sensed that his latest affair was something quite different. She was probably tired of the competition anyway and was not prepared to put up with having to handle her husband having a more serious relationship.

With his wife potentially off the scene, so to speak, Shmel's roving eye had a new lease of life. Not that his wife had ever been able to stop him looking and roving, but I suppose from his point of view, it was like being released from an invisible tie and he was going to make the most of it. But then there was me, although, unlike his ex-wife, who had chosen to break the ties. I, as yet, had not been able to attach an invisible tie to him, so he saw fit to do as he pleased.

When Shmel was finally free of the marriage shackles, I frequently had cause to think that as well as looking, he was actually sampling other women. Call it female intuition if you like, but my sixth sense would often bug me. I felt that he was constantly picking unnecessary arguments and rows, which I soon learned was yet another tell-tale sign of his insatiable urge to wander.

A Brush with the Loo… It was during one of the school holiday periods that mum had been kind enough to offer to have the children for a week. They loved staying with her in the seaside town of Brighton and it gave Shmel and I a golden opportunity to have a quiet, cosy week on our own. But this time it wasn't to be, for as fast as I had taken the children to mothers on the Saturday, we had an argument about nothing on the Monday, ending up with him storming off and me slamming the door behind him.

By the following Friday, having spent four days completely alone I was feeling so bored and fed up that I rang mum to say that instead of picking the children up as arranged on Sunday and taking them home the same day I would come the day before and stay overnight. Mum, of course, was delighted as she always loved to see me and have me stay over. I had not heard from Shmel since our latest row, so I didn't contact him to let him know what I was doing, I just packed an overnight bag and on Saturday lunchtime I headed off towards mums.

Because I was so convinced that Shmel was cheating on me, instead of going my usual way to Brighton, I decided to take a different route that would take me into London and right near to where he had his bed-sit. He had told me so many lies recently that I had reached a point where I couldn't believe anything he said to me at all. So, just to satisfy my own curiosity, I thought I might be able to see what he was really up to and in so doing learn the truth for myself. I cannot remember much about the journey into London as my mind was saturated with thoughts of this horrible little man who was giving me so much grief. Yet somehow, I found myself going over Vauxhall Bridge, from where I made a quick detour and eventually drew up and parked down the side street, next to the hotel in Regents Park that housed his permanent one-room bed-sit. I sat outside in the car for a while, trying to think of a way to get in to see him. I suddenly came up with an idea and decided to ring him on my mobile and make up an excuse.

"Hi, Shmel, it's me, Shar, I am on my way to Brighton to pick up the kids and as I was passing I was wondering if I could drop in to see you and perhaps use your loo?"

Well, the shock he must have had when he realised I was near his place certainly sounded in his voice. He hummed and hawed, not knowing quite what to say and after making a couple of feeble excuses he hurriedly said goodbye and put the phone down on me. I kept my cool, as I was determined not to be put off so I got out of my car and walked along until I reached the hotel that was situated on the corner of the road. I went into the plush hotel foyer and called his room from the house-phone, saying that I was really sorry to drop in on him like this but I hated using public toilets and was getting a bit desperate. He panicked somewhat and started coming out with the most ridiculous excuses in order to put me off, but all these excuses acted like a red rag to a bull and it made me all the more determined to get up to his room at any cost. In the end I just told him I would be coming up to see him and with that I put down the phone.

I hesitated a few moments gathering myself together and then slowly started to walk over towards the lift. Suddenly the lift doors burst open and he came rushing out to see me. He was freshly shaven and was wearing an open necked shirt and shorts, while on his face he wore the guiltiest expression I had ever seen. He was all in a flap and tried to engage me in pointless chat, but I suggested we go upstairs to his bed-sit to talk, for if nothing else, I was now very anxious to use the toilet. He desperately tried to put me off again, saying that his bathroom wasn't tidy and that he had to go out urgently, etc. When I flatly insisted on going up to his room he suddenly did what was usual for him and that was to take flight. He gave me some half-hearted excuse about not having time to go back upstairs as he had to go to one of his video shops urgently. Leaving me standing there, he immediately took off out of the hotel, jumped into his car that was parked outside and shot off like a rocket.

This naturally made me all the more suspicious. Unfortunately, I didn't have a key to his room so I decided that my best approach would be to appeal to the Spanish security guard who was standing in the foyer. I smiled sweetly as I walked over to the guard and with all the charm I could muster I explained, very politely, that my fiancé had not had time to let me up into his bed-sit and as I needed to go to the toilet, desperately, perhaps he would be kind enough to let me go up there. I had to exaggerate a little about my relationship with Shmel otherwise I knew for sure the guard would not let me in. I managed to convince him that my need was very urgent and that my 'fiancé' had given his permission and although wary at first, the security guard kindly said that he would let me in, but that he would have to accompany me to the room. I had no problem with that of course, so after the guard had found the spare key from behind the reception desk, we headed for the lift. Upon our arrival at the second floor I followed the security guard along to Shmel's room. My heartbeat quickened as he fumbled with the key. When the door was finally opened, I walked straight over to the bathroom and turned the door handle but, just as I expected, it was bolted from within. The sweetness fell from my face instantly and my whole attitude changed from that of an angel to one of a demon. I attacked the bathroom door in a desperate attempt to open it, shouting, "Open the door! Open this door NOW!" at the top of my voice.

Immediately, the security guard became flustered, realising that he had opened the door on a very large can of worms. I screamed and shouted at whoever was locked in the loo, threatening, that if they did not come out I would smash the door down with my bare fists. The poor security man didn't know what to do, he tried to pull me away from the bathroom door in a vain attempt to calm the situation down, but he was absolutely and totally wasting his time and effort, as I yelled at him that I was not leaving and would not be satisfied until I found out who the scrubber was in the toilet.

It must have taken around ten minutes of hysterical ranting and raving and wrestling with the security guard before a clicking of the lock meant that all was to be revealed. The security guard and I stood stock still as the handle of the bathroom door turned and slowly a very coy, half dressed woman appeared from behind. My mouth dropped open as I recognised the face of a woman who I knew was quite willing to accommodate any one of Shmel's pals whenever it suited. I was well aware of this woman's reputation as she had accompanied us to Las Vegas as a partner to one of his associates and she was more than generous with her favours there. I wasn't aware at the time – but I later learned she had indeed been another one of Shmel's past girlfriends... Men, huh!

This latest brush with one of Shmel's cast off women was just another one of a long line of incidents that made me feel so terribly depressed, that I would sit for days at a time doing little else but stew over the life I was leading with this man.

The Armani Attack... One lovely sunny day when I was alone and feeling particularly dejected and pissed off with him; I snapped, as my South American temper suddenly got the better of me. I stomped about my apartment trying to think of a way to give vent to my feelings. Storming into my bedroom I grabbed up the dressing gown that I had left lying on the bed and dragged open the wardrobe door and was just about to toss it in when hanging there, right in front of my angry eyes was Shmel's brand new, grey, Armani suit. My dressing gown slipped from my fingers and fell to the floor as I took hold of the sleeve of the jacket and ran my hand over the smooth, expensive cloth… as I did; I felt my anger surge up like a tidal wave. I had been so provoked recently by his insatiable womanising and all the lies he had been telling me that I felt the need to do something quite drastic, anything, in order to get my own back on him.

I walked over to my dressing table drawer like a zombie and took out a long pair of scissors. Snapping the steel blades together a couple of times and seeing the blades glint in the sunshine that streamed through my bedroom windows I stood and wondered… would I, could I? The sharp blades of the scissors ground together and cut easily into the sleeve of the jacket. Whether it was the sound of material being sliced or maybe it was my vivid imagination that induced such a vicious attack on such a lifeless item I cannot say, but I must admit, I felt absolutely wonderful when my job had been well and truly done.

Sitting down on the edge of my bed, staring at the sad sight of a once beautiful Armani suit shredded like the fringe on a lap-dancers scanty outfit all seemed rather sad, but then I was glad, for it had certainly gone someway towards soothing my temper. Unfortunately, I still didn't feel completely fulfilled so I looked around to see what else I could do. My eyes then fell upon his treasured 18ct gold Cartier watch that was lying innocently on my beside cabinet. I picked it up and slowly carried it through the hall and into the kitchen where I put it carefully on the counter. Taking a sturdy chopping board from the cupboard I carefully placed the watch down on it, I then reached under the sink to where I kept some general household tools and took out a hammer… Just then the telephone rang. I snatched it from its cradle and snarled, "Hello."

"Oh, hi, it's me darling, Shmel," he said in his 'I'm here again' voice.

Well, I knew damn well who it was, didn't I!

"Just thought I would give you a call to see how you were keeping."

Well, as you can imagine, I let him have it straight from the hip, I was spitting fire.

My voice resounded around the apartment as we argued back and forth, until I was so goaded by his smarmy talk and pathetic excuses that I threatened to smash the hammer down on the face of his beloved watch.

It took three or four sharp blows in quick succession before splinters of glass and bits of metal flew away from the chopping board.

"Don't! Don't!" He yelled down the telephone. I could hear the horror in his voice that had swiftly risen to screeching pitch when he realised that I was actually carrying out my threat. But it was all too late; his watch, like him was kaput, finished.

I slammed the telephone down and as I did the hammer slowly slid to the floor from my trembling hand. I plumped down on a stool that was standing nearby, deflated and spent. I collapsed heavily on the counter shaking and crying. My temper had got the better of me and I had done my worst. Was I really satisfied now? No, only sad. And instead of feeling rewarded, loneliness enveloped me.

I must have sat for what was an age, some hours even, before I felt strong enough to pull myself together. Once my trembling hands and the fury in my heart had diminished I had to take stock of the consequences of my manic loss of control.

I looked forlornly at the chopping board that lay on the table, still covered with the pieces of watch parts now entangled and twisted. I bent down and carefully picked up the few small fragments of broken glass that had fallen to the floor and then went round the kitchen, carefully looking for, and finding, a few other tiny slivers of shattered glass. I knew that I had to be extra careful for my children's sake as they were in the habit of walking around barefoot.

His precious gold Cartier watch that must have cost him at least two thousand pounds plus, (which was a lot of money in those days) now in twisted, shattered pieces was worth nothing other than its own weight in gold. I went through into the lounge and over to the writing bureau where I took out a small white envelope, and taking it into the kitchen I carefully guided the fragments of watch, including the battered gold case and damaged bracelet, into the envelope and moistening the edge of it with my tongue I stuck it down. The watch was worthless now, yet owing to its pedigree, I felt it still needed some deal of respect paid to it. I laid the sealed envelope on the kitchen table and walked dismally back into the bedroom. The bed was unusually dishevelled, my dressing gown was still lying crumpled on the floor where I had dropped it and the wardrobe door stood wide open. I glanced into the wardrobe and there, all askew on its shaped, wooden-hanger was the grey Armani suit, shredded and pitiful. The shears that I had used to decimate the suit lay open on the floor. I picked them up and closed the blades together carefully, being sure to replace them safely back in my dressing table drawer.

I walked back over to the wardrobe and stood there looking at the suit, not quite knowing how to proceed. I had committed the unthinkable, but had no notion of how I should follow up my actions. I sat there quietly on the bottom of my bed looking at the tangled mess and can remember thinking that this was the kind of story you sometimes read in a woman's magazine while enjoying a hot, delicious cappuccino. But, as there was no magazine to hand and no frothy cappuccino for me to sip, I had to face the fact that this was real life and I was going to have to move on, but where to and how to go about it. I had no idea.

-:: *The Attack* ::-

The Tangled Delivery... I put my problem on hold for a while until I could really think straight. The apartment seemed unusually quiet and I began to wonder where, exactly, Shmel had telephoned me from and where he might be now. As a rule, when we had rowed and were not speaking, he would go running back to his wife for comfort and although they were now divorced, I suddenly had visions of him still running back there, winging and moaning, and telling her all about his troubles and her, taking it all in and lapping it up.

That was it! The idea came to me in a flash. After all, if she had him pouring out all the dross about what a wicked cow I was, etc., etc., and if she was taking it all in and sympathising with him, (as per-usual) she might just as well have his ravaged suit and battered watch as well. So without any more ado, I rushed into the kitchen, grabbed a plastic shopping bag from a drawer under the counter and dashed back into the bedroom. I dragged the dangling suit from its wooden hanger and in so doing, sent the hanger crashing noisily to the floor. Kicking the hanger to one side I bundled the suit up, and dumped it unceremoniously into the bag making sure to tuck in all the loose flaps and ragged ends of cloth. I turned back and grabbed my own coat out of the wardrobe; I thrust my arm in one sleeve then threw it across my shoulders like a cloak. Still trying to manipulate the Armani bundle, I managed to put my other arm into the sleeve of my coat as I ran through the hall and back into the kitchen, where I scooped up the envelope that held the watch parts. I heard the bits of watch jangle together as I rammed it into the plastic carrier, then snatching up my bag and car keys I headed for the street door.

It didn't take too long before I turned the car into the cul-de-sac where Shmel's ex-wife lived with his three grown up children. As I swung my car into the lavish driveway, I was quite surprised when I noticed that his car wasn't parked outside the house after all. As I pulled up, I spotted his ex looking through her bedroom window and I guessed that on hearing a car approaching the driveway she came nearer to see who it was, as she now pulled the curtain wide and peered out at me. I wasn't quite sure whether or not to abandon my idea when I saw that Shmel wasn't there at the house, but then I decided that Shmel or no Shmel it was too late, I was there at the house and determined to deliver the goods. Getting out of the car, I gathered the plastic bundle from the back seat, slammed the door shut and with bundle in hand, stood up to my full height and smartly marched the bag and its ragged contents up to her front door. I duly dumped the bag on the doorstep then, brushing my hands together as though ridding them of some tacky rubbish, I hitched my purse strap up and onto my shoulder and was about to turn back towards the car when I heard the front door unlatch. It was Anne, she opened the door fully and stood there looking at me…

"Your ex-husbands stuff." I said vehemently, as I looked down and pointed to the bundle. She followed my gaze without a word. When she looked back at me I had a notion to brazenly introduce myself properly, for although she had seen me just once, last year, late that evening in the video shop, Shmel had made sure to keep a good distance between us ever since. So with head high I looked her straight in the eye and said, "I am Shar, the woman your husband has been having an affair with for the last year."

I suppose, thinking back, I expected her to go into some kind of frenzy, or at least look shocked or angry but she didn't. In fact, she didn't even look disturbed. She just continued to look at me until with a resigned toss of her head said, "Well, you're not the only one, *dear*!"

I shrugged and walked defiantly back to my car, trying hard not to look deflated. Quite honestly, I admired her spunk; I have always had a great admiration for people who are straight and honest, and I also have a great deal of respect for people who are not thrown every time life kicks them in the teeth.

I walked around the bonnet of my car towards the driving seat and opened the door, but before I got in, I remained standing for a moment and looked over the top of the car and across at the woman who had been cheated on so many times, that it just didn't seem to hurt any more. I called across to her and suggested that we would have to meet properly some time and that she might like to join me for a tea or coffee. She half smiled a yes and turned away back into the house, leaving the bundle still adorning the doorstep. She closed her street door shut as I got into the seat of the car. With my delivery made, I turned the ignition key and drove off home...

Some weeks went by with no sign or word from Shmel; it was just as though he had disappeared off the face of the earth. My temper had abated by now and I had calmed right down. Although I had become somewhat resigned to the way my relationship was going with this man, I remained defiant. I thought a lot about my life and the life we were leading and it fascinated me when I thought about his ex-wife's attitude. I would often wonder how she had managed to cope for so long with this man's strange behaviour and still remain sane.

Like her, the major problem I had with Shmel was his roving eye and the fact that he would try to familiarise himself with any woman who came near him, it was as though women had built-in magnets that would draw him to them. At times it seemed that he just couldn't help himself, he would make eyes at any woman. He didn't seem to care if they were old or young, attractive or ugly, to him they were women and almost all women were of interest to him. It wasn't until he met someone like his ex-wife, or me, that he became determined to maintain a longer relationship. Nevertheless, no matter what excuses I make for him, his continual fraternizing with the opposite sex would infuriate me beyond belief.

When I was going through one of my 'moods' with him, we would inevitably row and he would go off for a few weeks and leave me alone to get over it and it was during one of these 'getting over it' periods that I would think often about his long suffering wife, who had at last given up and divorced him. I was determined to get to know her better, if for nothing else other than curiosity and to find out what made this woman tick.

A few weeks later Shmel came back on the scene again, but in the meantime, the apartment that my brothers had bought and helped me furnish had been sold and it was hoped that in due course any money received would be returned to the bank, as unbeknown by me at the time, they had borrowed against the apartment for business reasons.

1990

Chapter 3 – The Ex-Ta-Tea.

Moving On Up... Whilst Shmel was enjoying the freedom from his long standing marriage and with my apartment now sold he helped me choose and move into my new rented house. It was a beautiful four bedroom detached house, tastefully furnished and very spacious. It was surrounded by a delightful garden which helped make the house feel secluded and very tranquil. At first I was very busy and much of my time was taken up reorganising the place in general and getting the children settled into their new schools. The new

house was beautiful; I just loved it as soon as I moved in and before long I felt very much at home. Shmel started to visit me a little more often, so all in all, I was very pleased with the arrangement. He would occasionally take me out to a theatre or cinema or we would go out for meals or perhaps just coffee. He was being very attentive, generous and amusing, and we had many a good laugh together.

Nevertheless, it wasn't long before we quickly dropped back into our old ways and it was during one of Shmel's disappearing acts and one of my 'cooling off' periods that I had an urge to contact 'the ex'.

The Ex-Ta-Tea... Not being able to resist the temptation any longer I decided to telephone Anne and invite her over to my new house for afternoon tea and a good heart-to-heart. When she arrived I took her coat, showed her into my plush lounge and offered her a seat. While she was making herself comfortable I went into the kitchen and made two fresh cups of Earl Grey tea. As I walked slowly back into the lounge with our two drinks on a tray I studied her a little more closely. She was quite a bit shorter than me, around 5" 3' I would guess. She had short, dark, beautifully groomed hair. She must have been in her early fifties at the time, and was still a very attractive woman. She was a little on the plump side now, not quite like the type of woman one might have thought Shmel would have wanted a long-standing relationship with, but she may have been very beautiful and trim when he first knew her, rather like a young Elizabeth Taylor, I imagined.

Over our cups of tea and in the comfort of my own house, we seemed to get on remarkably well, considering the fact that we were rivals, of a sort. She told me that she had been married to Shmel for around twenty-three years. Her ex-husband, she informed me, was a habitual womaniser and that he had had so many affairs they ceased to bother her in the end. She said that she had a house she was very happy in, clothes and money, so what more could she possibly want? Apparently, Shmel had set her up many years before in a beautiful, four bedroom, detached house, in a smart, upmarket area of Cockfosters. Expenditure for the house and all the bills incurred were paid by him, so she more or less wanted for nothing. Our conversation was quite revealing, as she most certainly knew her ex-husband far better than I did, but then she had been with him (well, in name at least) for so much longer.

At one point during the conversation she informed me that far from being upset or hurt by Shmel's lifestyle, she had actually maintained quite a good relationship with him, given that for many years now she had made a point of not sleeping with him, in case she contracted AIDS. I tried very hard not to appear the least bit shocked at this repeated damning statement, as I realised that she was just being facetious and showing off in front of a woman who must have appeared painfully naïve that time outside the video shop, especially when she compared her own knowledge of Shmel's past, to mine. We talked of many things and both agreed that this man we were, or should I say, *had* been sharing was not particularly prone to discretion and would often leave tell-tale signs of his transgressions. She told me how once, when tidying up, she saw something down the side of an armchair and that upon sliding the cushion from the seat, there nestling in the crease between that and the arm of the chair was an envelope with two used tickets to Switzerland. When Anne confronted him, by throwing the tickets down on the table in front of him, he told her that he had recently spent a holiday with an Austrian woman with whom he had been living, on and off with, for around eighteen years. He assured his wife that it was the last holiday he was spending with this woman as the relationship was now over and the holiday was a way of saying, 'Thank you very much and good bye.' It had been the 'swan song,' the big 'kiss off' for the Viennese-waltzer, we both giggled rather pathetically. After this we carried on talking about close, intimate things for a long time and both agreed that besides Shmel we had quite a lot in common.

This was to be the first of many such get-togethers, as over the course of the next few years we were to become quite good friends.

Shmel's Problem... For many years Shmel had suffered from a relatively common, but nonetheless miserable skin complaint. It was often aggravated by emotional problems such as worry, fear and anxiety, but it was made considerably worse by the sordid lifestyle, unbeknown to me at the time, that he was leading throughout our relationship. During my years with him, he would occasionally go to his doctor for additional medication or to see if there was anything new on offer that might relieve him of the unsightly, irritable and at times, painful symptoms. On one occasion when his skin had been particularly bad for a while his doctor advised him to, "Go seek the sun," as the sun apparently, is a great healer. Without hesitation, Shmel told me to pack our cases as we were heading for Israel and the Dead Sea within the week. I did as I was bid and we set out on a healing holiday.

The Wife Swap... The holiday started out very relaxing. The outward journey was good and the hotel in which we were to spend the week was very classy and comfortable. I also thought that the week would prove to be even more enjoyable after we met and became friendly with another couple who were staying in the same hotel.

They were a good-looking pair. She was quite short with long auburn hair, while the guy was tall, fair and very attractive. After a couple of contented days, either splashing around and sunning ourselves by the pool, or enjoying pleasant evenings spent in the lounge or on the terrace, the guy happened to make a pass at me. Well, I wasn't quite sure if it *was* a pass at first, as I thought it might have been little more than over-friendliness. You know what it's like on holiday? Because people are thrown together for only a week or two at most, they become friends much quicker owing to the fact that it is all going to end just as fast.

Shmel wasn't slow in picking up the indiscreet 'pass', helped along of course, by the guy's general body language towards me when we all talked and laughed together. Consequently, when we had said goodnight and had returned to our room that evening Shmel very eagerly remarked on the attention this man had been giving me. I of course brushed the suggestion aside saying it was nothing more than friendliness, but Shmel insisted that the guy fancied me. Naturally, I was quite pleased that a man would find me attractive, just as most women would, but it worried me to think that Shmel didn't seem to mind one bit. Instead of being very jealous, (which I considered would be the most normal reaction of a lover) he enthusiastically suggested that, as he quite fancied the woman, we might be able to do a wife-swap. I laughed his suggestion off at first but when I realised he was serious, I was shocked and totally incensed at his unbelievable proposition and declined the offer out of hand. I was thoroughly disgusted.

As you can well imagine I was absolutely furious with Shmel and his wife-swapping idea. For one thing I was *not* his wife and in actual fact, I was *not* on offer. I was still my own person and in charge of my own life, or so I believed. In the normal way I would have had a flaming row with him and he would have gone scuttling off to telephone his ex-wife of umpteen years, or to one of the mistresses he had on the go, but it was very hot and as there were only a few days left of our holiday I thought it would have been too difficult to launch into our usual way of going on, so I just went quiet and seethed.

I was later to be told by Anne, over one of our special cups of tea, that he tried exactly the same trick with her. She took great delight in telling me about the time they went to Portugal on a holiday and after pursuing a couple for some time Shmel suggested a wife-swap and like me, Anne declined the offer.

Poor bugger, I thought. He didn't seem to have much luck in the wife-swapping stakes.

My Israeli Taunt... The day after the wife-swap proposition we went on a trip into the town. Israel is a beautiful place, steeped in history and legend and quite different from anywhere I had ever been before or indeed, since. Most young Israeli men are absolutely gorgeous; many of them are tall, swarthy and dusky with defined-chiselled features. Their dark eyes smoulder in the intense heat of the sun and when they look at you they seem to be able to invade not only your body but your deepest innermost thoughts as well.

While walking through the busy, dusty streets that were swarming with people, I became acutely aware of the looks that many of the indigenous men were giving me. For, although I have a very light complexion my hair is a rich, dark colour, full-bodied and was quite long at the time. My hairdresser had often remarked on the strength and texture of my hair, saying that it had to be one of my best features. I have often thought of the time I spent in Israel and have since wondered that if having continental blood pumping through my veins, Israeli men might have felt an underlying affinity with this particular holiday maker.

I occasionally glanced at Shmel, who was sauntering along beside me. He obviously couldn't detect the looks of disdain I was dishing out to him from behind my sunglasses as he would smile at me from time to time, having completely forgotten the wife-swapping incident whereas, I was still stewing and trying to think of a way to get back at him. We carried on walking along the busy streets, window shopping and just taking in the essence of this remarkable country, when he suggested we go into a small café for some refreshments.

While waiting for our coffee to be served, I grabbed the opportunity to gaze into the eyes of some gorgeous hunk of a man who was sitting nearby and who had turned to look at me. I held his gaze and he continued to stare at me while Shmel was busy looking at the menu. The handsome Israeli guy gave me a furtive smile and cast his eyes over towards Shmel, but seeing he was preoccupied, he looked back at me and I was still smiling.

'You are so handsome.' I mouthed silently to him.

His eyes widened and his smile broadened and as he didn't put up any kind of objection to the overtures I was making to him. I said in a whispered voice, "You're so good looking!" I could tell by the look on his face that he didn't altogether understand what I was saying, although, I suspect he had a reasonably good guess and he liked it. He laughed quietly and turning around said something in Ivrit to his companion. At which they both looked back at me grinning broadly.

I flashed my eyes at them and slyly smiled.

By now Shmel had sensed that something was up and he gave me a very quizzical look. I saw him look at me from the corner of my eye so I blatantly pursed my lips towards this smiling hunk and his pal and whispered, yet again, "You're so handsome, you're gorgeous!"

Shmel's look of bewilderment faded as he cottoned on to what I was up to. He turned around and looked at these two smiling guys and then, looking back at me, said rather grumpily, "Okay, okay, okay."

I had gotten my own back on him even if it was only just a little bit; I felt that if I could show him how embarrassing it was to have your partner make advances to other people while you were with them it might have taught him a sharp lesson, but unfortunately it didn't, and... I sure got my comeuppance the following day.

The Wee Escort... We were booked to go on an all day coach trip that would take us to some of the most popular tourist sights in Israel. While waiting for the coach to arrive at the hotel, Shmel happened to take a liking to a twenty-year-old girl who was in our party, but travelling alone. He chatted her up and seemed to go out of his way, purposely, to make sure that she was well looked after. He even managed to book her a seat at our table for lunch, despite me showing off with him most of the day over it. He relished in making me feel uncomfortable.

Looking back, I will never understand why he treated me so, but I suppose he had no real respect for women and even less for the faithful ones. He completely ruined my day by taking an unnecessary interest in this young woman's welfare, as I considered she was quite capable of taking care of herself, yet he insisted on cosseting her every movement.

After visiting a couple of interesting tourist sights we eventually stopped for lunch at a prearranged restaurant and it was here that he insisted the girl sat with us for the meal. He fussed and flapped about her as though she was something extra special by making sure she was happy with her seat and then her meal. Although he made sure I was okay, it was obvious that he fancied this girl and she was just lovin'it, she just loved every moment of it – Poor bitch, I thought.

After the meal that Shmel paid for, the girl of course, was more than grateful and after making a pointless fuss about paying her share, she gratefully accepted the freebee after which, she twittered incessantly to her benefactor while I kept looking at my watch wishing the time away so that we could get back on board the coach. Although it seemed an age, eventually, my watch told me it was time to get up and go, so I gathered up my things as quickly as possible and made a move.

It was just a short walk back to our coach and I was only too glad to climb aboard so that we could get away from the girl and her incessant chatter. Once we were all seated the coach started off.

When we had been going for some fifteen minutes or so the girl suddenly got up and made her way down the isle of the coach towards the front. I saw her speak to the driver and it appeared that she needed to go to the loo. He didn't look too happy about her request, as we had only just left a restaurant that had ample toilet and washing facilities. Nevertheless, I saw him say something to her and after a minute or so the coach started to slow down. We were some way out of town by now and there were no convenient toilets around so it seemed that the only handy place for her to go would be in some thick bushes that ran along the dusty roadside. Once the coach had come to a complete standstill the doors opened and she got off. I watched through the window of the coach and saw the girl go over to the side of the road and carefully pick her way into a large clump of bushes, behind which, she eventually disappeared from view.

Shmel, who had been watching this mini drama unfold alongside me, suddenly jumped to his feet and made a dash for the coach door saying as he went, that he had better go to the toilet as well. I sat in my seat, totally amazed that he would be so unbelievably indiscreet as to follow a woman he obviously fancied to the toilet, or rather, to the bushes. But he did.

Reading this, you may well think I was just being paranoid, but if you knew Shmel the way I knew him, you would realise that he took every single opportunity to check out any female he came within a mile of. I sat in my seat despondent and miserable; there was absolutely nothing I could do with this man of mine. He was an established womaniser and as much as I tried so hard to ignore this infuriating habit, I couldn't.

He had such an unusual way with women and I had fallen for his way too. I must have been spell-bound or mesmerised by him; otherwise I would have given up and left him long before I did. He seemed to have an invisible hold over me… I often wondered why he wanted me. Almost all of the other women he encountered he would just use them and go, but me? For some reason or the other, I could not shake him off and in turn, he would not let me go.

Needless to say this girl and Shmel returned from the bushes after what seemed an eternity, but was actually about five or six minutes and resumed their seats. I cannot tell you for sure what happened in the bushes and of course I cannot prove anything, but, from my knowledge of his antics and from the flushed look on the girls face I can only assume that she had paid very well for the way this weird little man had looked after her all day and for the meal and drink he had bought her.

The Bed-sit Mail… The holiday quickly came to an end and we packed our cases and left the hotel. We were soon heading for the local international airport with plenty of time to spare. Foolishly I got into the queue with some of the other people who we had met on holiday and while I was passing the time of day with them, Shmel performed his usual trick of buzzing off, leaving me to check in. I seemed to fall for it every time we went away. As soon as we were settled in the queue he would wander off. It only took a couple of trips away to realise that while I was checking in, he would be checking out any tasty dish that may have been standing around. He also had a 'thing' about air hostesses. I often wondered if that was what he found attractive about me, the fact that I was an ex-air hostess. Perhaps tall, uniformed women turned him on, but little did he realise that most of the air hostesses were well and truly turned off by guys like him. Needless to say we argued profusely about his antics with other women and how he managed to ruin a measly, seven-day, healing holiday just because he couldn't keep his eyes off them.

When we eventually arrived home in England, although he would normally drive me straight home to my house before returning to his London bed-sit, on this particular occasion he didn't. Whilst driving on our way back through the city he said that rather than take me straight home he wanted to pop into his bed-sit to check his mail and perhaps, he said, I would like a coffee. Well! That didn't happen too often, so I said okay. Mind you, the fact that I didn't go up to his bed-sit very often was probably my own fault, as once I had seen his poky little hideaway I never really relished the thought of going there very much although, I would go occasionally if he invited me up for a coffee.

I don't know what it was about the place but I never felt very comfortable there, ever. For one thing it was very small and for me, it seemed to be a little old fashioned. It consisted of just one room with a bathroom attached and it had one of those strange, put-you-up beds that fitted into the wall, creating a handy situation whereby… If you can imagine a man asking a girl up to his place for a drink or to look at his etchings and just when she was expecting it least of all, at the press of a button and with a twang and a mighty clonk, a ready made bed would appear 'Just like that!' Hopefully, the innocent maiden would be so surprised, shocked and overwhelmed she would swoon into the man's arms and with a bit of luck, into his bed. Yuk!

The doorman touched his cap and gave us a smile as we went into the hotel. We went straight over to the reception desk where the usual guy gave us a welcoming smile.

"Had a good time?" he said, as he turned around and brought a number of letters from Shmel's mail-box.

"Yeah, great, thanks." Shmel replied, taking the letters. We turned towards the lift.

"Glad to see you back." The receptionist smiled.

Once upstairs, Shmel dumped his mail on the small table just inside the door and went over to the kitchen area and filled the coffee percolator. He reached into a small cupboard and got out a pack of ground coffee and while he was setting up the percolator I casually walked around the room, which took me the whole of one minute and I ended up standing back by the little table that held his stack of letters. The letters had fanned out, the way they do, and one particular letter had written in bold black letters, right across the front, a headline for a dating agency. I picked the letter up and when Shmel walked back over to me, I waved the letter at him and asked him what it was. He had a quick glance at the letter then gave me some off-hand reply saying that he often received junk mail such as that, but I could see that it was a confidential letter written to him personally. I was very doubtful about his explanation, as I was not *that* naïve and I most certainly knew what junk mail looked like and this definitely did not look like junk. I heaved a great sigh and dropped the letter back onto the pile and turned away. I was already tired and fed up as you can imagine. We had just returned from a miserable holiday and all I really wanted to do was get home to my own house and see my children again. We drank our coffee, and eventually he got around to taking me home. Once home and when my cases had been deposited in the hall he presumably, went off back to the bed-sit, although, to be honest, I really didn't care where he had gone, I was just delighted to be back with my children who had been left with one of my lovely friends; it was nice to feel safe and really loved again.

Safe, that is, in the knowledge that my children loved me because I was their mother and weren't likely to go eyeing-up a substitute mother the way Shmel eyed-up substitute girlfriends.

Whiteleys in Bayswater... Once home, I guessed I wouldn't be seeing Shmel for a while so it gave me the perfect opportunity to go out for a meal with Anne. I rang her up to ask if she would like to come out with me on the following Friday and she replied saying that she would be delighted to accompany me to a restaurant in Whiteleys, Bayswater.

We had just enjoyed a good girlie chat and a quiet meal and were just finishing it off with a coffee when I was chatted up by a very handsome Swiss Banker. We exchanged telephone numbers and he said he would keep in touch. He told me that he travelled through England, Switzerland and Tenerife frequently and I felt that I had a very good chance of getting to know this guy and who knows? A promising relationship could have been forthcoming, but just when I thought I might have scored with someone new, that very same night Shmel got in touch with me and came back on the scene ruining any chance of me having, perhaps, a fresh start with someone new who might have given me real and lasting happiness.

My Operation... Throughout the year of 1990 I had been experiencing quite a lot of worrying gynaecological problems. Not being the type to mess about when it came to health matters Shmel had already signed me and the children up to a health insurance scheme, so he advised me to go and consult a private doctor. I was also seeing a lot of Anne at the time and when I confided in her regarding my problems she kindly introduced me to her own doctor in Wimpole Street, London. After the consultation, plus numerous tests, I was told that I was in need of a total hysterectomy.

On the advice of the doctor I was taken into hospital quite quickly and the hysterectomy was performed. Naturally, I was very upset at the prospect of an operation and the eventual outcome but in retrospect, I realised that it was needed and indeed, crucial to my future health and wellbeing. I was hospitalised in a private room in the Portland Hospital for a week. Now I'm not going to say that Shmel didn't visit me regularly, because he did, but his visits were rather bland and uninteresting; they appeared to be carried out more from a sense of duty than from a real and genuine concern. On the third day of my stay in hospital, he came in all dolled up sporting a very large cigar, telling me he was going straight from the hospital to attend a party organised by his ex-wife. I couldn't understand, for the life of me, why he would want to go to such an event and told him so. But in spite of anything said or how I felt

I knew he would go whether I liked it or not, so I resigned myself to resting so that I could concentrate fully, on getting well as soon as possible.

I never could make out why he would want to go to his ex's party especially while I was unwell and recovering from a major operation, until later, when a friend informed me that Shmel felt it was a golden opportunity for him to hand out specially printed business cards notifying all the young women there that he was a film producer! Huh! What a joke…

My Loan Mistake… They say that everyone has their ups and downs in life and at that moment in time Shmel's life was way down in a dip, or so it appeared. While I was laid up in hospital recovering from my operation, his ex-wife's luxurious four bedroom house in the stockbroker-belt of Hertfordshire was in the process of being re-possessed. Obviously, he said, he didn't want his ex and his children to be without their home so he persuaded me to take out a huge loan to cover the mortgage. He had spoken to me earlier in the year about some problems he was having trying to keep up the repayments on the property and now, things had taken a turn for the worse. His businesses had hit a bit of a slump and as the majority of his money was tied up in the video shops he suggested that perhaps I could take out a loan in order to tide him over. He assured me it would only be for a short while before his video businesses perked up again. In the meantime, he said that he would help me pay back the loan, as and when he could.

Still feeling depressed and unwell, I agreed to his proposal as I couldn't tolerate seeing anyone without their home, especially after all the problems I had encountered when I divorced my first husband. I took it for granted that the loan would only be for a short period as I was convinced that Shmel would pay it back swiftly; I assured myself there was no need to worry. I was therefore horrified when I eventually found out that his ex-wife's house had indeed been re-possessed owing to payment arrears and after questioning Shmel in depth, I was given to understand that he had blown the money I had borrowed for him elsewhere, and as I was unable to repay the loan myself, much to my utter dismay, I was declared bankrupt.

Trying hard to be positive, I have to say that my operation was a complete success even though I picked up an infection which meant having to spend more time in hospital than expected. Nevertheless, the specialist gave me the all clear, even though I still had quite a bit of discomfort and pain when I eventually returned home to my family.

For the next few weeks everything seemed to go to pieces around me and I wasn't seeing Shmel very much either. During that time he told me that he was busy setting up a new business venture with an associate he had recently become acquainted with. He had come up with this business idea which involved him writing and producing a video magazine. To help him get his idea off the ground he went into partnership with a guy who looked remarkably like the American film star Steven Seagal. Although I wasn't seeing him very much he did keep in touch with me regularly by telephone, I could only assume therefore, that he was desperately trying to find a way to get me, as well as himself, out of the financial difficulty we were in. In some ways I felt rather sorry for Shmel as he always seemed to try so hard to please everyone and do well, yet somehow, real success always managed to elude him.

A week or so after I had been discharged from hospital and was convalescing at home, Shmel telephoned me one evening from the London Hospital in Whitechapel to say that he would not be able to see me, yet again, that night as he had escorted the secretary from their newly formed business into hospital as she was suffering from stomach pains. He said that he was going to have to make sure she was alright and that she got home safely and he would see me when he could. I put the phone down and held my head in my hands and wept, I found it hard to believe that he could be so insensitive as to telephone me, for no other reason but to tell me that he was caring for some other woman in hospital while I was in pain, depressed and feeling very lonely, I couldn't do anything about it at the time but believe me, I vowed to get my own back on him somehow, some day, all I had to do was bide my time and most importantly, get well.

1991

Chapter 4 – The Decline.

Health Matters... 1991 found me very ill and even more depressed than I had ever been, in my life. I was forty and my health had plummeted as never before. I don't know why it was, but hitting the big four-0 was a bit of a life-stopper for me. I would often think and still do that if women could avoid being forty I am sure we would all be that much happier knowing that we would not have to endure the difficulties most of us are prone to, upon reaching that dreaded age.

To add to my affliction and problems upon hitting this particular birthday, the hysterectomy I had to have, plus the infection I fell victim to straight afterwards, all took its toll on my poor body. And, although a couple of months down the line I was, in effect, better and from my doctor's point of view, had fully recovered from the operation, my body didn't appear to have grasped the message and the mental scars had scarcely began to heal. I truly believe that my body was in a state of aggravated shock from all that had occurred in my life up to that time.

I have heard it said and feel sure it is true, that it takes around two years to recover fully from a pregnancy and the birth of a child and that it takes two years or so to grieve fully for a close family member who has died. It probably takes around the same amount of time to get back on your feet again after a divorce and it no doubt takes around two years to become fully familiar and totally at home in a new house. Therefore, looking at it from a comparable, but opposing point of view, it must have been around two years or so from my first meeting with Shmel that my body started to react violently to the aggravation I had been under for most of that time.

Shmel and I had first met in the early part of the summer of 1988 and by 1990 my body had gone into a kind of disturbing state of distress, for soon after I had recovered, from the hysterectomy I started to gain weight. Okay, okay, I know it is not *that* unusual for women to gain weight after a similar gynaecological trauma, but then, to add to my body's sudden upset, upheaval and weight gain, I was having to cope with this massive menopausal jolt, on a par with running headlong into a ten-ton elephant who refused to move out of the way. What with night sweats, when I would awake suddenly in the night feeling like a burning volcano with its boiling lava overflowing profusely. Or just when I went to talk to someone I suddenly went a violent red and proceeded to leak, copiously, like a colander when it had just had a saucepan of boiling peas emptied into it. How embarrassing is that? Then there was the feeling I sometimes got in my hands, arms and legs, just as though a million ants were crawling all over me. Ugh! I constantly felt as though all my energy had disappeared, never to be found again, for I was lethargic and feeling exhausted most of the time.

The S.S. Break-up... While desperately trying to nurse my sad body back to some semblance of normality Shmel's partnership with his Steven Seagal look-a-like pal, that had started off so promising, had well and truly gone down the chute, for although the two appeared to get on remarkably well at first, this ill fated venture was to put an end to all that. It transpired, or so I was later told by a mutual friend, that once the new business had been set up and everything started to take off, the unlikely pair fell out, big time.

Shmel had this dreadful habit of winning people over by charming the socks off them and just when all seemed to be going along nicely he would turn nasty or find fault, when they were least expecting it.

People like me, his ex-wife, and a few other women no doubt, who loved him in some way or other took the failings along with the man, but most people, men in particular would not, consequently, problems were bound to arise. Inevitably then, a few months into Shmel's new business venture, he and this 6' hunk of a man had a big verbal punch-up. Now, from what you know of Shmel, you will have surely realised that he wasn't a one for physical violence of any kind, but when I heard about the big row he and S.S. had I like to visualise this pretend scene in my mind's eye?

I can just see S.S. standing 6' plus in his stocking-feet and Shmel standing the whole of 5' plus, and that was with his shoes on. I like to imagine Shmel completely losing his rag over something quite mundane and lashing out. I can just 'see' his arms and legs flaying about with his head down and S.S., having reached out, placing a huge hand over the top of Shmel's head in order to keep him at bay until the angry little aggressor had worn himself out then, without any hint of ceremony, S.S. promptly tossing him out of the office and landing in a heap on the dusty pavement.

For real now! Can you not see the secretary and the other office staff splitting their sides with laughter? Especially when Shmel, still hot under the collar and all patchy-red from his skin problem, stalked off down the road all heated up, with nothing in hand to dowse the flames? Shmel, poor soul, was destined to fail, for once off the scene the company has since become a very successful business with a very healthy turnover. Shmel, on the other hand, who thought up the idea in the first place, never stopped whinging and saying how *he* could and should have had some of the action. And no doubt he could and should have, if he had not been 'Shmel the loser'…

Notice To Quit… Within a month or so of me returning home after being discharged from the hospital, having been made bankrupt and Shmel having being unceremoniously thrown out of his business partnership, I was given notice to quit my lovely house. I was devastated. The landlord was very nice of course and gave me a lot of old spiel about letting property being a real big problem to him; consequently, he said he had no other choice, but to put my rented house on the market. I felt desperate when he gave me just one month to vacate my home.

In my miserable state, I imagined my life being lost somewhere along the same path as that of the tinker and drifter, constantly being moved on from one place to another. I imagined my children and I having to live out of boxes and suitcases, with no real and permanent hook on which to hang our hats. I would sit for ages nursing my depression and regretting ever having sold the apartment that my brothers had been generous enough to have set me up in before I embarked on this tenuous relationship. It didn't bother me too much knowing that my lovely apartment belonged to the bank; it would have just been comforting for me, at this time, to know that there was no landlord to give me notice to quit. At the end of the day, I had in effect; given up the place of my own free will and was now living to regret it very deeply.

The New Woman… And where was Shmel all this time? You might well ask. He had done his usual disappearing act and was nowhere to be found, although, he was still supplying me with a generous amount of money.

It wasn't actually true when I implied that he was completely *off* the scene, the fact being, he was not completely *on* the scene either, if you get my meaning. Or, to put it bluntly, he was not sleeping with me at the time. He would pop in now and again, ask after my welfare and update me with some bits and pieces of news. He would then bid me farewell and leave me some money. He seemed to have lost all interest in me as the love of his life, or his sex partner, but then again, I tried telling myself that he was leaving me alone so that I could fully recover from my operation without having to bear any pressure from him. Looking back, I suppose he was doing me a great favour, but at the time I couldn't see it like that and certainly didn't appreciate it. In fact, his lack of presence aggravated me to the extent where I kept wondering exactly whose presence he *was* in.

By this time Shmel had ceased running home to his ex-wife, as, since being divorced she had found herself a new boyfriend. I felt really pleased about her new relationship. For having got to know her a lot better and learning more about her life with Shmel, I had developed a great deal of admiration for her. She was feminine but sturdy; small in stature, but tough. I suppose, living with Shmel for so many years, she had been forced to develop the strong side of her character in order to protect herself and her feelings from this lecherous womaniser. Meanwhile, as the days and weeks wore on, my weight escalated beyond my wildest nightmares and at one point I tipped the scales at eighteen stone.

While I was recuperating and piling on the pounds, Shmel took up with someone new. It seems that after being thrown out of his office and not having this new business venture to concentrate on he must have kicked around for a few weeks not quite knowing what to do. Looking at life from his point of view (if that's possible) he must have felt that he was on a bit of a hiding to nothing. He was newly divorced, and there was no going back to his ex as she had found herself a new man. I was laid up, feeling like nothing on earth and not one bit eager to start up any kind of sexual relationship. He was up to his eyebrows in debt, struggling to keep up the repayments on umpteen houses, apartments and other monies he had borrowed from all over the place. His video businesses were going through a very bad patch, as the cinema had made a big, new comeback. People, it appeared were finding it more pleasurable looking at the big screen as opposed to the small one (or so he kept telling me). And to crown it all, he had been dumped by his mate S.S., so all in all, it must have seemed to him that his life was hardly worth living.

Shmel must have thought deeply about his very existence and decided that, rather than throw himself off the nearest railway bridge and into the path of an oncoming express train, it would be far better to throw himself into bed with a woman, no matter who it was or what she was like, so that is exactly what he did.

Apparently, a woman happened to dial the number of his London hotel bed-sit by mistake…Mmm! After her apologising profusely and he accepting, he asked her if she would like to meet him in the foyer of the hotel for a coffee or whatever. She of course said yes and within next to no time they were lost in love and sex, a commodity he may well have been missing out on for a few weeks. He made sure to keep well away from everyone else while he enjoyed what was on offer morning, noon and night. His new woman turned out to be a thirty-year-old who had two children and a history of drug abuse. Knowing him, he was probably only trying her out with an eye to his future plans, as there was no way he would keep a relationship going for any length of time with a drug-taking slapper.

As ill and depressed as I had been, I had to pack up my belongings and find a new place to live. Shmel quickly got sick of his new flatmate and after taking her contact details he sent her packing. I was not aware of his 'bit on the side' at the time, but I was enlightened, at the first opportunity by a so called - friend.

There were people we both knew who would take great delight and found pleasure in, passing on all the latest gossip about Shmel's transgressions. It never failed to amaze me how these people, who were supposed to be friends, loved to watch the pain and anguish spread across my face when I heard that my partner had been cheating on me, yet again. No matter how hard I tried to hide it, there was nothing more painful than having my feelings of love and pride dashed to the ground in public. Consequently, I never did ask Shmel about the woman he had while I was feeling so ill, I just didn't want to know, I started to do what his ex-wife did, which was to ignore it as much as possible and hope that in the fullness of time it would all go away.

The New House... Nevertheless, once Shmel's latest conquest had gone, he was back on the scene again and together we found a delightfully furnished house in a smart area of Snaresbrook. It lay in a secluded cul-de-sac overlooking a junior school. The new house gave me plenty to think about and do, plus a reason to pull myself together. I also started to work hard to get rid of the ugly fat that I had accumulated so quickly and so easily around my ailing body. Luckily, I was still under the guidance of my doctor and after studying all the wretched problems I had been encountering of late he decided to put me on a course of H.R.T. and fortunately, that assisted in my effort to get well quicker and lose some weight.

Around this time Shmel booked up a number of holidays that I must admit were good, not only for my flagging morale but for my continued recuperation too. Inevitably, I would be allotted the task of checking in the luggage while he checked out the air hostesses or indeed any girls that were around, but quite frankly, I gave up getting too annoyed about this tiresome habit and managed to get on with what I was doing in spite of it. I knew it would take months to get back to my old self so I tried hard to remain calm and composed while taking full advantage of the holidays he provided for me. I never questioned him about affording the holidays as, surprisingly enough, although his businesses were going through a very slack phase they still seemed to be providing enough money for him to buy cars, clothes and anything else he wanted, so meeting the expense of luxury holidays was taken for granted, in fact, I never had to worry about money at all. Anything I wanted he would buy, get or give me, with the exception of his true love and faithfulness, of course.

My Italian Fling… I was absolutely delighted when one day Shmel came over and told me to pack as we were going away to Italy. By the time our departure day had arrived, excitement at the prospect of going was running high, as Italy is one of my favourite parts of the world, I just love it, plus the fact that I was now feeling much brighter than I had for ages. My weight was not quite as low as it could have been, but at least I was controlling it which made me feel happier and more positive about myself.

On the afternoon of our departure to Italy, we went through the usual routine whereby, upon arriving at the airport terminal Shmel would abandon me with the luggage while he went off to explore the airport talent. The only bright spot of the wait was when nearing the check-in desk, Shmel decided to make an appearance to 'help' me with the heavy cases. An elderly couple who were standing immediately behind us asked what part of Italy I and 'my father' were going to. Shmel was not one bit amused at this remark but I must admit that a very satisfying smile spread across my face as we were called over to the next vacant desk. Eventually my 'father' and I boarded the aeroplane, found our seats and settled ourselves down. For once, Shmel had decided to occupy the seat nearest to the window. I wasn't too fussed about the seat anyway as I usually preferred to read rather than gaze out at the clouds. Once the plane had taken off, I got out my book, but, before getting really stuck into the third chapter I glanced around. Shmel was looking out of the window, so rather than talk to the back of his head I stayed quiet. The aircraft was full as usual, but he always tried to book business class, where at least we had a little bit more leg room and as Shmel had shorter legs than me, I always got him to put any hand luggage I wanted to keep handy under the seat in front of him so that I would at least, have a little bit more room in which to put my feet. I never felt guilty about doing this as he always dumped the baggage onto me at the airport, so for him to have a small amount of inconvenience on the actual flight was, I thought, only just and fair.

Whilst looking around the cabin I happened to catch sight of a young Italian guy sitting in the next row from me across the aisle. I could tell he was tall as he sat high in his seat and I could see almost all of his face over the head of the pretty girl who was sitting alongside him. She was busily reading, with her nose in the in-flight magazine, choosing some expensive perfume for her young man to buy, I expect. I sat for a moment, looking at this guy's beautifully groomed hair, glowing so black and gleaming under the overhead spotlights. He looked up and caught my eye and we kept eye-contact for a few moments more than is usual for complete strangers. I thought I noted the faintest hint of a sparkle there, but perhaps it was the spotlights, which I know can often create a false impression.

I can vaguely recall Shmel mumbling something about some adverse weather that was expected to create a small amount of disturbance during our flight that had been announced by the captain just prior to takeoff. I didn't take too much notice of his remark, although I do remember grunting a reply. Shortly after the aeroplane had levelled off and had reached its cruising speed, I opened up my book again to chapter three, but before looking at the first word I sneaked a quick glance across at my handsome Italian and there he was, already looking back at me.

I smiled a faint smile, similar to the faint sparkle I thought I saw in his eye earlier and then looked down at my book. I must admit, I tried really hard to read my book, well, I was reading the words, but you know what it's like when you are reading words but your brain fails to assemble them in any kind of coherent order. My thoughts kept taking me along avenues I didn't want to go down, or perhaps, I *did* want to go down these avenues? I don't know. All I knew at the time was that I became particularly disturbed and excited during the flight.

I constantly turned to look at this guy. I just couldn't help it. It must have been some kind of unexplainable, chemistry between us which I found a little embarrassing, as each time I looked across at him, he was looking at me in return. We more or less carried on like this during most of the flight, except, of course, when we were eating or drinking and our thoughts were otherwise engaged. At one point, when his girlfriend was talking to him, I sneaked a glance across and I saw him flash his eyes away from the item she was showing him in a woman's magazine, and cast a fleeting look over her head towards me.

A couple of hours into the flight Shmel, who had been unusually quiet, mentioned that it would not be too long before the plane started to come out of its cruising speed in order to start the slow descent. The in-flight food and drink had now been cleared away and all that was left was for the air hostesses to do their final run with the duty free merchandise. I was well aware of their timing, from my air hostess days and I knew it would be a good ten minutes yet before the D.F. run started. I decided that this would be a good time to go to the powder room. The toilet in the business section of the plane was positioned discreetly behind a thick, heavy, blue curtain. I spotted my Italian guy briefly as I stood up, but I didn't think about anything very much as I walked towards the curtain.

I flicked the curtain to one side and just as I stepped behind it and was about to take hold of the toilet door I felt a firm, strong hand grasp my upper arm. It all happened so quickly. I was spun around and there facing me was my Italian. I gasped, and before I could speak, he took hold of both my arms firmly and sought my parted lips with his. We kissed passionately for a matter of seconds, even though it seemed to last forever. He released me and drew back, still looking into my eyes. He said nothing, and I stood in stunned silence. I did not speak Italian and I assume, he didn't speak English, but then, what was there to speak about? He slowly lowered his eyes, clenched his jaw, turned and walked away, leaving me standing there speechless, while the heavy curtain swayed gently from his departure. My emotions ran riot. I was so surprised, I realised of course, that we had been engaging in a fleeting affair with our eyes, but this was ridiculous, this was just about the very last thing in the world I expected to happen. My hand went up to my cheek and I felt hot and flushed, so I flicked my hair back and opened the neck of my white top in an effort to cool down quickly. Scarcely a quarter-of-an-inch thickness of blue material had separated us from the other passengers. Rows and rows of unsuspecting travellers were sitting there minding their own business. Shmel looked relaxed, sitting there with his ear-phones in place listening to the in-flight radio. The Italian's lady-friend was lying back with her eyes closed. And, there we were, discreetly hidden behind an innocent curtain, making love.

I stood for a few moments trying to compose myself, desperate to cool off, before I eventually pushed the curtain away and walked back down the short aisle to my seat. I tried very hard to look absolutely normal and to avoid looking across at my Italian lover who was now sitting down next to his lady with his own eyes closed. I took up my seat next to Shmel, who I thought gave me a rather strange look as I sat down. Perhaps it was guilt that made me think that or perhaps it was my racing heart that made me see looks that weren't really there. I settled myself as quickly as possible and took up my book again, but I never did get around to reading the third chapter, well, not on the flight anyway, it also occurred to me later, that I had completely forgotten to visit the loo after all that, but I can assure you, I have never forgotten my Italian affair.

Thinking back and if I am being completely honest with myself now, I am sure Shmel must have guessed what had happened that late afternoon behind the curtain. My temperature had shot up so fast that it blew my thermostat and I am sure I must have tottered back to my seat appearing to be a little the worse for drink. Perhaps if I *had* been drinking it wouldn't have shown up quite so much, but as neither Shmel nor I drank alcohol, he would have instinctively known that something unusual had happened. I have already told you that he was very astute and didn't miss much, so I now think that it was highly likely he must have seen, well, almost seen, what had happened. He no doubt clocked the fact that I kept looking around and if he followed my line of vision he must have seen the Italian guy looking back at me. With this going on most of the journey it is obvious to me now, that he would have watched me going off towards the loo and when he saw the guy jump up quickly and follow me down the aisle. Well…

Then, can you imagine Shmel seeing this mini rumble behind the curtain and then the curtain flick open as the guy quickly returned to his seat all fired up, then a few moments later seeing me totter back to my seat, hair pushed back, shirt open, with a rosy glow on my face and perhaps my lipstick smudged? Oh dear! It's all so embarrassing for me now; I just want to die every time I think about it.

Still, at the time it was very pleasing, rather romantic and it made me feel very special and extra satisfied, believing I had got one over on Shmel. However, having told you my little secret, I must say that for all the years I was to spend with Shmel he never once mentioned my Italian and he never once threw the episode back in my face, despite the turbulence that I, as opposed to the weather, might have created on the plane.

Passing Ships… Shortly after my Italian 'affair,' Shmel took me on another holiday to the beautiful island of Malta. On this occasion, a long standing friend of his had invited us to attend his son's wedding. We decided to travel out a few days earlier than necessary so that we had some time in which to relax and perhaps do some shopping before the big day arrived.

We booked into a very classy hotel and spent most of the first day lazing around the pool. The next morning I had a good look around and although the hotel appeared to have everything we could possible want, I decided to take myself off to the local shops. Shmel was thoughtful enough to ask me if I wanted his company but I said no, as I just adore looking around on my own at times, so, telling him that I wouldn't be too long, I set off.

It was a beautiful day, just perfect for a bit of shopping, so I took a leisurely stroll along the cobbled street that led down to the local village. I stopped here and there to look in the shop windows and browsed around a book shop or two, as I needed to get a greeting card and I thought a book would make a welcome gift for a girlfriend whose birthday was coming up soon. The morning wore on and the sun rose higher in the sky and I soon began to feel very hot and tired so I stopped at the next hotel I came to.

The Hilton Hotel was a large modern building set in a beautiful location overlooking the sea, it was also the perfect spot for me to have a coffee. I made my way up the few steps that led to huge, heavy, glass doors that were opened for me by the concierge. I thanked him then headed straight for the coffee shop, which was situated to one side of the foyer. As I walked past the reception desk, I noticed a very handsome guy in an airline captain's uniform standing there chatting to one of the receptionists. I don't think I am a flirty person by nature but I did stare at him somewhat, as thoughts of my father, and how handsome he used to look in his pilots uniform came flooding back to me. The captain turned and caught me looking at him so, I quickly cast my eyes away and carried on into the coffee shop. I ordered myself a drink and just as I took a seat the handsome pilot came over and asked if he could join me for coffee. I was rather surprised at his sudden appearance, but I looked up at him and smiled. He obviously took my smile to mean yes, so he sat down opposite me. We chatted easily and very casually, during which time our coffees were served. I really enjoyed talking to the captain, it was so good to speak of 'aircraft' and hear the familiar, pilot-type, jargon again and I took the opportunity to tell him a few snippets about my father.

We were not together very long before we finished our drinks and I said that I was going to have to start back to my hotel. He asked me which hotel I was staying in and I told him it was the large hotel up the hill a little way. He said he had been pleased to meet me and hoped perhaps, we might meet again soon, by which time I had picked up my things and said goodbye. Once out of the hotel, I turned and started to walk back. Looking at my watch I could see that I had been out far longer than anticipated. I looked ahead and could see our hotel some way off in the distance towering over the top of some quaint little shops. I knew it wouldn't take me too long to get back if I hurried so I quickened my footsteps. Suddenly, I saw a familiar figure heading towards me, it was Shmel. I was instantly annoyed to think he would come looking for me just because I had gone out on my own for a little while. He was still some way off as yet and had shown no signs of having seen me and as I didn't particularly want him to find me, I suddenly had an idea and taking advantage of some handy cover I managed to squeeze myself in-between some tall bushes that were lining this particular little section of pavement. I stood quite still and peeked between the lush greenery as he gradually headed towards me.

I smiled sneakily to myself, as I watched him come closer and closer to my hiding place, but it was obvious that I had concealed myself well, as he seemed totally unaware of my presence in the bushes. Then suddenly, to my great surprise I saw my handsome captain walk past my hiding place. He was frowning and looking ahead in the direction I had told him I would be going. Surely, I thought, surely *he* wasn't looking for me as well? I couldn't believe it. Shmel and the captain walked closer and closer towards each other and as they crossed each other's path I found it quite amusing to see them pass like ships in the night, both looking for the same harbour and fortunately for me, both missing it.

As soon as they were both out of sight I made a quick dash for my hotel, making sure to take a different route back. I managed to look quite calm and casual when Shmel eventually returned, some three quarters of an hour later, looking all hot, bothered and rather cross because he hadn't been able to find me. Little did he know how quickly I had returned to the hotel, cooled down and composed myself after having had a luxurious dip in the pool and a good giggle at his expense.

We spent the next day quietly, just lazing around. He didn't mention my shopping expedition and I most certainly didn't mention my coffee with the captain. We had a reasonably early night (because Shmel was tired after his long and unsuccessful hike) and of course, the next day was destined to be a very demanding one.

The Malta Wedding... We had been invited out to Malta to attend and help celebrate the wedding of the son of one of Shmel's long-standing friends and it was to be an extremely classy affair. The wedding breakfast was to be held in a smart, local, countryside club, which was all very swish. I had to be sure to look my very best, not only for my own self esteem but for Shmel, as it always made him feel great and very confident when he had a beautiful woman on his arm. Not that I am saying I am beautiful of course, but whatever good features I might have possessed I was sure going to make the most of them.

The next day, wearing one of my favourite designer outfits, I thought I looked really great. In fact, even Shmel remarked on my appearance saying, "Wow! Shar, you look absolutely stunning."

We had a wonderful time at the wedding and the country club reception was superb, everything seemed to go perfectly to plan. The wedding ceremony itself was just beautiful. It was so sincere and the happy couple were head-over-heels in love, you could see by the way they looked at each other. Being a bit of a softy at heart and a total romantic, I was very moved by it all. The couple were delightful, the setting was serene and everything about the day was just perfect, or so I thought... It wasn't until I noticed Shmel up to his old tricks of chatting up anything in a skirt that the magic of the day started to wear a bit thin. I couldn't believe that he would be bothered to chase after anyone else while I was there. After all, I had received so many comments that day, all totally spontaneous of course, as quite a few women as well as men had commented on my looks and attire. How could I possibly look so nice, so stylish and so desirable, as one kind gentleman put it, when Shmel was ignoring me by chatting up other women?

The day had started off so wonderful and here was I, in all my finery, now feeling so utterly depressed and lonely. Everyone seemed to have someone. Me? Well, I stood alone for a lot of the time and had to rely on strangers to talk to and was eventually, more than pleased to leave the place and get back to our hotel. We had only planned to stay in Malta for a week, thank God.

Needless to say, we were not on speaking terms for the rest of the stay and spent most of the journey home in silence.

Once back in England, Shmel went straight back to his hotel bed-sit after he had dropped me and the luggage off at my home. I really felt that I had had enough and was thoroughly fed up with the way he treated me so I decided that there was little else for me to do but end our miserable relationship.

Pants On Landing ... Shmel did not dare show his face for a few weeks and then, as usual, he turned up on my doorstep one morning, early. He came out with all of his usual explanations and excuses, but I was sick of hearing them and our early morning meeting soon developed into a hearty slanging match. We rowed continuously for a good fifteen minutes until I lost my temper altogether. I charged up into the bedroom, with him following of course, our exchanges became even more heated. As neither one of us was prone to physical violence, rather than vent my aggression out on him, I headed instead for my wardrobe where some of his clothes were hanging. I threw open the wardrobe doors and scooped up as many of his clothes as possible and unceremoniously marched them across the room and threw them out of the open window. He went into an anxious flap, waving his arms around in a vain effort to stop me doing my worst, but I was wound-up to such an extent that I went for whatever I could find. I dragged open my cupboards and drawers, grabbing at his pants, socks, shirts and ties, nothing was safe, nothing was sacred, it all had to go and the nearest exit was my bedroom window.

Unfortunately, at that time, my house overlooked a junior school and all this occurred around eight thirty in the morning just as most of the school children were arriving. The kids and their parents thought it was great fun seeing someone's underpants and socks flying through the air so early in the day. They could obviously tell that a major row was in progress, especially when I went to the window with yet another pile of clothes. I could see the upturned faces staring at me, many of the onlookers were giggling and smiling and some were covering their mouths in astonishment as the clothes continued to burst out of the window before fluttering down onto the grass verge below.

When at last my anger gave way to tears I leaned on the window ledge, exhausted. Tears ran down my face as I tried to check my rapid breathing and calm down. I had lost all control again. How could this man cause such feelings of anger and resentment within me? How could anyone have such a hold over my emotional state? You may of course think that I must have been completely mad for putting up with him, but after having been in this... this, so-called, relationship for about three and a half years, what could I do? I was in love with him and I continually dreamed of the day when we would, perhaps, have some kind of normal life, similar to the life I had when young.

I came from a very solid background; my parents had been together for years and were very close. They idolised my two brothers and were over the moon when I was born. In fact, mum would often say, that my dad was so excited to have a daughter that when he went to the local town hall to register my birth he spelt the name incorrectly and that is how I became Sharman instead of Sharmaine, but that was never to be a problem to them, as the old proverb always reminds us that: '*A rose by any other name still smells as sweet*.' My parents and brothers loved me; they were always there and would do anything for me, so it was only natural that I would want Shmel to be the same. Why couldn't he love me the way my parents and brothers did?

Looking back on our strange liaison, it would often occur to me that Shmel must have suffered from some form of male P.M.T. for, all the time he was with me he alternated in this strange type of life-pattern. For three weeks of the month he was caring, loving and very amusing, then for no apparent reason, he would pick a fight or do something else that would undoubtedly upset me. He seemed to spoil for an argument or row at regular intervals; it became very obvious that at times he needed a separation and some breathing space. Whether his behaviour was intentional so that he felt justified to pursue a new love or perhaps go off with one of his many girlfriends I didn't know at the time. I would often try to be honest with myself and look at our life realistically, for I knew that, living with this man was never going to be easy or normal in fact, I knew in my heart it would never last, it just couldn't – No way.

My Girl Friends... I was fortunate enough to have some very good friends around me at that time. I was quite friendly with Anne and I would often invite her over for coffee and a chat. She was always good for a laugh and the laugh was usually at Shmel's expense. Also, there were my faithful friends, girlfriends I had been close to for years. They would constantly try to warn me against Shmel, saying that he wasn't worth all the upsets he caused me and that I was worthy of someone better. Deep down I knew they were right, but I was in love with the man and they were fully aware of that fact. Time and time again they would try to comfort me and bolster my flagging ego, especially when Shmel was on one of his annual walk-a-bouts. But they were resigned to the fact that I loved him and knew that by trying to put me off him, they were doing little else but wasting their precious time and effort.

During one particular separation, a friend suggested that I should try to get out a bit more. "You're never going to find anyone decent if you sit here licking your wounds all the time, you should get out there and find someone new!" And she was right of course.

It was very difficult to find enough enthusiasm to start going out again without Shmel, but after a while and with a great deal of gentle persuasion from my faithful friends I did. Nowhere very grand of course, but I was getting out a bit more. Late one night on my way home from a friends house, I bought myself a popular daily newspaper. I knew I wouldn't be going out now for at least a couple of days and thought this might be a good opportunity for me to catch up on some of the news.

In between looking after the children and doing the general household chores I sat reading most of the next day and in so doing I happened to come across a dating column on the back page with a more, up-market advert that caught my eye.

'**Find your New Love.**' It said in bold print. '**Why wait a moment longer?**'

'Call today, many professional and highly qualified men and women looking for love and a permanent relationship.' So I called!

My Gentle Date… I had to answer quite a lot of questions and give in-depth personal details about myself so that the agency could introduce me to a suitable partner, but once I had put the telephone down I felt rather relieved that I had taken at least one step away from Shmel. At the time, I didn't realise what a glutton for punishment I must have been, for by the end of the week I was booked to go on yet another blind date, this time to meet a gentleman in a well known London Hotel on the Embankment. When making the final arrangements for our meeting I described a distinctive camel coat that I would be wearing so that he would easily recognise me.

It's hard to describe how I was feeling that day. I wasn't really nervous or excited, or even very hopeful; I think I was more surprised, if anything, to find myself actually going through with this meeting. It would have been so much easier to stay at home and not have to go through the tedious rigmarole of meeting up with and getting to know someone new. It is quite difficult for me to explain my actions, but I probably only went through with this meeting because I hate letting people down and if nothing else, I still had some small amount of integrity left.

The day of our meeting dawned and I duly arrived at the hotel with plenty of time to spare. I stood in the foyer for a few moments then decided to go over to the reception desk and ask if anyone had asked for me by name but on reflection, I changed my mind – I thought it would be better to let him find me so I slowly made my way over towards one of the plush armchairs that stood to one side of the reception area. Looking around, I was very impressed with the hotel as it was really beautiful. It was exquisitely decorated and there where large, tasteful, flower arrangements standing about the place. There where huge, crystal chandeliers that hung high in the ornate ceiling and as I looked down from one of the glittering chandeliers, I was confronted by a smiling, handsome gentleman.

"Err, excuse me, are you the lady I….?"

To save him any embarrassment I broke in saying, "Yes, and you are Mr. David Greenham I assume?"

His smile broadened as we shook hands warmly. I can tell you for true, I was very impressed with my date.

He looked to be in his early forties, very smartly dressed and extremely well groomed. He was just a little taller than me and quite broad in the shoulders and I couldn't help but notice how well spoken he was when he introduced himself to me properly. We laughed when he told me how he had been looking around for a lady in a camel coat, wondering what she might be like and how relieved he was when he saw me. This meant, of course, that he must have arrived at the hotel in good time too, something I admire very much in people. I am never late if at all possible and respect people who are also good timekeepers.

He led me through to a beautifully laid out tea room where we were shown to a small intimate table. The waiter brought us tea in a classic, white and gold, bone-china tea pot, with matching milk jug, sugar bowl, cups, saucers and silver spoons, accompanied by a small plate of finger pastries, nothing too fancy, more refined, I would say! A quintet of musicians played at one end of the tea room, mainly light classical music. Indeed, everything that afternoon was extremely civilised and elegant.

Mr Greenham was especially polite and knew just how to treat a lady. He had helped me off with my coat and carefully handed it to a waiter before we sat down and he launched into general chatter straight away so that I didn't feel uneasy. He asked me first what prompted me to sign up with the agency. I thought it best to be perfectly honest so I told him that I had two children and had been divorced for some years and although I had been seeing someone for a while, he was proving to be a little unreliable so I thought of giving a reputable agency a try. He said he understood and that he too had been divorced as his marriage hadn't worked out the way he would have liked. He said he had two teenage children, a son and a daughter and although he saw them as often as he could he felt he needed someone with whom he could share the major part of his life with, so he too thought he would try an agency. We both seemed to want the same sort of things in life so I felt very comfortable with him.

Once we had finished our drinks and he had sampled a pastry or two, my date raised his hand towards the waiter who came over almost immediately with the bill on a small silver platter. He cast a swift glance at the bill and replaced it on the tray and as I got up from my seat and turned to walk away, I saw him take out a smooth, black leather wallet from his hip pocket and toss a folded twenty pound note onto the little tray. So, either it was an extremely expensive tea or Mr Greenham was very generous. I felt very happy as he quickly followed me up after having retrieved my coat from the cloakroom. He then took hold of my elbow firmly and escorted me out of the tea-room and into the plush lounge.

We each took a seat by some impressive, ceiling to floor windows overlooking a small outdoor garden. The sun was shining through a willowy silver birch, creating some dappled shade. I had not felt this good for an age. He sat in one armchair and I sat in another, slightly turned towards each other. A small, round, highly-polished, mahogany table stood in front of us, down beside which I placed my handbag. I laid my camel coat over the arm of my chair and settled myself down. He asked if I would like a glass of wine or a coffee, but I smiled and declined the offer. We both sat back in our seats, calm and relaxed. He was quietly spoken but very precise. We both made comments on the little outdoor garden saying how delightful it was and then we commented on the comfort of the hotel. He then asked me about myself. I told him a few general things; you know the kind of things I mean? Then, just as I finished what I was saying, he took over the conversation and told me a little about himself and his work.

He was very interesting and quite amusing, and he made me feel very much at ease. It was nice to see him concentrating fully on what I was saying when I was talking, and it was very noticeable how, apart from an occasional glance at the garden his attention was focussed entirely on me, a pleasant change from most of the conversations I had with Shmel when we were out. Only once did I see him look around and that was when someone called out from across the foyer, in fact, we both looked up, then realising it was not for either of us we looked straight back at each other. We must have been chatting for at least another hour before I looked at my watch and decided it was time for me to make my way home.

He said that he had had a very enjoyable afternoon and asked me if he could see me again. I said it would be a pleasure, so he suggested that I join him the very next day. He told me he was a lawyer, a Q.C. in fact and that I could meet him at lunchtime in the court house where he was to stand in for the judge. Taking a business card from his wallet he wrote down the address of the court house were we planned to meet. I happily agreed, saying that I would have to make arrangements to get my children picked up from school and given tea by a friend of course, but as that wouldn't be a problem, I said that I looked forward to meeting him again. I put the business card away, safely in my handbag and thanked him.

"Well, I'll see you tomorrow then!" he smiled as we shook hands warmly and in a very gentlemanly manner he leaned forward and kissed me on the cheek. I picked up my coat and threw it over my arm and with my bag in hand I took my leave, turning a couple of times to wave farewell. I had had a truly pleasant afternoon.

Who Needs A Psychiatrist?... You will not be one bit surprised when I tell you that I never did meet my gentleman friend the next day or any day since, as Shmel got in touch with me that very same evening. It was just as though he knew instinctively when I was on the verge of straying. I hadn't seen or heard from Shmel for weeks, but once he did telephone me it seemed as though he was suddenly on the phone every five minutes. It is not an exaggeration to say that he was extremely persistent if he wanted something. No matter how annoyed I was with him or how off-hand, if Shmel decided it was time to have me back, he would not stop until I was his. He would think nothing of telephoning me constantly day in and day out, telling me how much he loved me and how much he missed me and how he couldn't wait to see me again. I loved his voice and he knew it and he would keep on talking to me, persuading me, urging me to go back with him again and again. He would wear me down mentally and physically. His onslaught on me was relentless once he had made up his mind and the fact that I loved him and needed the love he could give me, I inevitably gave into his charm and seduction. I had lost and he had won. I had lost my gentle date and missed what could have developed into a very satisfactory relationship and Shmel? Well… He had won me over, yet again.

About this time I was becoming increasingly worried about my weight problem. None of my clothes fitted me and it was almost impossible for me to fasten most of the waist-bands on my skirts and trousers. I would look despondently at my beautiful designer clothes hanging lifeless in my wardrobe and long to be slim again. I would often feel that there was no accounting for my weight gain as I was eating exactly the same as in the past and had never had such a worrying and frustrating problem before and yet I knew for sure it was the result of the hysterectomy I had undergone during the early part of the year. I had been assured by the doctor that once my body had become accustomed to the biological changes everything would be alright and my weight would return to normal, but I felt very frustrated by it and couldn't wait to get back to my former self.

Unfortunately, instead of my weight stabilising as I had hoped, it rapidly reached new and unbelievable proportions, so I started to look around for help. I checked out all the fad diets of the day and tried everything else I could think of but nothing seemed to make one ounce of difference. Eventually, I was referred to a private clinic by my doctor. Shmel thought this was an excellent idea and encouraged me to go. The clinic was the Amelia Moorhen Eating Disorder Hospital in Lersott Crescent, London, NW1.

Shmel drove me there the morning I was to be admitted and we both felt quite pleased and relieved that something was going to be done at last. Checking myself into the private hospital with a small holdall of personal stuff, I became almost instantly disturbed by the general state of the place. The room allotted to me for the next seven days was in no better condition, in fact, to say it was grubby and scruffy, is being polite.

During my stay in hospital, I had organised for my mother to live at the house so that she could care for the children so there were no problems for me there. Waiting for Shmel to leave was my biggest problem, as I needed to contact my mother to inform her of my predicament, for I had decided that there was no way on earth I would stay at this place for a full seven days as it was too dirty; I even noticed traces of dried blood on my bed-sheets. Ugh!

It transpired that the hospital had been set up some years earlier for people who were mainly suffering from anorexia and bulimia and I saw no one besides myself suffering with obesity. The clinic seemed to be full of people who were starving, thin and emaciated, which made me look gross and even fatter, than I actually was.

Upon my arrival at the clinic I was assessed by the specialist and given a plan to follow in order to assist me to manage my weight more successfully. My set program also included regular sessions with the house psychiatrist. During my first session with the analyst I was encouraged, with the help of a relaxation technique to 'let go' all my troubles and talk them out in an effort to get to the root of my problem. I did 'let go' plenty, telling him about my recent health problems and also the serious problems I was having with my two-timing partner. Consequently, at the end of the session the doctor put down his pen, took off his glasses, leaned back in his chair and said,"Frankly, I don't think you have the sort of eating disorder that we can prescribe medication for. I believe you are in the wrong kind of hospital, indeed, if anyone needs to be in hospital talking to a psychiatrist, it must surely be your boyfriend."

The doctor continued to say, that he thought Shmel must have many deep-seated issues that needed to be addressed and it was he who had the problems and not me. Naturally, I was delighted with his diagnosis, but the doctor did conclude that my metabolism was probably out of sync., owing to my recent hysterectomy and if I watched my diet closely, sooner or later my body's metabolic rate would settle down resulting in a more manageable and steady weight, as opposed to the worrying yo-yo problems I had been encountering of late.

That afternoon Anne came in to visit me. I told her all about the dreadful state of the hospital, the condition of some of the other patients and I recounted the remarks made by the psychiatrist. Anne said she fully understood what the doctor had said about Shmel and thoroughly agreed with him. Moments later Anne dived down into her bag and produced a pack of four delicious-looking, sugar-coated, yummy, jam doughnuts and in the privacy of my grubby room we ate them with great relish.

When Anne had left and I was alone once more I became ever more isolated owing to the peculiar atmosphere about the place, for when I did venture out of my room and saw some of the other inmates most of them appeared to be distant, indifferent and uncommunicative, some seemed confused and positively 'spaced out', so I tended to keep myself to myself and stayed in my own room as much as possible.

The Coincidence… Although I thought that my short stay of just two days in the 'eating disorder' clinic was a waste of everyone's time, especially my own, I must admit that I did feel a little comforted by being told yet again, that my weight would eventually stabilise. With those words still ringing in my ears I was delighted to discharge myself and return home. Shmel it seems was back in my life, for a while at least, while my weight continued to fluctuate, mainly in the upward direction, making me feel unwell and very miserable. Perhaps it was my physical state that made me feel so depressed. I was constantly worrying about my health and although Shmel could work his magic on me when he was around, he was of no help during the days we were apart, especially when I was left alone battling with my weight problem and the fatigue I was plagued with.

I became extremely fretful and anxious and must have exhausted the Harley Street doctors by the amount of times I went to see them, so I was very fortunate when one afternoon, by mere coincidence, I met a resident doctor at one of the surgeries at the Whipps Cross Hospital, in Leyton, who had treated my son for a problem some years before. We exchanged pleasantries and he casually asked after my health in general. I poured out my troubles to him unashamedly and after listening quite intently, he suggested that I should, perhaps, have my blood tested for diabetes and thyroid dysfunction. I thanked him for his help and then booked up to have these tests done as soon as possible and in due course I was informed of the results.

I am not quite sure whether I was relieved or worried when both tests-results came back positive, but it sure helped me to understand the problems I had been experiencing with my weight-gain, the awful tiredness and the despair I had endured for so long. Thankfully, once my problems had been identified I was immediately called back to the Harley Street surgery where I was told that my medical condition could be treated quickly and easily, and I was duly given medication that started to change my life and health almost immediately. Fortunately, it wasn't too long before I began to feel much better in myself, I was starting to feel like the old Shar again, until that was, I noticed a mole on my leg that had quite suddenly turned a menacing colour and had become rather irregular in shape. Back to the doctor I had to go and after a series of tests I was told that I had a skin melanoma that would have to be removed sooner, rather than later.

Once again I became mentally traumatised, fretting about my children having to be constantly looked after by my mum, friends or childminders, while I was going through agonies worrying about what would happen if my skin cancer should spread, plus all the other anxieties and fears that accompany this dreaded condition. Needless to say, by this time, I was getting little or no support from Shmel, who always seemed to disappear off the scene just when I needed him most.

Française Doute... During these long months of worry, when I was trying to come to terms with a multitude of illnesses, I took the opportunity to go on a couple of holiday breaks to France with Anne and her boyfriend. The trips were pleasant enough and I was glad of the rest and companionship. Anne and I got on very well considering I was in a relationship with her former husband, although, it did take me a time to fathom out exactly what kind of relationship, or should I say friendship, we did have. For most of the time it was very good and rewarding but there were times when she would seem a little distant and cold, to say the least. I used to worry about this somewhat, but I did know and fully understood how and why women can be difficult to comprehend at certain times, owing to the fact that their hormones can play havoc with their general temperament, so I more or less put it down to that, I knew full well what it was like trying to tackle the dreaded menopausal phase...

Eventually though, I learned that when Shmel and I had rowed and were not on speaking terms instead of running back to Anne as in the past, he would go skulking back to his bed-sit and from there he would contact her by phone and tell her stories about me in a bid to blacken my character. He would take every opportunity to tittle-tattle about me, rather like an old woman gossiping over the garden fence to her nosy neighbour. It was something he always did, apparently, in order to make himself appear good in the eyes of others, especially his ex. This would explain why, at times, Anne would go cold on me and appear to melt away into the background.

Thinking about it rationally, I would imagine that she didn't particularly want to be drawn into her ex-husband's arguments, which I suppose is understandable, as it could have made things rather awkward between us, for Shmel and I argued far too frequently for comfort. Whereas, in contrast, when Shmel and I were on speaking terms and everything was hunky dory, she would be all over me like a dose of chickenpox, wanting to catch up on all the gore, I suppose.

C'est la vie!

1992

Chapter 5 – Changes.

The Name Game... Never having been the type of person who indulged in casual affairs, I felt a great need to be settled so I would often discuss with Shmel the way our love affair was going and say how important it was for me to have a more permanent relationship with him. I wasn't too sure if he was ever taken with the idea at all, but we had been dating for about four years by now and I was growing ever more impatient to be settled.

I may have been a little old fashioned, for sure, but I had always felt rather uncomfortable with our relationship the way it was, so eventually I decided to have my surname and the surnames of my children changed to his by deed pole. Once it became official, I felt a whole lot better about us as a 'family', I also thought that there was a possibility that my children would be able to relate to him better if they could think of him as their daddy.

The Proposal of Marriage... Whether it was this that prompted Shmel to reconsider our relationship is difficult to say, but believe it or not, shortly after changing my surname to his, Shmel decided that we would most *definitely* get married eventually. I was absolutely delighted, because he knew I hated the way we were living; it wasn't one thing or the other. I would often tell him how much I yearned to have a normal life with a husband and kids.

When I remarked on the matter of getting engaged Shmel said that naturally we would, and as his cousin worked as a jeweller in Hatton Garden he said he would take me there one afternoon so that we could discuss and decide on the type of engagement ring I would like.

I love diamonds, but instead of going for the traditional solitaire I decided to have a square cut diamond with baguette shaped diamonds either side. The design was considered in great detail and eventually finalised with my ring measurement being taken, all I had to do then was wait until the ring was ready to be picked up. At this time I was very happy and truly believed that I was in the process of acquiring what my heart so desired.

I made arrangements to have an engagement party at my home in Redbridge. I didn't want anything too big so I just invited a few members of the family and some friends. There was my mum, of course and Anne and Dave. There were my two teenage children and Shmel's three youngsters, who were in their early twenties. Our engagement party was not a lavish affair, just a pleasant day with the family, during which, Shmel officially proposed and gave me the ring. It looked so beautiful on my finger; the ring itself wasn't overly large but was stunning and very classy, just by looking at it you could tell it was worth a pretty penny. The presentation of the ring completed the celebration and made everything perfect for me. The only thing that marred my day was the fact that neither of my brothers would come to help me celebrate as they both knew of Shmel's reputation and certainly didn't approve of their sister being with this man, let alone getting engaged to him. They had warned me on many occasions of Shmel's turbulent past, but at the time I thought, perhaps, having a good and loyal wife who would give him everything he could possibly want, there was every chance he might change for the better and that eventually, my brothers would be pleased and proud to consider him as an important member of our family.

Shmel's Family... Being officially engaged went a long way to making me feel more like part of Shmel's family. He had four children in all, a son from his first marriage, who he never saw and three children from his long marriage to Anne. There was also his mother.

None of us really got on very well. Not that I am an unfriendly person, in fact, I love people and I am usually keen and eager to be friends, but I always felt that there was a weighty barrier separating us. I never could understand why this should be, but I did eventually find out that whenever Shmel and I had rowed he would not only telephone Anne and tittle-tattle to her, but he would also seek out his mother and tell her all about our personal affairs, which would make me appear like a shrew or some kind of she-devil that he could not control. Shmel had this canny ability to twist events and conversations around so that only *he* appeared in a good light. Knowing this to be so, I cannot really blame his family for disliking me so much, as they could only go by all the bad things Shmel told them about me, which I can only assume must have been pretty awful.

Naturally, his mother would pass these stories onto Shmel's children causing them to dislike me also. All except, for his youngest son, who managed to stay unbelievably neutral and accept me for who I truly was. Despite trying on every occasion possible to close the gap between us, I made no headway at all with the son and his daughter who had a very poor and off-hand attitude towards me. Nevertheless, I tried to remain calm and resigned myself to the fact that rather than be friends we would have to learn to tolerate each other. As for Shmel's mother, I had been taught from young to treat my elders with the utmost respect, so I automatically made every effort at all times to show her the kind of respect she deserved.

Having come from a very stable and conventional background where love and respect had been instilled into us from small children, I truly hoped that one day our two families would be able to meet, talk and be friends. I longed for the day when Shmel and I would be able to welcome anyone from either of our families into our home. I'd often try to imagine a family member knocking on the door, and coming in for a nice cup of tea and a pleasant chat. I would perhaps, envisage inviting them all over to dinner on occasions so that they could sample my cooking, because even though I say it myself, I am quite an accomplished cook and always try to present a well laden and attractive table. Unfortunately, the reality of it all was that it was never going to happen, although at the time I was ever hopeful.

Now that we were engaged, I begged Shmel to give up his bed-sit, the pokey hotel room he had rented for many years in the West End of London. I so wanted us to be a proper family and live the way normal families lived. What I really wanted was for Shmel to give up his bed-sit willingly and move in with me and my children permanently. At the time he was still only staying with me one or two nights a week which for me, wasn't enough. I wanted Shmel to entrust himself to me, body and soul.

The Nose Job... Although I wanted Shmel to live with me in a proper manner I did have a major problem with him, especially when he did stay overnight and that was his very loud snoring. I would find it almost impossible to go to sleep while the dreadful din he made was going on. On many occasions, I would give up and try to get some sleep on the sofa in the other room, where, I could still hear the noise, but at least it was a little more tolerable. The longer we were together the more I realised that this problem he, or should I say *we* had, would have to be resolved somehow if I was to ever going to get some restful nights with him. I spoke about this problem often and he would always say something like, "Well, I can't help it, it's just one of those things, it's a good job I have my bed-sit, at least you can get a few good nights rest."

But that is what I *didn't* want; I didn't want him to have an excuse to keep the bed-sit, it seemed that no matter what I said or did, he most definitely would not give up his private space without a fight.

However, I must give him his due and say that; he *did* try everything possible to reduce the snoring and whatever I bought for him he would try out. But despite the fact that I would always be on the lookout for anything new coming onto the market, I never found anything that would do the trick and shut him up. As a very last resort, I suggested he might think about having surgery. We talked a lot about it and I finally persuaded him to go and consult a specialist about his problem. The doctor checked him out thoroughly and said there *was* an operation they could perform that worked quite well for the majority of patients, so with an ever increasing amount of gentle persuasion from me he decided to go for it. He was quite terrified during the days leading up to the operation and I never quite knew if he was fearful of the surgery procedure or whether he was afraid that if the operation *did* cure his problem I would then insist that he gave up his bed-sit so that we could live together like a proper couple.

Eventually the operation went ahead and in the days that followed, Shmel did little else but whinge and whine and feel sorry for himself. He also kept complaining about how painful it had all been for him, so I went out of my way to make an extra fuss of him and I made every effort to give him lots of sympathy. But, after going through all that and having to put up with weeks of his moaning and groaning, to my dismay, the operation made absolutely no difference at all and I felt very saddened to conclude we would never be able to share our double bed for the whole night. On top of which, Shmel was extremely angry with me for having insisted he go through all the pain and trouble for nothing. I must admit, that it was me who put a lot of pressure on him to do this and towards the end I virtually insisted he went through with the operation, but I swear to this day, it was meant for the sole purpose of enriching our relationship.

Unfortunately, I never did get to spend many full nights with Shmel. I can even recall most vividly, going away with him for four days to a very swish hotel and spending every night sleeping in the sunken bath!

The Hampstead Apartment... Shmel was very secretive and would avoid, whenever possible, confiding in me as to what he did or where he went, but on the other hand, he wasn't very discreet either and it was not one bit unusual for him to leave letters, tickets or receipts lying around the place for anyone to see.

By now we had been going out together for over four years so I was quite surprised to learn, quite by chance, about an apartment in Hampstead that he had hitherto, kept under wraps. I knew he liked space, in fact he liked a lot of space and that's why I believed he wanted me to get rid of the lovely apartment bought for me by my brothers and move into larger accommodation. I often felt very confused by the way Shmel conducted his life, as I could quite understand him going off for weeks at a time when I was in a smallish apartment, but he would do exactly the same after we had acquired and settled into a larger rented house. As he always appeared to detest small places I was more than surprised when I found out about this additional rented apartment that he had acquired in Hampstead. I couldn't understand why on earth he wanted yet *another* place, besides the bed-sit he already rented in London.

It was absolutely no use whatsoever asking him for an explanation as to why he did the things he did, so I used to invent explanations in order to justify his actions to myself. What I figured was, as the London bed-sit was quite small he may have become bored with it at times and perhaps needed somewhere else with a different outlook and that it may have been just a little bit roomier. This self-explanation kept me reasonably happy for a while, until one day he wanted to collect something from the Hampstead pad. It was when we happened to be out for a drive in the car one day, when he suddenly said that he would stop at his place to pick up something. When he eventually pulled up outside his new abode, I took the opportunity to go in there with him, only to find, to my amazement, that it wasn't a particularly big or smart place after all. When I asked him why on earth he wanted yet *another* place, especial a non-descript one at that, even he had to admit that it was a complete waste of money, not that he lacked money of course, as despite the general slump in business, his video shops seemed to be doing remarkably well at the time; even so, I couldn't see any reason why he should throw his hard earned cash down the drain.

As time went by I had to resign myself to the fact that we were never going to live like a 'normal' couple. I also had to come to terms with the fact that his snoring had not been alleviated by the surgery he had undergone, and that the likelihood of it ever being cured was bleak. I'd often get terribly depressed about it all, especially the way in which things had worked out between us, but at times like that I would force myself to look around at all my possessions and my life in general. Having been set up and now settled in a lovely house with my two children I was very happy, so when comparing my life to that of many other people I considered myself to be very fortunate. Other than the fact that my partner only spent a couple of nights with me each week, I was content at home, there was plenty of money coming my way therefore, there was little for me to moan about as most things in my life were fine and dandy.

Eventually I gave up and against my better judgment, I decided to stop bugging him about living with me properly; I felt that I had no other choice than to resign myself to our unusual lifestyle.

1993

Chapter 6 – The Legacy.

A RAT by Any Other Name... Mum and I were very close and we made a point of always keeping each other updated with most of our personal affairs, plus any important family news going the rounds, in fact, we were happy in each others company and got on remarkably well. Somehow though, she never actually came to terms with my engagement to Shmel. She really didn't like him very much, didn't trust him and most certainly didn't like the way he treated me.

My mother is a very good judge of character and she would often say things like, "Shar, this man is no good for you," or, "You're a lovely girl; you could have done so much better for yourself."

I ignored her warnings, of course, as I was determined to make a real go of it with my man. I thought perhaps she was annoyed with me because I had become engaged to Shmel and had changed our surnames to his. From mum's point of view, any major changes such as official name changes and the fact that I now had an engagement ring meant that there was definitely a wedding on the cards and I don't think she really wanted that for me. If it had been with anyone else, I am sure she would have been very happy, but with Shmel, no way!

She always did try to get on with him and tolerate him for my sake, but deep down, I now believe she had grown to dislike him fervently. She could see right through him and as a mother she found it very painful to observe the way he used me and took me for granted. On one occasion when I happened to be going through a particularly bad patch with him, mum called him a rat. And strangely enough, that name has stuck with him ever since. Even now, most members of my family and almost all of my friends, when enquiring after him, will refer to Shmel as the RAT and on hearing that expression, there is never any mistake as to whom they are talking about.

The Snub... For most of his adult life, Shmel had suffered badly with a miserable complaint, whereby his skin, especially on his face, head and hands would become very scaly, itchy and sore. Because of this he had to go for regular checkups to the London Hospital in Whitechapel. Sometimes I would be able to go too, but on one occasion when I couldn't, he came home that afternoon very upset and depressed.

When I saw how miserable he was on this particular day I asked him what the problem was and why he looked so down. He proceeded to tell me that while he was sitting in the hospital waiting room that morning he had noticed a young man in his late thirties with the very same problem as he. He sat looking at the young man for an age; for he thought the guy looked familiar and that he vaguely recognised him, although, he couldn't think from where. He said that he so wanted to go over to this man and talk to him about the debilitating problem they were both suffering with, but decided against it as he was acutely aware of the embarrassment that this condition causes. The man's appointment was scheduled before Shmel's and when eventually a nurse called the young man in, to Shmel's surprise he had the same forename as his first born son, a son that he hadn't seen in years. Shmel was left alone in the waiting room having to come to terms with the fact that he had been sitting in the same room as his own son all that time without realising it.

Shmel had already told me that he had been married to a young girl many years before. Apparently, the marriage was quite brief as he had met Anne soon after and had decided to divorce his young wife. Unfortunately, a child had already been conceived between Shmel and his first wife, but the divorce went ahead, even though she was deeply and madly in love with him. Shmel said, naturally, he regretted having to divorce his first wife, especially as she was pregnant, but he was in love with Anne and it was just one of those things.

Evidently, the broken-hearted, young, mother-to-be gave birth to a baby boy a few months later and Shmel did get to see his son on occasions as the child was growing up. Eventually, the young girl re-married and on so doing, she cut all ties with her son's father and her new husband adopted the boy and brought him up as his own, which resulted in Shmel losing touch with the boy he had grown to love. Shmel deeply regretted never having known his son properly and longed to put matters right. So why was he so upset after having met his long lost son at last? Well...

He told me that after his son had gone in to see the doctor he failed to reappear, by which time Shmel had been called in by a nurse for his assessment. While being examined by his doctor, Shmel asked after the young man who had been treated before him and the doctor was able to confirm Shmel's conclusions. The doctor also told him that the young man had been admitted onto one of the wards to have extensive treatment on his skin. Shmel told the doctor that he knew how painful that was and that he would like to go up to the ward to commiserate with the man. Shmel was so thrilled at meeting his son at last, that once his own appointment had concluded he quickly made his way up to the ward where his son was being treated, only to be told by the nursing sister that the man had given her strict instructions not to allow anyone in to see him, no one at all!

Shmel fought back the tears as he related his sad story to me. He said that he was absolutely gutted to think that his son didn't want to acknowledge or even speak to him. But after all, if he had only ever given his son a painful skin complaint he couldn't really have expected him to start playing happy families after an absence of around thirty years could he?

Today: It seems obvious that Shmel's son must have recognised him instantly from photographs his mother had shown him and probably decided that he didn't want to become involved with his father again as....
Four years after Shmel's first meeting with his son, he was to meet him again at the same London Hospital. Determined, this time, to become acquainted with him, Shmel chatted to his son saying that he would like to take him out to dinner and introduce him to his half brothers and sister in a hope that they could meet and all become friends in time. Eventually, his son gave him a business card just before they parted.

Shmel, of course, was delighted and the next day he rang the number on the card umpteen times unsuccessfully, only to discover that the number was obsolete. Shmel has since had to live with the distressing fact that, other than another chance meeting, he was never going to have the pleasure of his son's acknowledgement and respect. My mum, it appears, was not the only one who disliked Shmel.

1994

Chapter 7 – A Fool Such as I

The Keeper... Shmel seldom discussed things with me or asked my opinion on anything really important and unbeknown to me, at the time, he had signed yet another contract for an apartment, this time in Southgate. This new pad was in his home territory, not very far away from his ex-marital home. It was some months before he let slip about the apartment, so I cannot be sure how long he had actually been a tenant. I think he must have forgotten that I didn't know about the apartment and once he had let the cat out of the bag he invited me round to see it.

I never really got used to Shmel's strange ways and sometimes felt that I didn't really know him at all. I would often remark to my mum or girlfriends saying that, the way he carried on, no one would ever believe I was his fiancée. At times, I found it difficult to accept myself and would often feel quite distant from him. There would be no use complaining though, as he was still looking after me and my children and giving me whatever I needed or wanted, financially, that was.

Little did I know, at the time, that it wasn't only me he was keeping? I will never know for sure how many women he had on the go during our relationship although, admittedly, I was beginning not to care very much so long as he was seeing me occasionally and giving me housekeeping money. By now I was getting used to the insecurities that surrounded our union. I had also accepted his strange gypsy-like wanderings that were now a part of my own way of life. I was still the faithful, loyal woman who would wait patiently until he decided to come to me again, forever hopeful that one day Shmel would see sense and settle down with me properly.

With regards to the 'new' apartment, I believe that once Shmel had come clean about this new place it didn't quite hold the same amount of mystery about it, for soon after I had been to see it, he released the tenancy. The apartment didn't go back to the letting agency though, as Shmel's ex-wife Anne decided to take it over from him, as it appeared that the apartment she moved into after her house had been repossessed back in late 1991 had been put up for sale.

Anne's Smart Apartment... The apartment Anne moved into when her house was repossessed was really lovely. It was made even more desirable once she had added her feminine touches. She had quite a few pieces of beautiful furniture and some very expensive statues, pictures and general items. I often went to see her there and we had many a good laugh. She even invited me and my children over for Christmas lunch the first year she was there, which was delightful; she gave us a wonderful day and made us very welcome. At that time, Shmel was nowhere to be seen. I had absolutely no idea where he was or who he was with and frankly, I didn't care at all.

The Shock Video... On one of my early trips to Anne's apartment, after we had indulged in a good girly chat over a cup of tea, our conversation gradually got around to Shmel. After relating some of his most recent antics, she suddenly said, quite mischievously that she has some 'things' for me to see. Being curious about anything to do with Shmel, I urged her to show them to me quickly.

She went into her bedroom and came out with a package and some items of clothing that looked like underwear. She teasingly shook out the undergarments which consisted of a skimpy G-string and matching bra and told me that when she was clearing out her house in order to pack for the move she found all of this stuff in the loft along with a video. Cheekily, she laid the items on the table, I pulled a face at the underwear and turned my nose up as I poked the bra with a finger and picked the panties up between my thumb and first finger. I then turned the video over in order to see the title but it didn't have one. Well, not a real one, it only had a white label with 'Shmel' written in pen on the spine.

Anne was extremely blasé about her little surprise and she seemed to take great pleasure in picking up the video and carrying it across to her player. She located the video into the slot, but hesitated a moment and looked round at me before pushing it fully into the machine. She continued to look at me while the video was running into the start. Naturally, Anne, had already seen the show, so she was more interested in watching my reaction to the sordid, amateurish sex video made by Shmel, showing him and his middle-aged Austrian mistress-come-girlfriend of the time, having sex. I was quite eager to see the video but as soon as the images appeared on the television screen, I was filled with mixed emotions. I was suddenly shocked, disgusted and horrified. I couldn't imagine what else I could possibly see or find out about this awful man with whom I was wasting my life.

Ashamed or What… Fortunately, the offending video tape was quite short and I felt that, once started, I had to bear the sickening scenes to the very end. Once the show had ended, Anne rewound the cassette before ejecting it from the machine after which she carefully put it away in a drawer. She made me promise not to mention the existence or contents of the tape to anyone, especially Shmel. And I never have, up until now. Why? Well for a start I have always felt extremely uncomfortable and ashamed of its existence and I found it difficult enough to think about, let alone talk about. Apart from which, I cringe every time the mental pictures come into my head as Shmel looked awful, even grotesque, lumping around with his girlfriend, even though the woman appeared to be reasonably attractive. The one question that kept bugging me though, was why would Anne ever want to keep an item such as that? A question I have never had answered, even to this day.

My Son's Barmitzvah… The relationship between my mother and Shmel was always strained to say the least, as he didn't like her very much. The feeling was mutual, of course, as she didn't like him either and each time she visited me, she would spend quite a lot of our precious 'chatting time' trying to put me off him. She could see he was no good for me as she thought he treated me abominably and would tell me so each time we got together.

A year before meeting Shmel my dad had died from the complications associated with diabetes and mum would fervently assure me that he would never have approved of our relationship. She often urged me strongly, to get rid of Shmel as he was a waste of my time but unfortunately; all the talking in the world could not put me off, I loved him and that was all there was to it. I was a fool, but then all those in love are fools, are they not?

Mum never really understood our relationship and the extent of the power that this man had over me, and I am somewhat embarrassed to admit that I could not resist him. If he told me to jump, I would jump, and if he beckoned to me, like a lamb I was sure to go to him.

At Christmas time, just prior to the New Year of 1994, my landlord made a rare visit to me. He had previously informed me by letter that he would be 'dropping by to see me' and as I wasn't in the habit of receiving a Christmas or New Year gift from him I feared the worst and I was right in my assumption, as he informed me then and there, that he was considering moving back into the house and that he was giving me one month in which to move out. Once again I was devastated at the thought of moving, I was desperately trying to recover fully from all my illnesses and felt that a move at this time would not be beneficial to my health.

Nevertheless, I had to go whether I liked it or not and because this notice to quit upset me so much and made me feel even more depressed than I did already, just for once, Shmel came up trumps and soon found me a new house. Once again the house was extremely nice and he worked hard to help me get set up. I was also glad of the help given to me at the time by Anne, her boyfriend and a few of my other friends, who enabled me to get established with all haste, and without whose help I could not have managed. Once settled in, my mum would come over and stay with me from time to time. We were a great comfort to each other, as I was still unwell and struggling to take care of the children. For her part, coming to terms with, and fully accepting the death of my father was still a long way off, or so it seemed.

My son Darren was now twelve years old, fast heading towards thirteen, when in our religion and true tradition of his forefathers he would officially become responsible for his own moral and spiritual conduct. In effect – A Man.

I was very much taken up with all the preparations that went towards organising my son's Barmitzvah party. Mum was amazing; she helped me such a lot. She had great experience in these matters, as she had witnessed two of her own sons reach and overcome this important stage in a man's life. Mum saw to it that my son attended Sunday School to learn the special prayers, and we both busied ourselves organising a grand celebration for all of our family and friends. Everything had to be just right, or as right as it could possibly be, for such an important occasion.

During all these hectic preparations the day to day relationship between Shmel and mum deteriorated at an alarming rate. He always needed and wanted to be the centre of attention *all* of the time and just because for once, he wasn't, he took to showing off with me and picking unnecessary arguments, which made things very difficult for us all.

The crunch came one day when I snapped after yet another disagreement over nothing, I decided that I couldn't take it any longer so I threatened to send him packing. What with all the organising and arrangements I had to see to, plus the fact that I was becoming very concerned and anxious, worrying about what the guests would make of his roving eye, frankly, I reached a point where I didn't relish having him at the party at all.

I must have made it so blatantly apparent that he was getting in the way and, realising that he was no longer welcome for the time being, Shmel took the hint and went. At the time I felt a great sense of relief as mum quickly resumed her usual demeanour, thank goodness, and I was able to calm down knowing I wouldn't be hurt by his attention to other women and hopefully, my son would have a wonderful day to remember.

My son's special day went without a hitch. He looked so handsome wearing the beautifully made suit that mother had bought him. Seeing my child become a man was very overwhelming for me, something I will cherish all my life and never forget.

The party was held at The Forum Hotel which was a very plush West-End establishment. It was a very lively, upbeat hotel, just perfect for a young man's special party. There was some form of jazz music being played most of the time, so if nothing else, we were assured that everyone would be kept amused and happy.

All Barmitzvah parties have a theme and my son chose the theme of aircraft. I had a special cake made in the shape of an aeroplane. The theme chosen by my son made it apparent to all our family and friends that his ambition was to follow in the footsteps of his grandfather and become an airline pilot. Mum was thrilled and delighted as you can well imagine while I, being his mother, was very proud. The day was so wonderful, I can't recall one single thought of Shmel crossing my mind, I just took this golden opportunity to enjoy myself and be very happy. I was made happier still in the knowledge that *he* wasn't around to upset, offend or humiliate me in front of all my family and friends.

After the row that occurred during the preparations for my son's party and his subsequent departure I did not hear from Shmel again. As the days slipped into weeks and the weeks grew into months, I began to think that I might have put him off for good and I had to come to terms with the fact that our relationship was over and that he may not be coming back to us ever again.

The Zip Drive… A good few months went by with no word from Shmel, until one day as I came out of my front door there, parked right opposite my house, was his car. Not being able to believe my eyes. I stood stock still, just staring and thinking, surely he hadn't come back to see me again, not after all these months.

The house I lived in was on a busy road, so I had to wait a minute or two before being able to cross safely. I couldn't resist getting a closer look at the car, just to prove I wasn't mistaken. The car was parked on a narrow slip road between two rows of houses, so I had to approach it with some amount of caution. I didn't quite know what to expect, but upon mounting the pavement and drawing closer I could see him sitting in the driver's seat.

As he saw me get closer he slowly let the car window down and called out to me, "Hi!" he said, looking straight into my eyes.

He leaned out of the window a little and asked me if I would like to join him. I hesitated then declined the offer and took a step back. Leaning out of the window a little further he said very quietly, "Please Shar, please join me, perhaps we could go for a short drive." His whole appearance was strange, not strange to look at physically; it was the way he spoke and his general manner. He looked subdued, quiet, even docile, not a bit like the rat-man I had become used to.

After having been initially taken aback by his sudden appearance, practically on my doorstep, I was reluctant, not knowing quite what to do, but I was quite intrigued by his request for my company and I was especially fascinated by his unusual approach towards me. I did try fighting the temptation, but eventually felt compelled to go with him, so rather half-heartedly I walked around the front of the car and as I did so he closed his window and then leant across the seat to unlatch the passenger door for me... Having got in and closed the door behind me, before I'd had time to reach behind for the seat-belt, he had already moved off. He turned sharply at the end of the road and accelerated away. He didn't look at me or say anything, he just kept looking ahead. I shuddered slightly, not feeling completely confident as to what I had let myself in for. What a fool I had been to have responded to his request. I could have kicked myself for being such an idiot, but then, pulling myself together sharply, I considered that the best thing to do was absolutely nothing other than sit tight and hope for the best.

Once out on the open road, we carried on driving in silence for a short while longer then, suddenly, he took his hand off the steering wheel, brushed it over his head and instead of placing his hand back onto the steering wheel he plunged it down into his crotch. Wondering what the hell he was doing I turned to look at him and sat totally gob-smacked as he deftly unzipped his fly and hooked out a rock-hard penis. My God! I couldn't believe my eyes; I must have looked rather like one of those large, eyes-lashed-surprised dollies that are sold in the local toy shops. Looking up at his face he grinned sneakily back at me, as we both looked down again at his best friend standing tall and proud, ready and aching to do his bidding.

How he carried on driving straight is a complete mystery, whilst I on the other hand, was having a mental seizure. In all the years we had been together I had never seen him do anything like that before. Quite honestly, I didn't know what to do. It was obvious that he was in great need of some TLC (Tender Loving Care) or maybe he needed some SSF (I will leave you to work that one out). Needless to say, I'm not going to let on what happened for that would be telling, wouldn't it?

I really couldn't make out what had come over him, he was either desperately hard up or perhaps, he had been missing me to the extent whereby, rather than tell me verbally how much he needed me, he had decided to demonstrate.

The zip-drive, as I like to call it, took us far into the evening by which time, he had recovered his composure and we were both feeling a little peckish. We pulled up outside a classy Chinese restaurant and booked in. We indulged ourselves in a long, lingering meal during which, we took the opportunity to catch up on the most recent events that had taken place throughout our long separation. Eventually, satisfied in all departments, he took me back home and dropped me off outside my house. He wished me good-night, saying how pleased he was to have made it up with me and that he was looking forward to seeing me again soon. I said goodbye and watched as he drove away. I saw him raise his hand to wave farewell, as he sharply turned the corner and disappeared out of sight.

I turned away and shuffled around in my bag looking for my house keys, I took hold of the bunch, found the Yale key and inserted it into the lock. I opened the door wide and as the light from my hallway flooded the path, I knew then that I had once again opened the door on yet another chapter of my life with Shmel.

A Little Flutter... Feeling rather overwhelmed by all that had happened earlier in the week; I gradually became a little deflated when everything settled down to normal. Unfortunately, Shmel didn't contact me after our zip-drive as I had anticipated he would, so I felt rather pleased when Anne and her boyfriend, paid me a visit and invited me out to dine with them at a well-known Casino in Southend-on-Sea.

I love and so enjoy the thrill of a little flutter so I jumped at the chance, saying yes, I'd be delighted to go with them. Anne called by to pick me up on the Saturday evening and we climbed into the back of the car while Dave drove. We had a great time going along, we laughed together and made all the usual wise-cracks that women make about men not much good for anything other that a bit of 'you know what' on a good day that is or, only having one brain cell and that was in their trousers, well...sometimes in their trousers! Laugh, well we laughed until we almost cried.

Anne was a really lovely lady and I had become very fond of her. She was more or less Shmel's age. He was around fifty-seven so she must have been about fifty-five. She could be quite stunning to look at. She was beautifully dressed on most occasions and although her figure was a little fuller than perhaps she would have liked it to have been, nonetheless, she was still a very attractive lady. Maybe it was because we both had fuller figures, our hair was roughly the same sort of colour and we both enjoyed a good laugh, that at times people mistook us for sisters.

It wasn't long before we arrived at the casino and after parking the car we went straight in for dinner. It was a bright and exciting place and the food was excellent too. We had a lovely meal and sat talking for a while before we decided it was time to go and blow some cash. We spent a good while going around the gaming tables. I love a little flutter, as already mentioned, but I tried to spread my money out so that it didn't all go at once. I always managed to lose my money the way most of the other punters did, therefore, I always allotted myself a certain amount to squander and once that had gone, I look for something else to do, or I just took the opportunity to relax.

Having spent about an hour at the tables, playing a game here and taking a chance there, I inevitably lost my stake money. Feeling a little disappointed as usual, for like everyone else, I like to have a little win now and again I had to resign myself to the fact it wasn't going to be my lucky night. It did cross my mind to change up a few more pounds, but with my luck...Oi! I thought better of it. Therefore, after deciding against spending any more of my money, I knew that there would still be the enjoyment of walking around with Anne and Dave or just mingling with the other punters.

After wandering around for some time watching the other players lose their money, I mentioned to Anne, who was still in the throws of losing hers, that I was going to find a seat somewhere, and she said that she wouldn't be much longer before she joined me. I couldn't see Dave anywhere around, but then, not being very interested in him anyway I didn't bother to look out for him I just picked up my bag and made my way through the gaming tables and down towards the end of the casino.

The back end of the casino was beautifully ornate with huge mirrors adorning the walls. Large settees were scattered here and there, that seemed to have been specially placed to comfort those who had lost all. There were a few people sitting in these seats, some looked very depressed and one looked quite the worse for drink.

As my feet were now aching from the new shoes I was wearing, I quickly found myself a seat and ordered some drinks from the waitress, I just sat relaxed, watching the action and waiting for the others to join me. After a while, hand in hand, Anne and Dave made their way over towards me, I smiled at them and gave them a cheery wave. Anne waved back and after sitting down she told me that Dave thought it was going to be his lucky night and hoped he might break the bank after having had a couple of lucky wins. Thinking he was being smart, Anne continued, he put the whole lot on a game of Black Jack and said goodbye, quicker than that, to his money. We laughed as Dave pulled a glummer than glum face, knowing, it was all part of the fun, or so we tried to convince ourselves, as we drowned our sorrows in long, icy-cold glasses of diet Coke and lots of laughs.

More of a Flap... We were still chit-chatting and laughing when I happened to turn and look down the aisle between the gaming tables when who should come walking towards me? Why, none other than Shmel the rat, who had not been around to see me since our zip-drive.

Immediately it occurred to me that Anne must have purposely enticed me here to the casino especially so that Shmel and I could meet up again. But no! For there, following up behind him was this thin, elderly lady wearing a mini-skirt, high heels and a figure-hugging jumper. Not being able to believe my eyes, yet again, in the same week. I thought, Oh my God! Don't tell me this is a 'girlfriend', she must have been sixty if she was a day. After all, even the best makeup in the world could not hide the tell-tale wrinkles that lay like rows of tiny beads around her scraggy neck.

She was, well, what I can say, she was almost indescribable. If you can imagine a little old lady in a teenage get-up... Well, as for myself, I was for the second time in a week, totally and unbelievably gob-smacked. Mind you, I wasn't quite as shocked as he was when he saw me, in fact, you could have pushed him over with the proverbial feather. I saw the look on his face when he realised it was me sitting at the end of the room, he didn't know which way to turn his head, especially when the old girl came up and hung all over his arm like a warn out fox-fur that had seen better days. In those few moments my mind must have somersaulted at least a dozen times, I didn't know what to think.

Was this one of Shmel's new lovers? Oh no! I couldn't believe it.

Did he plan this in order to show her off to me? Oh no! I didn't believe that, either.

Did Anne know about his intended visit to the casino and purposely invited me there to watch the fireworks? No, surely not.

Was it pure coincidence?

There were so many questions rushing through my mind all at once, even I couldn't keep up with them. Then the hurt started to seep into my thoughts, the pain of seeing Shmel with someone else, especially someone so old and used up. Aching with embarrassment, I was left wondering how he could even *think* about being seen around with this old biddy, when he had me, his fiancée, who was only too readily available and constantly at his beck and call.

I could have handled it better for sure, if his new woman had been a beautiful young girl, fresh and vivacious, but to be replaced with an old hag was to me, repulsive and humiliating.

Once I had recovered my composure, well at least recovered it to the point where I could think straight again, I picked up my bag and told Anne I was leaving. As I jumped to my feet Shmel gave me a weak smile. The old hag was so oblivious of it all, it was quite pathetic. He managed to manoeuvre her to one side, keeping her well out of my way as I stormed past them. He must have become suddenly anxious, as he knew of my temper and he wouldn't have been quite sure how I might have reacted. But there was no need for him to have worried, for I made my way directly to the cloakroom where I quickly collected my wrap, only too eager to make my way out of the casino and into the cool, fresh and reviving sea-air.

Anne and Dave hurried out after me and we made our way home in silence. I didn't know and still don't know whether Anne was aware of Shmel's latest conquest, but if she had known she had kept it very quiet. They both knew how hurt I was and there was no mistaking my obvious pain as tears stained my face. I closed my weary eyes and laid back on the car seat and thought that although people often mistook Anne and myself for sisters, I had obviously not become as hardened to the knocks and the facts of life with Shmel as she had. Therefore, I had no option but to presume that this had to be the end of Shmel and I as an item, and no mistake.

The Reckoning… Three whole months went by without a word and I resigned myself to the fact that my time with Shmel had expired for good and that I would eventually have to sort myself out. Fortunately, he was still paying the rent on my house but I knew for a fact that this situation could not and would not last much longer. As time went by, I would jump a little each time the telephone rang for I was realistic enough to know that when Shmel pulled the plug on me there was no way I could afford the rent on my house and would have to move out and find a much cheaper place in which to live.

The thought of all the upheaval involved in moving again would depress me so much, that each time a thought surfaced I would try to push it to the back of my mind, but no matter how hard I tried, those thoughts were never too far away.

One afternoon, having just come back from doing a little grocery shopping I had dumped my bags on the table and was just taking my coat off when the telephone rang, "Hi!" I said, with a cheery voice."

"Hi! Shar it's me…" And then, silence.

Initially I froze. The blatant audacity of this horrible man to telephone me right out of the blue, he had unbelievable bravado.

I flew into an uncontrollable rage and yelled down the phone, telling him to get off the phone and leave me alone.

He kept telling me to calm down and listen to what he had to say. But not wanting to hear what he had to say, I kept telling him to get off the phone, just go away. After all, he had such a cheek to ring me yet again, after all this time and after all the hurt he had caused me.

He kept apologising and saying he was sorry and that he didn't mean to hurt my feelings. He gave me some old spiel about his latest conquest, I really don't remember what he said for sure and it was probably all lies anyway. He kept on talking, his voice becoming calmer, more persuasive while I desperately tried to get my brain into gear. Initially, I took up with this man because he seemed to have lots of money, something I was without and in great need of. Not that I particularly wanted the money for myself; it was mainly in the hope that my children would be able to enjoy a better and more secure future. And now, because of my children I had to try and think rationally and make the right decisions, as the last thing in the world I wanted to do was put their futures in jeopardy.

Shmel was always generous with his money and treated me well financially. When he had money he would give it to me, or rather, leave it in a jar on the sideboard. He would think nothing of leaving me hundreds of pounds at a time and as he also paid the rent on my house, I had absolutely no money worries at all, but then on the other hand, I did feel very beholding to him. It could appear to the outsider that Shmel asked for very little in return for what he gave me. The odd rumble, a good blow-job now and again, kisses and caresses the type of request that any man might ask for, without expecting to give *anything* in return at all. To other people it appeared that Shmel paid well, in fact, very well for my favours. As ever, the only major problem with our relationship was his roving eye and the fact that I could not handle it. Also, I don't particularly want to go over old territory again, but I was truly in love with him and I wanted him to commit himself to me wholly.

Today: If our relationship had been straightforward, such as: I will give you sex and you will give me money, things would have been so much easier, but it wasn't like that at all for me. Admittedly, I went out with Shmel in the first place to help me secure my own and my children's futures, but like all the best laid plans, they somehow went astray. I didn't honestly take into account the fact that my love for this man would come into the equation. Let's face it, when you lend your body to a man, you can just take it back, give it a good wash, walk away with your money and get on with your life. But when you give your heart and your feelings to someone you cannot take them back so easily. You cannot take your feelings and wash the mud off or take your heart back, shower it down and go, can you?

This, then, was the problem I had to come to terms with. And this is what I was weighing up during the time Shmel was talking to me, trying to persuade me to go back with him, and forgive him. I had to ask myself if I could coldly go where I had never been before, to live a lie, to give as little as possible whilst taking all there was on offer. Would I be able to turn my innermost feelings off at will? And have the gut-courage to play Shmel at his own game and win? After all, Anne appeared to have succeeded, but then, I wasn't Anne and had no intention of ever becoming just another one of Shmel's cast-offs.

When my thoughts came back to the moment, Shmel's voice was still purring in my ear, telling me how much he missed me and that he would never do anything like that again. All the while, he was trying to persuade me to allow him into my life again, as he was lost without me, blah, blah, blah. With my mind now calm, his voice was soothing and sensual as he flaunted his magic charm, making me once again powerless and with no more strength left to fight him off I relented and gave in to him. Somehow managing to convince myself that deep down he really *did* love me and that is why he pursued me so ardently. Why would any man, especially a man with the wherewithal to have almost any woman he wanted still be chasing after me? Why would he bother to telephone me morning, noon and night if he were not besotted with me? No man bothers with a woman he doesn't love, after all, women are little but two a penny to a man with money.

Today: I now know that while kidding myself that he loved only me, he was servicing, as well as keeping at least three or four other women at the same time. It has since transpired that he had set each of us up in a house within a short distance of each other. He must have had delusions of grandeur, believing he was some great sultan with his harem of women, all in close proximity to each other and ready to attend to his every need. But, unlike the sultans of old who just walked into the harem and chose a woman for the night, Shmel had to work a bit harder than that, for it seemed that when he fancied one of his women he had to hurt, upset or row with the one he was with so that he could pop across to the next one. Poor soul, he should have lived a few centuries ago!

1995

Chapter 8 – A Friendship Ends.

The New BMW… After yet another spell apart at
the end of last year, 1995 found us back together
again – for a while at least and not knowing quite
how to please me, Shmel decided to buy me a
new car. The car that my mother had bought for
me some years earlier now needed quite a bit of
work done on it so rather than spend a couple of
thousand pounds on an old car, Shmel took me
out to get a new one. There were so many cars
and makes to choose from, but eventually to help
bolster my flagging confidence I decided to go for
one of the small BMW series. At least, the new car would be streamlined,
slim and beautiful, unlike its new owner.

The Book Launch… During the summer of that year Shmel was invited
to a book launch, and I went along as his escort. It was a fabulous party
organised for the introduction of a new book called 'Good as Gold' written
by one of the richest men in this country Mr Ralph Gold who was at the time
living with a lady who Shmel had known many years previously. The author
was and still is, along with his brother David, the owner of the 'Ann Summers'
outlet that sells sexy lingerie, adult gadgets and toys.

It was a very lavish affair set in a huge and sumptuous countryside
mansion. There were valets on hand waiting to park the guest's cars and
once our car had been taken we made our entrance, only to be greeted by the
author himself and his partner. I must be honest and say that the lady looked
stunning in a most beautiful designer dress in my own favourite colour of
lilac. She looked and acted the perfect hostess and companion for her man.
She knew of Shmel from days gone by and knew me vaguely and although this
time she acknowledged me straight away, we didn't actually indulge in any
kind of conversation, we just said polite hello's and moved into a banqueting
room along with the other guests. We were handed drinks and offered select
and appetising snacks by waitresses who were constantly milling around the
room. There was absolutely no expense spared to delight the guests, none
whatsoever.

Among the vast number of invitees was the well-known 'King of Porn' himself, Mr. Dave Sullivan, also amongst the crowd of guests I noticed a very famous boxing promoter. We mingled with friends and associates for some time, while getting acquainted with many of the people I didn't know and just thoroughly enjoyed the small talk that people indulge in on occasions such as these. Once everyone had arrived, the launch ceremony itself took place and we all watched as photographs were taken of the author with his book. This went on for some time as the photographers took pictures from almost every angle in order to get the perfect shots.

Eventually, the photo-shoot was over and it was time for the host to thank his guests for coming (as if they wouldn't have turned up for such an occasion). He then said that there was plenty of food and drink for everyone and that later there would be some entertainment for our amusement. When the guests had had their fill, people were requested to move back a little, while a small stage was assembled and laid down. Once the makeshift stage was ready, two 'Page 3' girls appeared and proceeded to sing and dance for us. The twin girls wore very scanty outfits from which their boobs were bursting forth. The all singing, all dancing girls did appear to be showing themselves off as artistically as their cumbersome boobs would allow, but I must admit that their performance was of no particular interest to me. Nevertheless, it was a truly wonderful event and I recall thinking that the host couldn't have put on a better show.

Still, despite the grandeur of it all, after a while the evening started to drag somewhat and quite frankly I became a little bored as some of the guests became a little incoherent owing to the amount of drink that was freely flowing and eagerly consumed. People seem to change so much after alcohol has entered into the blood stream and where one can enjoy the varied conversations of the sober, drink-induced conversations can leave a lot to be desired, I suppose not being a drinker has its drawbacks and I freely admit that this is one of them. Even so, having just backed away from one such drink related 'conversation' I decided to search for Shmel in order to suggest we make our way back home. Unfortunately, my search was in vain as he was nowhere to be found. I scanned the crowded room looking for his white beard and moustache, unsuccessfully. His disappearance meant that I became rapidly suspicious and I started to form mental pictures of him frolicking with some female or other in a corner somewhere.

Not having seen him for some time, I started to ask around in the hope that someone else might have seen where he had sneaked off to. The first few people I asked gave me little but blank stares in answer to my questions. Eventually, someone said that they had seen him and pointed vaguely towards the stage. I moved as quickly as I could through the crowds of laughing, happy guests and there, making a complete idiot of himself was my darling fiancé. His clothes now sweaty and askew and his face glowing red as he sat ogling the twin girls on stage, sweat was running off his beard as the heat coming from the stage spotlights made him look sticky and dishevelled.

I winced to myself when I looked at him sitting there on the edge of the stage, peering at the dancers as they moved sensuously and provocatively. He was acting as though he was a mere youth of fourteen and had never seen anything like it before! Many of those in the audience were laughing – at him, I felt sure. I just wanted to sink back into the nearest corner. I was embarrassed, ashamed and very sad that this much looked-forward-to event should have deteriorated into this…

Eventually the dancing girls made their exit and the makeshift stage was taken away so that general dancing for guests could commence. Shmel, still hot and bothered made his way over to me. I was absolutely furious with him and he knew it. I angrily suggested that we take our leave and make our way home. He tried to persuade me to stay on a little longer for he guessed that he would be in for a big row as soon as we hit the road. I didn't really want to leave without him so I reluctantly found a seat and sat down with him, anyway, the room had now been cleared. Dance music had already started up and couples were taking to the floor. Suddenly, Shmel jumped to his feet again and to my surprise he made his way over to a couple who were dancing close together. Apparently, Shmel knew the guy but seemed more eager to make the acquaintance of his partner, a tall, slim, long-haired, sexy beauty who was no doubt a model come girlfriend. I watched as Shmel encircled the couple and danced around with them. They obviously didn't want his intervention but on a night like this, people have to grin and bear those who are invasive. I suppose Shmel was hoping that his friend would release the girl for a while so that he could have a hold of something different.

I knew from the past that I would not be able to drag him away from it all. So I moved quietly out of the room towards the entrance hall and retrieved my coat from a waitress who stood looking bored and tired at the door. She gave me a weary, forced, smile as she handed me my coat, the type of smile that I could not find in my heart to return. I just mumbled a low, 'Thanks.' and took my leave… Shmel, obviously not having much luck with the dancing couple, must have seen me depart, so he caught up with me and followed me out to our waiting car and in silence; we made our weary way home.

The Decline of Our Friendship… Once I had managed to get over the embarrassment that Shmel had caused me at the book launch, he said he would take me to Malta for a week, but instead of going on our own he decided to invite Anne and Dave to join us. I wasn't too sure how this arrangement would work, but as we all got on relatively well I convinced myself that the holiday would be fine.

We were all booked into the same four-star hotel, and were happy to arrive and get settled into our relative rooms. It was a lovely hotel and I was looking forward to a good weeks rest with plenty of laughs. At first all seemed to be going well except, that was, for the evenings, when we would either sit around in the small, attractive, outdoor-courtyard or in the cosy lounge.

Everything would start off alright but whatever we talked about, the conversation would gradually end up with Anne and Shmel reminiscing on their past. I realised of course that Anne and Shmel went back a lot of years and that they had spent many happy times on the beautiful island of Malta, not only as a couple but as a family, added to which, they had a mutual friend who lived on the island permanently, a friend they were both very fond of.

Nevertheless, this constant reminiscing got on my nerves and made me feel miserable, as each evening we had to sit and listen to endless stories that Dave and I knew very little or absolutely nothing about. It all came to a head when Shmel invited his friend over to the hotel to share an evening with us.

On this particular evening we all made ourselves comfortable in one corner of the lounge and sat chatting happily. After a short while Shmel's friend walked in. We all rose to our feet, as we were delighted to see him. He was smiling broadly as he walked towards us with arms outstretched. He greeted Shmel and shook hands with him warmly. He turned to me and took my hand graciously and slightly brushed my cheek with a brief kiss. He then turned to Anne and took her into a warm embrace. I watched them as he encircled her with his arms and smiling, he held her close and closed his eyes it was obvious that he was extremely fond of her. When he released her he took hold of both her hands and said, "Well, how are you? It is so lovely to see you again, I have missed you very much."

Anne smiled and replied saying that it had been *so* long and that she had missed him too. He released her hands and they both turned slightly as Anne introduced her friend to Dave. They shook hands briefly and both said how pleased they were to meet each other.

We all sat down and launched into rapid conversation. Shmel and Anne spoke most of the time as they were more familiar with this man than either Dave, who hadn't met him before, or I, who had only met him once when he invited us over to his son's wedding in 1991. Nevertheless, we all made an effort to converse with him, he was such a pleasant man. I asked him how his son and his wife were getting along and he smiled politely and said that they were both fine and very happy.

After a while Dave suggested getting us all a drink. We thought that was a good idea and after telling him what we wanted he went off. It was obvious that he was feeling a bit left out, I know I certainly was, especially as Shmel and Anne went deeper and deeper into conversation with their friend, mainly talking about old times and past events. The evening wore on and apart from the odd word or brief remark, Dave and I spent a wasted evening gazing into thin air. Personally, I thought it was extremely rude and rather thoughtless of the ex's to spend practically the whole evening talking about matters that neither of their partners could join in with.

By the time Shmel's friend had taken his leave and we had made our weary way back to our room I was bored, fed up and thoroughly pissed off. I was only grateful that we would be returning home the next afternoon and that I would not have to suffer yet another evening of reminiscing. I laid awake for hours that night, thinking about the weird relationship we had with each other, but I suppose it was only to be expected that petty frustrations, annoyances and jealousies would arise in our situation. I would feel quite annoyed with Anne if she spent too much time chatting to Shmel and I could only conclude that she must have felt the same emotions as I, when she saw me with the man she still considered to be her husband.

Anne the Troublemaker... I suppose it was inevitable really, but after this latest holiday the relationship between Anne and I gradually petered out. I must admit that it took me a very long time to get over her delight in showing me the sleazy, sex video of Shmel and his middle-aged, Austrian girlfriend.

At the time I was forced to put on a brave face in front of her and had made every effort to come to terms with the disgusting video by telling myself that the film had been made many years before I had met Shmel and that most of us do stupid and outrageous things when we are younger. But at the time, I can remember thinking how upsetting and uncalled for it had been to purposely try and hurt my feelings as much as she had. I tried very hard to pretend I didn't care, but I *did* care and she knew it.

Having always been a trusting soul, taking people at face value, I was having serious doubts about the true quality of the friendship that Anne had shown towards me all this time. And I could only conclude that she befriended me purposely so that in time, she could get her own back, for having been the one serious threat that had finalised the breakdown of her already precarious marriage to the RAT. Nevertheless, I didn't want to lose her friendship altogether so we continued to contact each other, but only on odd occasions.

I can remember inviting Anne over to tea one afternoon, after not having seen her for months, when she spent most of the time telling me about a holiday her and Dave spent with Shmel and his elderly lady friend in Paris, during one of Shmel's long spells apart from me. Anne made a point of saying what a wonderful time they all had and then took great delight informing me of how Shmel and 'Minnie' spent most of the holiday in their room...

I became ever more mindful of the fact that on every occasion possible Anne would revel in telling me something unseemly about my fiancé. It became very obvious that our so-called friendship was never going to be quite the same as it had been during the early years no matter how hard I tried. Eventually our once, close relationship trailed off altogether, after all thinking back, we were not *real* friends, we were just two women vying for the love and loyalty of one man.

I realised of course, that Anne and her ex-husband shared a lot of history, a history that no one could deny her of, yet it would be something that would be denied to me in the future. I was really quite sorry when our friendship finally ended but I suppose that any kind of relationship between us must have been considered bizarre to the outsider.

The Bridge Player... Shmel was a very good bridge player and would often spend an afternoon in a popular West End bridge club, mainly frequented by very influential, middle-aged men and women. At one time I did try to learn to play the game but couldn't quite take to it. I never could find the time to concentrate fully on the game and although it could be enjoyable for a real enthusiast, it became quite obvious that most of the people went to the bridge club more for the social life and in order to meet their pals. Shmel knew a lot of people and liked to be with the affluent and prominent, therefore it was very beneficial for him to be part of the scene.

The Widow-Woman... It was at the bridge club he met 'Minnie' an elderly widow, I believe. Not that she was wealthy or influential, indeed, she was quite the contrary. She lived, in a small, one bedroom apartment in a more run of the mill area and worked part-time in a jewellers shop. I was told by someone (who I will introduce you to a little later on) that she drove the type of clapped out car that would have made almost any second-hand car dealer choke on his door-step sandwich with laughter. But you will be hearing more about this lady in due course. For the moment it will suffice to tell you that this woman was in her sixties and was apparently his standby girlfriend, meaning, whenever he wasn't with me or with any fancy-bit he might have casually picked up, he would turn to her for comfort.

The Set-Up... I would often become so depressed about my relationship with Shmel that I took to questioning myself constantly, thinking perhaps it was my own fault that things were not right between us. Maybe I was handling it all wrong, but I couldn't think how or what I was doing to cause these problems. I would then think that perhaps my imagination was playing tricks on me and I was seeing women and events that weren't really there.

One evening out of pure desperation I thought about setting my fiancé up. I wasn't going to see him that particular evening as he had already told me that he was going back to his bed-sit in London to have an early night. Unbeknown to him, I had arranged to have a girlfriend come over for a meal that evening and while indulging in a couple of diet Cokes and a good laugh, between us we cooked up this cunning plan to test him out. After we had eaten and I had cleared away I got my girlfriend to phone Shmel, firstly to see if he was actually in his bed-sit and if he was, she could then speak to him and apologise for having dialled the wrong number, as a ploy, to see what he would say.

My girlfriend was well aware of the problems I had with him so she was only too happy to help me execute my plan. I knew Shmel wouldn't recognise her voice as I made a point of keeping my friends well away from him. (No prizes for guessing why!)

She dialled his number from the lounge and I picked up the kitchen extension ready to listen to every word and after a couple of rings he answered the phone.

"Oh! Hello is that Jerome?" My friend said in a slow, puzzled voice... She was great!

"No, I'm afraid not. *Who* did you say you wanted?" I heard Shmel say, in an equally puzzled voice.

"Oh!" Replied my girlfriend quickly, "I do apologise, I must have hit a wrong number." She winked at me and pulled a face.

I beckoned to my friend, eagerly, to start up a conversation with him.

"I wanted to speak to my brother, I am so... sorry." She giggled down the phone and looked across at me. She was doing a wonderful job.

His voice came over the extension.

"That's perfectly alright, I am glad you made the mistake, you have such a lovely speaking voice."

My friend giggled again and made some accommodating remark. She looked across at me, but her smile was beginning to fade.

His voice had already dropped down a gear or two into a soothing, persuading mode. "Are you free this evening...because I'm here all alone watching a video and I thought perhaps you might fancy joining me?"

My friend looked across at me and gasped silently, she realised Shmel had taken the bait and fallen into the trap.

With those soft words still ringing in my ear, I took over and belted down the telephone extension saying, "How dare you! How dare you, I set you up, this is my girlfriend you are talking to. She did not dial a wrong number, she dialled your number on purpose, just to see what you would say, you bastard, you RAT, I screamed and yelled at him.

He very quickly tried to sooth my anger down by saying that he guessed it was a joke and that he only went along with it to tease me. He threw the ball back into my court by saying. "What do you think I am eh, a schmuck or something?"

But it was all too late; it had proved beyond doubt what a despicable little man he was. What a bastard, what a schmuck! I was shocked and distraught, to think he would pick up someone, anyone, that quickly and that easily.

My poor friend was aghast and very upset for me and was sorry that she had been a party to my obvious distress. I comforted her by saying that it only went to prove what I already knew, which was, my fiancé was nothing but an outrageous womaniser who cared for no one but himself, and that it only went to show that he had no kind of loyalty to me whatsoever.

Today: My worst fears had been realised, I felt betrayed and deceived. He had tried to get out of it by lying to me; he hadn't even the grace or decency to own up. He even came out with his usual, boring comment, saying that... "He spoke to everybody, whether man or woman." But from my point of view, just like a rat from the sewer he scurried about sampling any piece of rotting cheese, whilst leaving a trail of stench and misery behind him. But of course, I knew that it wouldn't be too long before he came back to me and because I needed him I, like a fool, would forgive and try to forget.

1996

Chapter 9 – Fun Time.

Some Good Times... When things were going along smoothly, I used to love going away for the week-end and Shmel would often choose a place at random while looking through a newspaper. He seemed to like going away for short breaks and although I loved going away on holiday too, I very much enjoyed going out for a drive and perhaps finding somewhere to spend the week-end. I always made sure that my children were well cared for and in safe hands so I felt free to indulge myself in these occasional fun times. I would be so happy when Shmel picked me up in the car and we would start out on a long drive. These journeys would sometimes lead us to some very up-market and expensive hotels where we would stop for a meal, or we could, just as easily, call in at a country pub for lunch.

One day we went out on one of our wandering drives and ended up at a hotel not too far away from where we lived, at a place called Dedham. This particular hotel, called 'Le Maison' was one of four, exquisitely decorated and superbly managed establishments. We liked the look of the place immediately so we checked in for the week-end.

The hotel was in fact a small mansion and each suite was decorated in the Georgian style. We loved the room we were given, the bathroom alone was the size of a small apartment, it had a sunken bath and jacuzzi, and was tiled throughout in black and white. The hotel didn't have an eatery actually attached to it, instead; 'La Talbooth' restaurant was situated someway off down the hill, so when we wanted to eat, a chauffer driven car took us to the hotel's superb dining room that served à la-carte cuisine. We certainly wouldn't have had to worry about having too much to drink, not that we drank alcohol at all, but it would have been just another bonus if we had. It was one of those wonderful hotels I would recommend to anyone and will always remember with affection.

There was no doubting the fact that Shmel and I had some really good times together, especially when he was in a pleasant and attentive mood. He would treat me very well, buying me whatever I wanted and would take me out for week-ends or away on holiday, and we had many a good laugh. I was very appreciative of everything that Shmel gave me and did for me and even when I didn't feel like it, I always tried to be bright and happy, although I never lost sight of the fact that, underlying the outward happiness, there was always a cauldron, brimming with boiling oil, ready to spill over. I already knew that he had other kept women and that he wasn't averse to having the odd bit on the side as well, but foolishly, I chose to remain blinkered, hoping that in time they would somehow all go away. When we were together, I would look at him at times and try to imagine him in the arms or company, even, of some other woman, but as stupid as is sounds, I couldn't. I just couldn't imagine him being with anyone else. When he was with me, he was mine and that was that.

Nail Splitting Stuff... I used to think that it was sod's law for whenever I started to feel a little safe in our relationship something would crop up to spoil the illusion, like the time I went to have my nails done.

I used to have my nails manicured regularly in a popular beauty shop quite near to where I lived. One day whilst having my nails refreshed, the technician happened to mention that there was a rumour going around that my dear fiancé was seeing one of her other clients. She asked me if I was aware of the situation and did I know the woman. I wasn't seeing Shmel at the time as we had argued a few weeks back. "Frankly," I told her, "I didn't know where he was or what he was up to." Although, just out of curiosity I asked her what this woman was like and was told that she was roughly the same age as Shmel, short and a little old fashioned. The nail technician also revealed the fact that her client and Shmel were off to Portugal for a week. It emerged that at the time, the new lady friend had a problem with one of her legs and Shmel had to push her about in a wheelchair all the week.

Some months later Shmel had the gall to tell me all about the holiday he spent in Portugal and told me how he had pushed this lady around in a wheelchair all the time. He said that they stayed in a villa once owned by one of his ex-girlfriends and that while they were there; they went swimming in the nude and, invited the ex-girlfriend to join in the fun. My mind boggled at the sight of these three, ungainly people prancing about in the altogether. I was past being upset about his wayward holidays or yet another woman. But I was upset to think that he would spend a whole week pushing someone around in a wheelchair after the many times he had left me unaided when I had needed his help.

The Rich Man's Bash... Although we both had mobiles I would never ring Shmel when he was on one of his walkabouts. I would only get in touch with him if I thought it was really important.

One day a letter fell on my front doormat and when I opened the envelope it was an invitation for Shmel and I to attend the birthday party of Mr Ralph Gold, the same man whose book launch we had attended the year previously. Knowing him the way I did, I realised that Shmel would have been furious if I hadn't informed him about the party, as he always loved to mingle and rub shoulders with the rich and famous. He was therefore delighted when I rang to tell him of the invitation and he was only too pleased to accept. We made arrangements then and there for him to pick me up on the day of the party.

It was mid July and a most beautiful day for the event. Shmel called for me in plenty of time. He was dressed in very smart casuals and I wore one of my designer outfits that I felt was fitting for the occasion.

We had a very pleasant two hour drive down to the venue. The party was to be held at the host's house and in the beautiful surrounding grounds. The setting was magnificent, but then it was to be expected as Mr Gold was rolling in money. The grounds had a private golf course, a lake and a winding drive that seemed endless. When we eventually pulled up outside the entrance to the house we were directed towards the boat-house that was situated on the river running alongside the vast estate.

We were greeted by the host and hostess and we mingled with the other guests, one being Jeremy Beadle the resident host of 'You've been framed' and the 1960s pop idol Adam Faith. The King of Porn, Mr. Dave Sullivan was there, a partner and a close friend, along with the rest of the jet-set, including another familiar face of a very famous boxing promoter and entrepreneur and many, lesser known people. Once drinks had been served we were all seated for a sumptuous meal. Entertainment was laid on for us, that I found most enjoyable and for once, just for once, Shmel behaved himself perfectly. Shmel behaving himself for a whole evening was most unusual, and the only reason I can think of for his impeccable behaviour was that there was no female that took his fancy.

The drive home from the birthday party was wonderful, cruising along through the beautiful, countryside, fresh, clean and peaceful. It was late and the stars were glimmering on a deep-blue, velvety backdrop. It was silent, so silent and I leaned back in my comfortable seat, tired, contented but very happy. The car was moving along smoothly and everything seemed just perfect, until suddenly, Shmel suggested that perhaps it might be a good idea for me to move out of the house I was living in and go somewhere like North

London. Apparently, he said, the rented properties were far superior and it was an area he was very familiar with.

Oh No! Not Another Move... My calm, peaceful aura was instantly shattered at his suggestion as the last thing I wanted to do at that moment in time was to uproot my children, yet again. For one, I didn't know the North of London very well, I had only been that way on a few occasions when I either visited Shmel's old marital home or the apartment that Anne now lived in.

I was suddenly very concerned about my children and the affect it would have on them, they were both coming up towards the age when they would be going to college and they also had well established friends that I didn't want them to be separated from. There was so much for me to take into consideration, only moments ago I had been thinking how wonderful it was for Shmel not to have ruined my evening by looking for some other woman, and here he was, looking instead for some other house.

We talked about moving for a while and eventually, I thought that perhaps, if Shmel was on his home-ground, his very own hunting ground, there might be the slight possibility that he would give up his London bed-sit and come to live with me properly. It would prove to be quite a big move for all of us but eventually, I felt it was something I had to do as a last ditch effort to cement our relationship.

While I was going about my business, trying to be the perfect mother and fiancée, the RAT was using his London bed-sit as a regular knocking shop. Shmel thought it was quite normal, as well as fun, to introduce any one of his friends, who may already be in lengthy and committed relationships, to his very own cast off's.

Shmel's Cast Off's?... Shmel introduced one particular friend to a foreign 'actress' and every Thursday (when she was in England) the friend would meet her in Shmel's bed-sit, and they would carry out a ritual whereby, the friend would feed his woman on smoked salmon and other goodies and after sharing a shower would spend the rest of the time fucking.

One Thursday afternoon when Shmel wasn't around and I was feeling lonely and very bored, I decided to drive to the London hotel where Shmel had his bed-sit to see exactly what was going on. I decided to wait outside until his friend, a man already known to me, arrived for his afternoon liaison. After parking my car across the road from the hotel I settled myself down for a lengthy wait, but fortunately, it wasn't too long before this man drove up and got out of his car with, what I could only guess was his special carrier bag full of goodies. After securing his car and having a quick look around, he hastily made his way into the hotel. I remained discreetly hidden behind the dashboard of my car, as I felt sure that if this man had seen me he would have had a heart attack and dropped dead on the spot.

Knowing him and to look at him you would never have dreamed in a million years that this man would have indulged in such a sordid and regular habit. After all, he had a delightful and unsuspecting partner of twenty-five years or so and should she have found out, she would have surely left him without a second's hesitation.

I only knew about this man and his ritual as from time to time Shmel would delight in telling me about other people's misdemeanours, although he would of course, swear me to secrecy. I knew Shmel was a very bad influence on his friend and when I rebuked him, as I often did, he would laugh at me and say that there was no man on earth who was faithful to one woman and any man given the slightest opportunity would take it and be damned.

Today: I would often lie in my part-vacant bed at night pondering on the man I loved and had committed myself to. He was so unlike the men in my background, the honourable and faithful men I had been brought up with and was used to. I often thought of my mum and dad and the normal, devoted and loving relationship they had shared all their married life and prayed that some day Shmel would give up the life he was leading and be dedicated only unto me.

A Very Happy Christmas... The Christmas of 1996 was coming along fast and as Shmel and I were together at this time, to celebrate, we decided to take a four day break in Bournemouth. We frequented the area quite a few times for no particular reason other than the fact that we just loved it there. The previous year we had stayed at a three star hotel in Boscombe called 'The Chine' that held a rosette rating for its fabulous à la carte menu and as we had enjoyed it so much we decided to go there again.

We invited mother to come and spend Christmas with us at the hotel as we felt it would make a nice change for her. She had been given the opportunity to go to my brother's house for a few days but she chose instead to come with us. She loved being with me and the children and by now the relationship between her and Shmel was one of mutual toleration, for she would do anything to keep the peace for me and at times like this she would try extra hard to be sociable.

I was feeling particularly good at that time, my weight was the lowest it had been for some years and I managed to squeeze into one of my better outfits. I can remember wearing a very expensive and classy fox-trimmed, animal print suit with a full length mink coat wrapped around me in order to keep the chilly evening air at bay when we ventured out. My children looked great too, in their modern gear, all bought from Selfridges as just a small part of their Christmas present.

Mum looked lovely as usual, she was beginning to look her old self again after years of grieving for my dad, and the day we picked her up to take her to the hotel, she looked like a million dollars and at least ten years younger than her real age. Shmel looked extra smart too; it was one of those happy occasions that went to make up for a lot of the unhappiness he caused me.

On the evening we arrived at the hotel we were greeted just like old friends, the staff were welcoming and friendly, we were also remembered and welcomed by some of the other guests who had frequented the same hotel each Christmas for years past. Just for once we all spent a wonderful holiday in a great atmosphere, with good friends and excellent service.

1997

Chapter 10 – The Wedding is On.

The Nutritionist... The Christmas of 1996 that Shmel and I spent with my mum was just wonderful. We had such a lovely break in Bournemouth, but on returning home I became thoroughly depressed about my spiralling weight problem, yet again. Since having had the hysterectomy in 1990 I had constantly struggled with my weight and felt that the doctors had been wrong when they assured me that my body would adjust because, quite honestly, it hadn't. I was not in control of my weight or able to cope with the pounds that piled on so easily.

Having always been tall and slim in the past, I yearned to return to my former self and would constantly go into the bedroom and look at the line of redundant designer outfits that hung neatly in my wardrobe, crying out to be worn.

I would often break down in tears especially after having been seriously dieting for a whole week only to find the scales registering the same weight as it had the week before. It seemed that no matter what I did, it wouldn't make one scrap of difference. I hated myself and the way I looked and was hurt and humiliated by the harsh words said to me by my most judgemental critic. Me!

Not knowing quite what to do, Shmel offered to give me some extra money so that I could get help from a highly sought-after nutritionist. Shmel was already leaving anything between four and five hundred pounds a week but decided to give me an extra couple of hundred for as long as it would take to help me with my problem.

This added cash enabled me to seek the professional help of the late Princess Diana's nutritionist Roderick Lane, who was reputed to be one of the top advisors in this country. I must have seen him on and off for months and although I had pleasing results at first, eventually my body refused to let go of the fat that had built up over the years and I would often stand on the scales only to find that the few pounds lost the week before had been hungrily grabbed back again. I would become so frustrated with my weight and my own body at times that I must have been unbearable to live with, so although

I was often hurt and infuriated with Shmel and his antics, I consoled myself, by believing that he must have loved me truly, otherwise he would never have stayed with me. I didn't realise at the time of course, that my weight would continue to yo-yo for some years to come.

The Spanish Clanger... Shmel had mentioned to me on a couple of occasions at least, that he was thinking of going into partnership with a lady called Carrie, the former wife of one of his friends who had moved to La Manga in Spain. She had become very friendly with a male chef and they thought that if they opened up a really, high-class restaurant over there in Spain they could easily make a killing. Shmel was very interested indeed in the idea; he was always attracted to anything that he thought could make him even more money than he already had.

It was during the early part of the year that we were both invited to La Manga to discuss the new business idea. I was very pleased that they included me and for asking me to attend. I was delighted to be incorporated in the various talks and proposals, added to which, I was tired and felt in need of a holiday.

We stayed in the five-star Marriott Hotel, which is a well known haunt for famous footballers, pro-tennis and golf players, especially when they are in training for a big and important event. The Marriott is a first class hotel in every sense of the word. Conveniently situated alongside the reception area was a small but very exclusive jewellery shop. I couldn't help but look at the exquisite and select items in the show cases every time I went by. My birthday was coming up and I thought how nice it would be if Shmel bought me a surprise gift.

Carrie and her partner Lee met us soon after we arrived in Spain and arranged for us all to have dinner every evening in a variety of local, top-class restaurants. Most of our days were spent looking at the area where the new business venture was to be set up. Shmel was heavily involved in this new project and would spend hours talking, discussing and making arrangements. At times I tended to get a little tired of all the discussions and the wrangling that went on and although I spent quite a lot of time with them, as I wasn't as involved in the project as I thought I would be and had no real say in anything either, I decided to stay out of the way whenever possible. Besides which, I quite enjoyed wandering around on my own shopping, sunning myself by the pool or just relaxing in the Marriott Hotel's plush lounge.

Towards the end of the holiday the partnership between Shmel, Carrie and her partner Lee had been cemented and Shmel handed over his third of the set-up money, which was around eight thousand pounds.

The new enterprise agreed upon meant that there was little left for us to do, so after a day relaxing together we prepared for the journey home. The following day, after having handed back the keys to our room and while waiting for the taxi to transport us to the airport, we decided to go into the hotel coffee shop for a drink. We ordered coffee and while we were waiting Shmel laid a small package on the table. A smile spread across my face as he nodded towards the package saying, "Happy Birthday Shar, it is your present."

I quickly picked up the package and opened it. I was so anxious to see my gift that I fumbled unnecessarily with the wrapping, but it was well worth the wait, as inside was a little blue box which held the most amazing gold and emerald knuckle duster ring that had been displayed in the front window of the exclusive jewellery shop in the hotel.

I was over the moon. I grabbed Shmel into my arms and gave him an almighty hug.

"Thank you." I said "Thank you so much, it's absolutely lovely, I love it, thank you." I kept repeating the words thank you and I love you, for at that moment in time, he made me feel very happy indeed.

Once home and for at least the next couple of months, the restaurant became our main topic of conversation. Shmel would often be on the phone to Carrie in Spain checking up to see if everything was going okay. But unfortunately, as the weeks slipped by, it began to emerge that things weren't going according to plan and within a short time the whole deal fell through. Naturally, Shmel was absolutely furious and he had many slanging matches with Carrie over the telephone before he finally managed to salvage just half of his stake money, a mere four thousand pounds. He was totally gutted. He had handed over his eight thousand pounds so easily and all he had managed to get back was half. For days he walked around depressed and miserable, fretting for the cash he was never going to see again.

Personally, I wasn't altogether surprised as I felt there was something rather dodgy about the whole deal in the first place. There were many things that didn't add up, but I felt obliged to go along for the ride as no matter what I might have said, Shmel wouldn't have taken any notice. He would seldom, if ever, confide in me with regards to his business interests. The only person he would talk to, or take advice from, was his eldest son from his marriage to Anne but in the main, he made business decisions by himself, for himself.

On this occasion he was fleeced of four thousand pounds and although gutted, he decided that four was better than none at all so he took the money and lost his friend Carrie. We later found out through the grapevine, that

Carrie had completely refurbished her apartment in Spain at a cost of around four thousand pounds. Hmm...

Lexus go to the Football Match... At the time I had to give Shmel his due, he was in with a lot of very rich and influential people, not as 'in' with them as he would have liked to have been of course, but he was close enough to some of them to gather up a few of the pickings that they occasionally gave away or dropped. Some of Shmel's business associates went back many years, to a time when the majority of them were struggling and jostling for a place in the sun. Unfortunately for Shmel, many of these men rose up and made a name for themselves along with mega-bucks and in so doing, left people like Shmel still striving to climb to the top. Nevertheless, he would try to rub shoulders with the rich and famous as often as possible, and would never turn down an invitation to a party, a business launch or opening, or indeed, any occasion where he thought they would all gather. When Shmel was invited to a function he would be absolutely delighted and would be in his glory, mingling with people such as football managers and players, nightclub owners, authors and the wealthy men he had done business with in previous years. He had never quite made it into their league of course, but just being in their presence helped to make him feel big and important! Poor soul...

On one such occasion we were invited to sit in the V.I.P. box with some very prominent and well-known people, such as the gentlemen already mentioned before, Mr Dave Sullivan and the Gold Brothers. We were there to watch Birmingham City, the team they owned, play a vital football match. This was about the time when Karren Brady, who was one of Dave Sullivan's directors for his Sports Newspapers, was made MD of the football-club at the tender age of twenty-four.

Shmel was over the moon, he had just become the proud possessor of the latest model, Lexus car, in fact, at that time he was one of the first to have this particular model in this country and we certainly attracted many a look of interest and envy when we drove around. He hadn't had the Lexus that long before we received the football match invitation, so driving all the way up North was to be its real maiden or at least its longest voyage so far.

The day we were due to mingle with the jet set in the V.I.P. box was freezing. Not wanting to appear cold, I decided to wear a gorgeous cashmere outfit, topped with my full-length mink coat. I must say how pleased I was that I had decided on this outfit, as not only did it help keep out the bitter cold, but mixing with all those wealthy people helped me to feel self-assured and confident. When the whistle blew for half time we all went down into two large, warm, rooms where hot soup and rolls had been laid on to help us through the second half of the match. This gave me a golden opportunity to say a few words to Karren, as for most of the match she was sitting at the front of the directors' box.

When at last the match was over and the final whistle had blown, we all went for a welcome, sit-down meal that had been especially prepared for the club owners and their guests. I must admit that football isn't my favourite sport no matter how famous the team or the managers and it really didn't matter to me whether the team won or lost, being part of the 'set' and the glamour of it all was the exciting part and it proved to be a wonderful and most memorable experience for both Shmel and I.

Saab Standard... Shmel had his fabulous new Lexus to drive, and my B.M.W. was now needing a small amount of work doing to it, so rather than fork out any money he decided, in his wisdom, that it would be more sensible to get me a new car. I must say that I wasn't at all impressed with his choice, for one thing he had not asked me what I would like and felt very annoyed that a decision had been made regardless of my own preferences. It was a case of, "Here's a new car, like it or lump it," and on this occasion I had to lump it.

The car he got for me was a Saab convertible, all very nice of course, if you like that type of car, but I didn't like driving it one little bit. I had to admit that it was a lovely *looking* car especially if I wanted to pose with the hood down, but personally, and if I had been given the choice, it would have been placed bottom of my list. I must stress though, that not liking the Saab was purely personal, as no matter how wonderful a car, is, that doesn't necessarily mean to say that it will suit everyone... and the Saab most certainly didn't suit me.

It's All Go... My eventual move to the other side of London took rather a long time to come to fruition and when Shmel finally found me a place we had to call on the assistance of our usual removal company. The removal company we always used was so familiar with the contents of my house, that they no longer had to come around to assess the cost of moving us, all they did instead, was to agree a date on which we should go.

That date was 31st August 1997. I will never forget that day as it was about the same time that Diana; the Princess of Wales was killed in a car crash in Paris. I can remember to this day, sitting on a storage box in my new house, crying my eyes out as I listened to the news bulletins on the radio.

The week I moved in was extremely hectic, not only did I have to sort out my belongings but most importantly, there was a new college to find for my son and a new school for my daughter. I had been very worried about this particular move and I must admit I wasn't looking forward to all the upheaval. Strangely enough though, within a couple of months we were all settled. The youngsters were surprisingly happy and liked their new schools and I was cheerful and getting used to living on the North side of London.

Shmel was still up to his old tricks of going off whenever it suited him and despite my pleas he made no attempt to give up his London bed-sit and move in with me for good, although, he did leave a couple of pairs of trousers hanging up in my wardrobe, and I did managed to find a little bit of space in one of my drawers in which to store a small amount of his underwear.

I very quickly resigned myself to the fact that he wasn't going to call this house his home. I also made a conscious point of never questioning him when he went on the missing list. It wasn't a case of not being interested in where he was or who he was with, it was for the simple fact that he had told me so many lies in the past, that I just didn't want to hear any more, therefore I refrained from asking.

I was well aware that he had kept a standby girlfriend for many years and even to this day, still cannot understand why he needed to have anyone else when he had me. I kept myself as attractive as possible, was still quite young looking, I was an excellent cook who kept a good home, intelligent, apart from which even if I say it myself, I was good in the sack. So why on earth would he want any other woman? Especially an old one or rough bits on the side I will never know; indeed, only God would know that.

The Wedding Plans... Even though I was very cross about the Saab and anxious about the move to a new rented house, at the time I had more to think about than a car as, believe it or not, Shmel had finally agreed to us getting married.

The wedding was set to be in April of the next year 1998

Today - I swear that I can hear you saying "Married - married? This woman must have been mad to even contemplate getting married to this man!" And you are so right, but at the time, I was caught up in this man's world and I had become locked into his way of living and unable to find a way out. Just like getting caught in any kind of muddy swamp, the more I struggled the deeper I sank. No matter how often I hoped and prayed that one day we would be able to lead a good and normal life together, my prayers were never to be answered. But what I continually failed to take into consideration was that this man was not normal or indeed, good, in the moral sense of the word.

Nevertheless, at the end of the day I was getting married! Yes! Getting married at last, I could hardly believe he had finally relented and given me the OKAY. It was I who had wanted this all the time, for being one who likes tradition, getting married was the right thing to do and now, all my dreams were to come true.

I was determined and made pretty sure that I wouldn't have a wedding similar to my first, it nearly broke my parents hearts for them to see me married in a registrars office, I am sure my mother, to this day, didn't consider my first marriage to have been sanctified as I hadn't been married in the Synagogue by the Rabbi. But this time, Mummy dear, I was going to do it right, by giving you everything you had ever wanted. You were going to be proud of me and it would be an event you would enjoy and never forget.

I was so in love with the idea of getting married and wearing a beautiful wedding dress and having all the other things associated with a proper wedding, my mind was in a maze and I would lay awake at night thinking about it and dreaming of the day!

I felt so lucky, for amongst my girlfriends was a lady who was an excellent organiser and she agreed to help me with the wedding. She was always full of good ideas and was just perfect for the job. She was a much travelled lady and would often return from a visit to America with the most fantastic and 'WOW' themes for parties, Barmitzvahs and weddings. I was determined that everything would be well co-ordinated right down to the smallest detail. The theme for my wedding was to be...Snow White and the Seven Dwarfs, as the lady who was planning my wedding had just brought me back from America the figurines of the lovable characters we all know so well. I spent the rest of the year planning, organising and thoroughly enjoying all the things that I thought would go towards the wedding of the year! Well, at least for my mum and myself.

The Mighty K.O.P... It was around this time, mid-1997, when I really began to believe that Shmel was well and truly on his way up in the world of business and finance, for not only had we been invited to a few more 'up market' functions than usual, we were finally invited to a Christmas party organised by the King of Porn himself none other than Mr Dave Sullivan. It appeared that he and Shmel went back a lot of years, from when they were both quite young. Shmel was in advertising and the K. of P. was just opening up his first sex shops in the East End of London. Shmel told me that the king would often contact him with regards to buying advertising space, in order to publicise his sex shops and Shmel would provide him with the goods. I never did find out what kind of relationship they really had, whether they were just business associates or whether they had been personal friends, I can only guess, but I did know that Shmel would have dearly loved to be closer to him than he actually was.

The King of Porn, this larger than life character, sure knew how to put on a party… He held a Christmas party every year and Shmel was desperate to be invited but never was until this year. Shmel was over the moon, the invitation card itself was something to be treasured, but the actual 'do' was really something else!

We made our way to Mr Sullivan's mansion in Essex, where the function was to be held. This amazing mansion had been described as the most expensive residence in the whole of London and Essex and to attempt to tell you what it was like would be impossible. It had to be seen to be believed and I could only describe it as magnificent, coupled with all the other superlative words you can think of.

When we arrived at the residence we were led into the hall and lounge area where canapés and drinks were freely accessible. We were introduced to some of the other guests who were already there and some who were just arriving. I must have stood around in some amount of awe at the grandeur of the place. I had never seen anywhere quite like it before, or since. Not really being a person who mingles that easily, especially with people I don't know very well, I hung back a little and allowed myself to take in all that was going on around me. After a short while, I looked around and noticed that Shmel was busy chatting to some influential-looking guys, so I decided to go and sit on a sumptuous cream sofa. After sitting there for a few moments an older lady who was already seated on the sofa spoke to me, I moved a little closer to her and we started to chat. It wasn't long before the lady introduced herself to me, as none other than the host's mother. She was a most delightful lady to speak to and after some small amount of general conversation she told me how her son had taken the trouble to have a lift especially installed in his house for her. She seemed to enjoy telling me how kind and thoughtful her son was and took great pleasure in pointing out where the lift was situated and how it worked. I spoke of my own mother to her so we suddenly found plenty to talk about and we only stopped talking when all the guests had arrived and we were informed that dinner was about to be served.

Whilst talking to this lovely lady I had been watching the arrival of many of the guests in all their amazing finery. Among the people attending were many well-known and familiar faces, not only people I had already met at functions we had attended in the past, but there were people I had not actually met before, but celebrities I recognised from television programs and sports events.

The gentleman whose book launch we had attended in 1995 was there with his partner and I actually sat opposite a very famous night-club owner,

Mr Peter Stringfellow, a man almost everyone would recognise, and with him was his attractive girlfriend of the time. The whole evening was a wonderful experience, and for me, one of the nicest gestures of all was when the host stood up and announced that if there was anyone at the dinner table that had to have a special diet, they only had to let the waiter or waitress know and the chef would prepare something special for them. There was superb entertainment provided for us throughout the evening. Needless to say, it was a very memorable evening, everything was just perfect and even Shmel behaved himself impeccably. All in all, I was extremely impressed and it was one of those superior functions I thoroughly enjoyed and will never forget.

The weeks seemed to hurtle by as we headed towards autumn. My thoughts were fully taken up with my wedding and just like all the famous fairytales of old, I wanted it to be just as fantastic and equally as magical. It really all began in earnest when I sent out the beautiful wedding invitations. Gold lettering on a heavy, cream, vellum paper was chosen and to add to the magic I put tiny gold confetti hearts inside each envelope so that upon opening, they would flutter around. I did try to warn most of my guests that there would be a surprise in the envelope as confetti was a relatively new idea. I cannot quite remember how many people we invited to the wedding reception as the numbers weren't important. We had plenty of money to spend on the wedding so we just invited whoever we wanted. Shmel of course, made sure he invited more guests than I did, but then he always had to go one better than me and although I was annoyed at the time, I really couldn't be bothered to get myself all in a state about it after all, he was paying! Anyway, Christmas was almost here and I felt that the New Year would be upon us before we could turn around.

Once the Christmas festivities and functions were well and truly over, I felt that my wedding had suddenly started to gallop towards me like a charging bull. I therefore began to plan, make arrangements, organise and double-check everything in great earnest.

We booked an excellent toast master to take charge of the wedding breakfast, who was young, good-looking and who was reputed to be able to keep any function under control. He did an excellent job at our wedding, and I was delighted to see this guy and his young wife on television's, 'Ready, Steady, Cook' program a year or so later challenging Ainsley Harriot and his team of chefs to cook some fish in a more exciting way,

Planning In Earnest... We notified our local Synagogue in Redbridge of our wedding date and at the same time arranged with the Rabbi to have the full works in order to ensure the most sincere wedding possible, something I truly believed would help to enrich our Holy Vows and married life.

Just to be cheeky, I asked the Rabbi if I could place a wooden box covered in gold material under the Jewish Wedding Canopy – The Chuppah – beneath which, the main and most important part of the wedding ceremony takes place. I explained that it would be so nice if Shmel appeared to be the same height as me but unfortunately, the Rabbi would not allow it – No way!

To complete the arrangements we booked an excellent group of musicians to play for all our guests at the wedding breakfast – So fingers crossed, all seemed to be going along nicely.

1998

Chapter 11 – For Better For Worse.

The Fairy Story Wedding... My wedding to Shmel was drawing ever nearer. Everything possible had been arranged and organised like a military operation. I wanted the whole thing to go to plan and for everything to be perfect on the day.

As already stated, the theme for my wedding was to be Snow-White and the Seven Dwarfs. I decided to have the banqueting room laid out with a large top table representing Snow White. With seven separate tables, each one representing one of the dwarfs. I thought the figurines, that had been given to me by my wedding planner would look great standing on the tables. The idea also appealed to me as Shmel's greying beard reminded me of the dwarfs in the old, but delightful Disney film. I can now see that this theme was chosen for all the wrong reasons, but at the time, I just thought it was apt.

My wedding dress, on the other hand was chosen with great love and care. I bought it for around fifteen hundred pounds from a local exclusive gown boutique in Hertfordshire and it was absolutely beautiful, even though I say it myself. It was made from a subtle, champagne coloured satin, edged with gold filigree lace. The bodice was tight fitting, off the shoulder, with gold lace puff sleeves. The skirt of the gown was made up of gold lace handkerchieves that helped give the gown an enchanted look. To complete the ensemble a very good friend made me a satin purse and headdress to match. My shoes were purchased from Gina's of Knightsbridge. I also made sure that my mum and my children all had completely new outfits.

Because my dear dad was no longer with us and both my brothers would be away on business, one of Shmel's long standing friends was chosen to escort me down the aisle besides having the honour of being best man. Both Shmel and his friend had chosen to wear black dinner suits with a gold matching waistcoat, and to complete their outfits they were having top hats and black patent shoes. What a turn on they would be?

The Wedding Bands… Just after my birthday in the February, Shmel took me along to Hatton Garden in the West End of London to choose our matching wedding rings.

As excited as I was, I became very confused in each of the jewellers we went into, looking at the vast array of wedding bands that were proffered for my consideration. Having too much choice, I felt, could be almost as bad as having no choice at all. Nevertheless, after visiting quite a number of establishments, one after the other, we finally set our hearts on heavy, matching 18ct gold and platinum rings. Shmel didn't mind what I chose so I finally settled for this particular ring as it was a good match for my engagement ring and sat alongside it perfectly. I came out of the jewellers so pleased, so excited and oh, so happy!

A Cruise Darling? … To finalise our wedding plans and to help make even more of my dreams come true, Shmel booked the honeymoon. He didn't discuss the honeymoon arrangements with me of course, but as Shmel had been on cruises before he thought, perhaps, a romantic cruise would be a good experience for me. He had often told me how people could dress up in all their finery during the day if they wished, although in the main, most people would only dress smartly for dinner in the evenings. I felt it would be such a wonderful opportunity for me to get all dolled up in my beautiful and expensive designer clothes and accessories that the prospect made me feel very excited. Consequently, not being completely satisfied with the wardrobe I already had and because of my fluctuating weight, I would often go down to a parade of shops nearby to purchase anything that took my fancy.

Along this parade of shops was a very well established travel agent with whom Shmel chose, booked and finalised our honeymoon. We were all set for a ten-day cruise around the Mediterranean. Yahoo! I could hardly wait.

The last arrangement to make was to book the photographer, who said that besides taking the traditional wedding photographs, he would video every moment of the wedding from start to the bitter-end, so that friends and family alike would have all the high-lights and a lasting memory of us all sharing in this very, very, special day.

Once news of our wedding started to get around I was absolutely delighted and very thrilled when Shmel came over one evening a few weeks before the wedding and presented me with an early wedding present from the property tycoon, Mr Nick Leslau, who at the time owned the Troccodero in London. The gift purchased from Tiffanys, was a silver, trinket box in the shape of an apple with a delicate and beautifully shaped leaf on the lid, it was truly delightful. – To this day it still adorns my display cabinet and will always be greatly treasured.

19th April 98 and All That… I had not slept that well for a good few nights before the big day, but I suppose I must have been suffering from pre-nuptial nerves. Eventually, the big day arrived and after I had bathed and got dressed in my fabulous wedding dress I had my make-up applied to perfection by a friend and at 11:30am the photographer turned up ready to start recording my very special day.

My mum looked beautiful and so happy, although I knew that behind her smile she held a great fear for my future with this man. She never usually hid the fact that she didn't like Shmel, but today she did. She looked and played the part of the proud and happy mother, just for me. From time to time I would notice her guard slip and I would look at her and find doubts and reservations welling up inside my own mind, but the wedding day was here and everything was booked and arranged. I was standing ready to face the world, so the show had to go on. I am sure that deep down, even deeper than the fears she held for me, she was happy because *I* was happy and she was especially pleased that this time I was to be married properly and in the eyes of God.

My day was completed by my teenage children, who stood confidently by my side and at one point made a lovely comment saying, "If you are happy Mum, so are we!"

My happiness was at its peak, things couldn't have been any better for what more could I have asked of life. The weather that day was absolutely beautiful, I had my close family who I loved dearly by my side, my children and my mother and in just a few hours I would have Shmel, my husband!

"The limousine is here for you!" I heard my mother call out above the sounds of people chatting and cameras flashing. I stood up tall, while my friends fussed around me, making sure that everything was just perfect then, as the video camera panned across to me, I took my first step towards the door and the waiting car.

The first small surprise I had was when I stooped slightly to get into the limousine, and who should be sitting there? Why, none other than my future mother-in-law. Nevertheless, it had already been arranged for my own mother and children to accompany me to the Synagogue so I greeted her respectfully and took my place in the limo. Once we had all settled ourselves in the car we moved off along the A406 - North Circular road. The stretch-limo windows were tinted so that I could see out, and I found it quite amusing to see other motorists staring in the windows in the hope of getting a glimpse of the occupants, the way they do when a car such as this glides up beside them. Sitting in my wedding gown with my family around me I felt so proud, I can remember thinking how much my dad would have loved to have been here with us on this day, I took hold of mum's hand and looked at her and I just knew she was thinking the same.

The journey didn't take that long and we soon turned into the driveway that took us down to the entrance of the Synagogue. Although people couldn't see into the limo as it gently glided down the driveway, it was very comforting for me to catch the first glimpse of my dear friends who were waiting to greet me.

Once the limo had come to a sedate halt, my family and my future mother-in-law stepped out; I stayed behind for a short while, as I wanted everyone to get settled before I made my grand appearance.

While the majority of our guests where making their way into the Synagogue and finding their seats, I carefully got out of the car, helped by Shmel's best man who was going to escort me down the aisle. We stopped for a few moments while the obligatory photos were taken, during which time the best man smiled at me and said how stunning I looked. He asked me if I was nervous and I replied saying that, apart from being a little shaky, I was just fine.

The photographers, now happy with the shots, moved aside and all went quiet as I turned to face my future. Taking hold of the best man's arm, we steadied ourselves for a moment or two and just as we were about to make a stately entrance I heard a dreadful din coming towards us from behind. Both the best man and I made a sharp turn to see what it was and there, coming down the driveway was an old, black, stretch limousine carrying none other than Shmel's family. Pop music was blaring from every aperture of the car and heads were popping in and out of the sun roof. I just couldn't believe what I was seeing. It was Shmel's three grown up children with their friends, laughing and shouting above the beat of the music. And although I was appalled; I was not overly surprised, as I might have guessed that his eldest son would be hell-bent on ruining my special day. Apart from the youngest son, the other two didn't like me at all, so why they wanted to come to my wedding I just cannot imagine. But then, I reminded myself that it was their father getting married and of course, it also presented them with the perfect opportunity to upset me.

On hearing the rumpus and seeing the disrespectful way in which they had approached this sacred and holy place, I completely lost my composure and tears welled up in my eyes. I dashed off to a side lobby that contained a ladies powder-room, swiftly followed by a couple of my dear friends who had been waiting just inside the entrance of the Synagogue and had seen what had happened. They both tried to comfort me by telling me not to take any notice of those bastards, as it was my day. They assured me that I looked very beautiful and suggested that I ignore them and rise above it all. Eventually, with this encouragement and knowing my friends were supporting me every step of the way I checked my make-up and once again confidently walked back to the entrance of the Synagogue, where the best man was still waiting. We smiled a little apprehensively at each other but, I took his arm with renewed poise and he respectfully escorted me to my place under the Chuppah and to where the Rabbi, Shmel, the two mothers and another one of Shmel's friends were dutifully waiting.

The ceremony proceeded, witnessed by a full congregation. Throughout the dignified ceremony our backs were turned towards our family and friends and although I was trying desperately to concentrate fully on the Rabbi and what he was saying and doing, I could not help but hear the constant damning remarks being made by Shmel's son. As hard as I tried, I could not ignore it and at least a couple of times I turned around and gave him looks of disgust and annoyance.

I stood composed and dignified as I made my holy vows and when the ring was placed on my finger I felt truly happy and completely satisfied at long last… The closing of the holy ceremony was followed by happy embraces and kisses and the traditional, breaking of glass under our heels whilst everyone called out Mazeltov, meaning good luck.

After signing the register we were off, back down the aisle to our awaiting limo that was to take us to the reception. I was now Shmel's wife and he was my husband. We walked to the car hand in hand; we looked affectionately into each others eyes.

"I love you." He said quietly.

"And I love you too."

I just knew, deep down in my heart, that this was going to be the beginning of a great and wonderful relationship between us. I was confident that Shmel would now settle down so that we could behave like a normal, happily-married couple.

Today: At the time I was convinced beyond any doubt that I was right, but my new husband was to prove me wrong!

The Reception… Shmel and I were the first people to arrive at Nan's Pantry in Ilford where the wedding breakfast was being held. Next to arrive were the two mums and my children. And then there was to be a short pause before the rest of the guests were due to arrive. This welcome break gave us all a small amount of space in which to relax and take stock of everything before Shmel and I took our places at the door, where traditionally, we received our guests as they arrived. By the time we had taken our places by the entrance our people started drifting in and they each greeted us in the usual Jewish style wishing us, Mazeltov! - Smiling happily, we thanked them and accepted the wedding presents they handed to us.

We spent around an hour greeting our family and friends, laughing, chatting and indulging in canapés and cocktails, before the guests finally started to be directed to their places ready for the sit-down meal. When everyone was seated, Shmel and I walked hand in hand up towards the top table accompanied by music and joyous hand clapping. We gracefully took our seats and waited for the meal to be served. While sitting there I looked excitedly and contentedly around the room. It had all been decorated so beautifully, with cream and gold, it all looked so classy and stylish. Everyone seemed thrilled, to see the figurines of the seven dwarfs standing sedately on the tables. They created many spontaneous jokes and much hearty laughter from my guests, which in turn meant much happiness for me, (even if Shmel wasn't too happy about it, but then, he had Snow White to look at, a virginal type of lady he wasn't, altogether, too familiar with). Also, I didn't care too much about what Shmel thought of it all... I thought it was great fun. The lady who organised our reception had certainly done us proud, in fact, she had excelled herself and I was extremely thankful and delighted.

We had arranged to have a four-course meal and it wasn't too long before the waitresses started to serve Shmel and I first, then the rest of the people sitting at the top table, then of course, the other guests. During the meal we had speeches, toasts and the exchanging of special gifts between Shmel and myself.

After the meal Shmel led me out onto the dance floor for the first dance, where he repeatedly told me how much he loved me. Despite my genuine happiness, I had to constantly guard against looking over towards the table where Shmel's youngsters had been seated, for they continually acted in a manner totally unbefitting a wedding reception. They were rude, insolent and loud for most of the time and I knew that they were desperately intent on ruining my day, but I wasn't going to allow that to happen, no matter what. I did speak to Shmel on a couple of occasions remarking on their lewd behaviour and as I found it offensive perhaps he would have a word with them, but he just laughed off my request and chose to ignore it.

He might have ignored his children's misconduct but my people didn't and for weeks following the wedding my family and friends would remark on their poor behaviour, continually reminding me of it and saying what an awful lot I had got myself mixed in with.

Despite his family, I had had a wonderful day but inevitably, my fairytale wedding was coming to an end and round 11:30pm it was time to cut into our magnificent four-tier, cream and gold wedding cake. Just for a few minutes there was silence in the banqueting hall while Shmel and I stood close together as photographers took pictures of us proudly holding the knife before making the first cut. The beautifully decorated cake was so huge that even after everyone had had a portion, it looked as if it had scarcely been touched, so I told the head waitress to slice and wrap the rest of the cake and I would decide what to do with it in the morning. By then it was midnight and time to say goodbye to the guests and to thank the many people who had helped me create for us, a near perfect day. Once all the guests had left, mum (bless her) and my children helped Shmel and I to gather up all the gifts, cards and keepsakes and eventually, tired and weary, we all made our way home.

Today: When I look back now on my amazing wedding that must have cost Shmel in excess of twenty-thousand pounds it is difficult to express how delighted and relieved I was that everything I organised went to plan and that there were no major hiccups. All I had to do from then on was to focus on my new position as the wife of a very, wealthy business man, a responsibility I was looking forward to handling with confidence and style.

And, just in case you might wonder what I did with my beautiful wedding cake, I took all that was left to the local hospital and gave it to the nurses on the children's ward. The duty-staff were delighted, everyone thanked me very much and wished me good luck - Mazeltov!

The Honey-gloom... Following my wonderful, fairytale wedding, the next few days were taken up preparing for my honeymoon and sorting out all the gifts and presents. We had some beautiful and thoughtful gifts given to us by friends and family alike and I spent quite a bit of time trying to find appropriate places around the house in which to set out the more personal items so that they could be seen in their best light. People are so kind and generous at these times, I was quite overwhelmed. Mum had come down from Brighton especially for the wedding and was due to spend a couple of weeks at the house, in order to look after the children while Shmel and I were away. Mum was not expected to act as a baby minder naturally, as both of my children were now teenagers, one being at school and the other at college. Nevertheless, they still needed someone to be there when they came home in the evening to make sure they had a good, wholesome dinner and someone around to look out for their general welfare. (Thank you Mum!)

I was so looking forward to our honeymoon, as this was to be my first cruise ever. Shmel of course, was a bit of an old hand at it as he had been on several cruises before, but it was to be a maiden voyage for me and after all the wonderful things he had told me about cruises I was so excited, I could scarcely think straight. I was convinced that the honeymoon would be an amazing experience and a complete success, just like my wedding day. Although, this time it would be even better, as my husband's 'delightful' family wouldn't be there to spoil it, thank God!

The day we were due to depart, I was ready, all packed and raring to go; I couldn't wait to get started. I spent most of the morning giving my youngsters loads of 'mumsie' type warnings and generally faffing around doing last minute bits and pieces. However, when the taxi driver pulled up outside the house and sounded his horn it made me jump.

"He's here, he's here." I said, grabbing up my bag and coat as Shmel opened the front door to him. While my new husband and the driver were sorting out the cases and loading up the boot of the taxi, I hurriedly said goodbye to mum for about the umpteenth time, then, with lots of waves and goodbye kisses all around I climbed into the back of the taxi with my darling husband.

We reached Heathrow Airport in plenty of time and after the usual formalities I rang to tell mum that we had arrived okay. We then spent the rest of the time ambling around the duty free and airport shops. We were scheduled to take the flight from Heathrow to Genoa in Italy, and then be transported by coach to the port where the cruise liner was tied up, waiting to take us around the Mediterranean.

The flight was only due to last a couple of hours, so we held hands quite a lot of the time and chit-chatted about this and that in general, mulling over the wedding and so on. I sat back occasionally and closed my eyes as I felt quite heady with joy and very safe, as Shmel had eyes only for me. I was content and very happy. We were well on our way to the holiday of a lifetime, the type of holiday that we would remember all our lives.

The aeroplane landed right on time at Genoa Airport and the air conditioned coach was dutifully waiting to take us to the port. We occupied a comfortable seat for the journey and relaxed back, thoroughly enjoying the picturesque scenery as we drove along. Eventually, some excited voices from behind alerted Shmel and I and we looked out of the window. We could just catch the odd glimpse of the blue Mediterranean when it came into view between gaps in the rugged landscape. I swore on my life, that I could hear and smell the sea even though we were in the coach. I knew for sure that it wouldn't be long before we drove into the harbour.

The coach slowly wound its way around the narrow roads until the harbour and docking area came into view. I excitedly looked this way and that, trying to see the ship that was to take us to paradise and back. But at the time, there was only one cranky-looking old vessel tied up, nothing whatsoever like the type of cruise liners I had seen displayed in holiday brochures and nothing at all like I had imagined, but then of course, this wasn't our ship. Perhaps, our holiday liner had been held up somewhere and we were going to have to wait around. God what a nuisance, what a pain! Still, not to worry, I was sure we would have been warned by the coach driver if they were expecting a problem or major delay.

I turned to look at Shmel and the ghastly look on his face said it all... This ancient-looking craft *was* ours, I decided in an instant, this definitely was *not* going to take us to paradise and back, but would more than likely take us to hell and back. The coach trundled along the cobbled road and turned into the harbour. The excited sounds that had been buzzing around the coach had disappeared, as people who had been so looking forward to a great holiday realised that they now had to re-evaluate their expectations. I had felt bitter disappointment at the first glance and knew that Shmel was fuming inside. I just couldn't imagine what had gone wrong.

Once the coach had stopped we all got off rather reluctantly, and stood around looking at this... this 'thing', that we were to spend our long-awaited holiday on.

With all our baggage unloaded from the bowels of the coach, the driver hastily climbed back into his seat, started up the engine and prepared to depart. I was just brushing the dust off my sleeve that had been thrown up by the departing coach - when a couple of the ship's representatives cheerfully came across to us with clipboards and pens, asking for our names.

"Ah, yes," a smiling rep. said as he crossed our names off his slip of paper. "You have suite number twelve, if you go down the gang-plank and up to the reception desk they will give you the keys."

We dismally made our way down from the jetty onto the M. V. Frimpton, leaving behind our luggage that was to be brought aboard by the staff. We collected the keys to the cabin and made our way down, on the port side. Because it was our honeymoon, Shmel had paid extra money for us to have a 'suite', huh! Well, if this was the 'suite', I didn't dare try to imagine what the standard cabins were like. Nevertheless, once everyone was on board, we sailed off into the unknown.

All at Sea... Our luggage was dutifully delivered by a very young-looking Asian boy shortly after we had found our cabin. Shmel tipped the lad and then we dolefully begun the dreary job of unpacking. Once we had sorted out our clothes and hung up what we could, we decided to go and explore our surroundings. We tried to look on the positive side of things, remembering the old saying that goes, something like – 'You cannot always judge a book by its cover.' We were hoping that the ship might look better on the inside than it did from the outside. Unfortunately, it wasn't to be, as neither Shmel nor I were in a good mood by now and nothing pleased us at all, plus, Shmel moaned and groaned about everything, which didn't help to cheer me up one bit although, on this occasion, I couldn't really blame him.

The little we saw of the other passengers whilst we were on our wanderings did little to brighten up our day, as they really didn't look our type, or the sort of people we were used to mixing with, in fact, we decided that we wouldn't particularly want to spend a day with any of them, let alone ten days. Added to our misery, it seemed that most of the people we passed were speaking in a foreign language. Although, just now and again we heard the strains of some good old English swear words and we were definitely *not* impressed with that either.

The décor of the ship left a lot to be desired and the few shops on the lower deck were little more than dire. I could tell by Shmel's general attitude along with the miserable look on his face, that this, so called holiday was destined to be a total disaster. As hard as he tried, and on this occasion I do believe he *did* try, he just couldn't hide his disappointment and annoyance. Once we got back to our 'suite', which amounted to one hard bed, a wardrobe with drawers that were tatty and damaged, and a grubby porthole, Shmel plumped down on the edge of the bed and proceeded to blame the travel company through which he had booked the holiday.

Apparently, Shmel had booked quite a few holidays through this particular agent in England, so he must have taken it for granted that the agent knew what he was looking for when it came to booking a very special holiday such as, his honeymoon. Like every other job of work, even travel agents must recognise and become familiar with their regular customers and I am sure they must become aware of their customers likes and dislikes and what they expect, especially someone like Shmel, who was well-to-do and didn't hide the fact.

Somewhere along the line there must have been some kind of misunderstanding and Shmel had been given to believe that this particular cruise to the Mediterranean was on a new ship. Thinking it was to be its 'maiden voyage' he jumped at the opportunity and it was only now that Shmel realised that the ship wasn't new, as in 'brand, spanking new' it was only 'new' to its owners, that of 'Garland Cruise Lines'.

Nevertheless, we were here, and there was nothing we could do about it. I didn't help matters, for as we cruised deeper into the Mediterranean Sea

I became very ill with sea-sickness. Consequently, most of the early part of the cruise found me in bed feeling extremely, urgghhh. During the first few days of our honeymoon trip the ship's doctor visited our cabin at least three times to check me over and give me injections to try and stop the sickness. Occasionally I would make an effort to accompany Shmel to dinner but unfortunately, this was also a disaster. For whoever organised the seating arrangements, sat us with a crowd of foreign-speaking people with whom we had no hope of conversing. Not being able to talk to anyone else at the table was extremely embarrassing. It was more difficult for Shmel, as he frequently had to dine without me. Eventually, not being able to stand yet another dumb meal, Shmel insisted we be relocated and put on a table with at least one other couple who spoke English.

This latest complaint endeared us to the captain of the ship, vessel or crate, whatever you'd like to call it, so much so, that we were probably considered to be the passengers from hell. Nevertheless, the complaints, from our point of view, were very relevant and totally justified. The relationship we managed to establish with the hierarchy of the ship became very apparent when we finally realised that we were definitely *not* going to be invited to sit at the captain's table for dinner. To think the captain didn't want to share our company in this traditional way was very upsetting and distressing for me. After all, I had packed all my new designer gear and was certainly not going to bother to dress up for my regular dinner pals. In fact, I reached a point where I thought all my beautiful designer wear was never going to be aired at all, well, not on this holiday and that was the truth!

Although my sickness abated somewhat, it usually managed to reappear to some degree when I occasionally made my way to dinner, as I found the food little more than disgusting. But, I will give full marks to the Asian waiters who did their utmost to please us.

Even though I was depressed and feeling very miserable most of the time I was looking forward to the much publicised - Midnight Feast - that was considered to be something extra special. Shmel had often mentioned this exciting event that he had attended on other cruises, saying that it was always a great evening with fabulous entertainment and a wonderful array of exotic foods. Unfortunately, I was so disappointed, for all we had was piped, supermarket-type music and *our* midnight feast consisted of plates and plates of curled-up sandwiches that looked as though they had seen better days, along with bite-sized lumps of plain cake. Ugh!

Four days into our cruise I decided that I had put up with enough and announced to Shmel, in no uncertain terms, that this holiday was definitely not for me. After all, I had already spent most of the time in my cubby-hole feeling sick and queasy and to top it all, a couple of days into the journey, I had accidentally walked into the shower door, badly gashing my head. You just can't imagine what I looked like when gazing into the mirror. A green, something or other, from out-of-space with a hole in the head! I was very quickly coming to the conclusion that this was definitely *not* the way to spend a romantic honeymoon... No way!

The Great Escape... The next port of call was to be Cadiz, so we took this golden opportunity to promptly, pack our bags. Not that we had as much to pack as we did when we first started out, as Shmel noticed whilst packing, that he had somehow 'lost' some of his possessions, amongst which were a smart pair of shorts, some underwear and a small radio. Mmm? Not that the loss of a few items of clothing worried us at the time, we were only too pleased to be leaving.

Shmel went to see the cruise liner's representative and told him to inform the captain that we would be departing the ship at Cadiz and that we would be contacting the tour operator in England in order to complain about the..., well, everything.

Not wanting to appear mean or seen to hold a grudge, we also informed the rep. that they could give our cabin, at no extra cost of course, to a decent English couple that we had befriended the day before. We hurried back and eagerly picked up our hand luggage from our cubby-hole and on the way back to the reception desk to hand in the keys, we happened to bump into the couple we had befriended. We were delighted to inform them that, as we were curtailing our holiday for personal reasons we had given our permission for them to be upgraded to our 'suite'. Well...They were absolutely delighted, as you can well imagine.

We arrived and docked at Cadiz on time and most of the passengers couldn't wait to disembark so that they could get away from the ship, albeit for just a few hours. We, on the other hand tottered down the gangplank with all our belongings, smiling and waving goodbye to some of the cabin staff and the few people we had made friends with.

"Good luck to them," I muttered to Shmel as we hit terra firma, "Rather them than me."

I was so pleased to be off the ship for good so that we could quickly put the last five days behind us. With renewed confidence I set forth in some of my fancy gear, ready to start my 'real' honeymoon.

We quickly managed to put plenty of distance between us and the moored vessel, and as we were walking towards the entrance of the harbour, we thought we would stop and take stock, so that we could decide what to do. We were in a foreign country, didn't speak the language and frankly, we had no idea where to go next. We obviously couldn't walk too far with our luggage so Shmel decided to head for the nearest road and hail a taxi, saying we would make our minds up from there.

With some amount of effort we summoned a taxi, and Shmel managed, after a style, to explain to a bored looking driver that we had disembarked, prematurely, from a newly arrived vessel and that we were looking for somewhere to stay for the night, a hotel perhaps? Obviously, Shmel's hand gestures hadn't explained things quite the way he had intended, for, after a hectic drive around the strange streets of Cadiz the driver promptly pulled up outside a car-hire establishment and gestured to us to get out. Mind you, at the time, we decided that hiring a car might not be such a bad idea after all, as we weren't that far from Marbella and we thought it would be a good idea to spend the rest of our honeymoon there.

But this idea was very quickly scuttled as, to start off with, Shmel wasn't too happy with the car they offered us and was even less happy with the amount of money they quoted for just the one day we were going to use it. I swear they must have seen us coming! We tried to explain that we didn't want to pay too much and that we weren't too impressed with the car they wanted to lend us either. We frantically mimed that we only wanted to hire the car for a day, just to get us to Marbella. But at that moment in time nobody in the world appeared to speak English or indeed, understand what we wanted, I became totally frustrated and Shmel was hopping mad.

We walked away from the car-hire company and stood in the middle of nowhere trying to decide what to do. Shmel didn't want to pay out any more money to a car-hire company or, for that matter, hotel and he grumbled, saying that he had already paid out enough for the cruise and that he was totally pissed off, fed up and furious with everything and everyone. We stood in the midst of our sad looking baggage and bags arguing about what to do. I could truly understand why my husband was so furious and annoyed, but after all, we couldn't stand there all day, we would have to do something and eventually we decided that we had no alternative option but to return to the cruise liner.

Fortunately, huh! The same taxi that brought us to this place was still waiting around so we called it over and gestured to the driver to take us back to the harbour. Shmel looked down at his watch and went into a bit of a panic as it appeared that the ship was due to sail within the next thirty minutes. We literally tossed our precious luggage into the boot of the taxi and I hurled myself into the back of the cab. Shmel poked the driver in the shoulder and gestured, by flapping both of his hands up and down, telling him to 'step on it pronto' to which, Shmel had hardly managed to get his foot in the car-door when the driver shot off like a bullet from a gun, hurling Shmel across my lap and plunging us both into the back of the seat. I had to hold on mighty tight to my hat (metaphorically speaking) as we sped along the bumpy roads and within a matter of minutes we were in sight of the harbour.

The taxi driver pulled up with a jolt, heaving us both forward in the process, so that we almost slipped off the seat. But, at least we were where we wanted to be, (that's a joke, by the way) and the moored liner was still in sight. I was just about to open the taxi door when Shmel grabbed hold of my arm and in so doing poked the taxi driver in the shoulder again saying that he wanted to be driven nearer to the ship. Well, I can tell you for true that the driver understood every word Shmel said for he grinned, shook his head, and held out his hand for the fare. After a few yes, yes, yes's and no, no, no's, Shmel gave up and, getting out of the cab he begrudgingly rammed a few notes into the driver's hand. Once I was out of the taxi the driver dragged our luggage out of the boot and dumped it onto the ground and drove off faster than that, leaving Shmel and I to get our cases and hand luggage back to the ship as quickly as possible.

Dash and Blow... We looked at our watches simultaneously, grabbed up our cases and hurtled off along the harbour and down towards the liner. We must have looked a sorry sight, trying to run along with our baggage on mini wheels, travelling at the speed of light, with our jackets flying in the breeze and my hair all dishevelled, Shmel, on the other hand didn't have that problem, but he was sweating like a pig and his face became extremely red from the unusual exertion.

We could see the seamen making ready to raise the anchor and we looked on with horror. Would we get to the ship on time? Would they pull in the gangplank just as we got there? These were the questions that were running through my mind as I sped along as best I could, waving my hand, in a hope that the captain of the vessel would see us and 'hold fast' until we got there. As luck would have it (if you can call it luck), we got to the ship with just a few minutes to spare. The crew-men were already busying themselves to cast off, so we frantically made a dash for the gangplank and dragged ourselves, luggage and all, as fast as we could up the rickety gangway.

'Thank God we made it in time', I thought, as the crew heaved in the heavy walkway. I was all puffed out and Shmel was panting like a dog. Nevertheless, we were back on board and we left our luggage dumped in a corner while we went and spoke to the rep. Oh dear! It was all so embarrassing having to explain that we couldn't find anywhere to go and unfortunately, had no other alternative but to return to the ship. Also, as sorry as we were, we had no other option but to disappoint the other couple who by now, had moved all their stuff into our suite and had to promptly move it all out again. Needless to say, the thwarted couple didn't speak to us for the rest of the trip.

But then that is life, and life can be a bitch!

-:: *Dash and Blow* ::-

I suppose looking back, we were quite fortunate that the captain allowed us back on board after having, more or less, told him to stuff his ship. But then, one always has to be prepared to back-track and eat humble pie when cornered or when one's back is against the wall. We spent the rest of the days wishing them away as quickly as possible. I continued being sick and ill for the rest of the journey and Shmel was as miserable as sin.

We were so pleased when the day arrived for us to start the journey back home, I could hardly wait to get onto the coach that was to take us back to the airport, and believe it or not, the ending befitted the holiday, as the day we left it was tipping down with rain and at one point our luggage went on the missing list. Because of my sickness I felt groggy and very wobbly even when I was on solid ground again. All in all, it was a 'once in a lifetime experience' of epic proportions, a holiday I will never forget, and it became our favourite topic of conversation for many months to come.

Home At Last… Shortly after we had arrived home from the honeymoon, my husband went to see the travel agent with whom he booked the fateful holiday, explaining forcefully about our dreadful experience. He made a special point of saying how extremely disappointed we had been that the holiday liner was so old and not the shiny new one we had been expecting. He explained that he was now hoping to be reimbursed to some extent, for our troubles. Of course, the travel agent didn't want to know and made all kinds of excuses, hinting that it was Shmel's fault for assuming that the vessel was brand new, instead of just new to the company. I think Shmel would have been happy and it would have gone some way towards appeasing him if the agent had offered to put us both up for a night in a hotel or something of equal value, but the travel company didn't want to show us any form of gesture of good will. After all, it was our honeymoon, for God's sake, not just your average holiday!

Shmel was so furious with the company and their lack of customer care that he decided to take them to court. He hired a solicitor and started proceedings, but after a short while he was strongly advised to drop the case as… "Quite honestly," the solicitor informed him. "You don't have a hope in hell of successfully suing 'Garland Cruises' and making anything out of it." So on that advice, Shmel did just that and dropped the case.

Shmel was incensed that a company could get away with ruining peoples' special holidays without having to account for their actions. What with Shmel's fury lasting for days, culminating in an embarrassing climb down, our honeymoon cruise became just another venture that had turned sour in his hands.

Nevertheless, with the wedding and honeymoon well and truly behind me, I tried to settle down to as normal a married life as possible. Not that my marriage was ever going to be normal as Shmel still wanted to live in his bed-sit, only staying with me a few nights each week. To be quite truthful, I soon realised that being married was going to make absolutely no difference to me whatsoever, as it turned out to be exactly the same as it was before I wed and unfortunately, this was how my life as Shmel's wife was to continue.

The Steak-Out… As the weeks passed we took to going out for a meal or two at the week-ends. One of our favourite places was a local steak house. Apart from the odd couple or party of people that might turn up on the off chance, more often than not, there would only be us regular customers who sat in our usual places. We always chose to sit in a quiet spot by the window, and near to us would regularly sit a trio of women, a grandmother, mother and daughter. Their faces became very familiar and we would often nod hello. One week when Shmel and I had rowed, I found out that he had gone to the restaurant as usual on his own and chatted up the thirty-year-old daughter eventually inviting her out for a meal. Trying his best to be discreet, he took her to an Indian restaurant and after the meal and seeing her home, apparently, he suggested they meet again, but unfortunately for him she politely declined the offer. Needless to say, we never saw the trio in our regular steak house again. I was used to the fact that whenever we were not speaking

Shmel would either go back to one of his old floozies or try to pick up some other woman, no matter who it was, just as long as it wore a skirt.

Ring, Ring who's Calling?... Despite our ups and downs I was still happily getting used to being Shmel's wife and having a wedding ring on my finger. After his most recent and dissatisfied effort to have a bit of a 'fling' we were soon speaking again and continued the habit of going out on a Friday and Saturday night. Even though I was a good cook and enjoyed preparing food, I have to admit, it was very pleasing to be able to take a break from the kitchen. At the same time, it allowed us to spend some quality time together. Shmel always liked a good restaurant and we would sit and enjoy a meal while catching up on the latest happenings.

There were at least three special restaurants we frequented; they were reliable haunts serving good food, in a pleasant atmosphere. The restaurateurs and staff knew us well and would often afford us that little bit of extra service that was so pleasing. We were, on the whole, good customers. We seldom complained, were quiet and gave a good tip. We would just sit and chit-chat in general, enjoying the excellent food, while minding our own business.

So it was one Friday evening after having made a reservation at a restaurant not far from where I was living. As usual, Shmel drove down from his London bed-sit to my house, arriving around 7:30pm. He pulled up outside, sounded his horn and on hearing him, I picked up my bag and coat, left the house, jumped into his waiting car and we took off.

I had booked into a restaurant that he particularly liked for that evening as I knew he relished the fine cuisine served there. Directly we arrived, he ordered our usual meals and we took our seats. Each time we went to a restaurant, because Shmel had to drive all the way from the centre of London, he would always dump his cigars, lighter and mobile-phone on the table and make a dash for the loo, during which time, I would make myself comfortable and perhaps pass a few minutes conversing with the restaurant owner or the staff. On this particular evening Shmel had only just disappeared into the toilet when his mobile rang. I wasn't in the habit of answering his phone as he didn't really appreciate it at all but on this occasion, as he had only just left the table, I picked up the phone, pressed the answer button and said. "Hello."

A strange woman's voice asked if she could speak to Shmel, I replied saying that he wasn't available at the moment but could I take a message. She said, rather flatly, that she was one of his 'working girls' and wanted to know her days and hours for the coming week. I was instantly stunned, but managed to hold my shock at bay while I said that my husband would ring her back as her number was on the screen. She thanked me and the mobile went dead, I pressed the button to end the call and sat looking at the innocent phone. I couldn't believe what I had just heard and was totally horrified. I recognised the term 'working girl' as another name for a prostitute and the sudden realisation of what this could mean sent a chilling bolt of shock through my bones.

Nothing but the Truth... I looked up from the phone in time to see Shmel walking back towards me still slightly adjusting his trouser belt. He smiled at me as I put the phone down on the table, my face must have been ashen although, in the dim lights of the restaurant he would not have seen it. But as he started to take his seat directly opposite me, it must have dawned on him that I had just withdrawn my hand from his mobile phone and after looking at it and then me, he realised that something had happened.

"Are you all right?" he inquired, looking at me a little puzzled.

"Your mobile rang and as you were in the loo, I had to answer it."

I could see straight away that he wasn't happy about that, but I continued, saying that it was one of his 'working girls' and she wanted to know her hours. He immediately averted his eyes away from mine and, pocketing his mobile he continued to look away. I tried to catch his eye but he avoided me by going straight for a jug of iced-water that was standing on the table and proceeded to pour some into my glass, after which, he picked up the menu and held it up in front of his face, creating a barrier between us.

I lifted my hand and deliberately pushed the menu slowly down onto the table and asked him in a controlled voice what was going on.

"Nothing, nothing." he replied, lifting the menu up again.

I immediately plunged the menu back down onto the table and repeated my question in a more controlled, even more determined, but still quiet voice. He knew I was not totally stupid and he could see that I had become aware of something very untoward. I watched as he squirmed in his seat and I saw a flush sweep across his face, despite the low lighting… I knew then and there, in that split second, that I had pulled the pin on a dirty grenade and that everything was about to blow sky high.

Shmel was in such a tight corner, there was little else he could do but come clean. This strange woman, in just a few, seemingly innocent words, had inadvertently blown the whistle on him and he had nowhere to run and nowhere to hide. So while I sat frozen to my seat, he launched into the sordid story that was to rock my trust, my marriage and my life. I had lost all sense of hunger by this time and the pangs of hunger I did have had turned to that of nausea.

He leaned forward and put both of his elbows on the table, he interlaced his fingers, rested his chin on them and started to explain in a very matter-of-fact voice how his video shops had been going down the pan for a long time and that he had eventually sold out to a huge company bearing a household name. He said that he hadn't made as much money from the deal as he had hoped, but because the video market had been somewhat slow for ages he had no other choice but to sell up at the price offered. On top of that, he told me how gutted he had been when his Steven Seagal look-a-like pal had kicked him out of the video magazine business since, after all, it had been his idea in the first place. Ahhhhhh!

He told me how much time he had wasted looking around at other business opportunities and, considering his age and the fact that no one would employ him now, quite honestly he said, he had just about run out of ideas when, all of a sudden - just like that! An opportunity came up for him to buy this adult sauna and massage parlour in London… Naturally, he didn't *want* to go into anything like that (bloody liar).

"God forbid" he said, it was the *last* thing he would have considered but, owing to the fact that he needed the money quite badly he decided to give it a go, at least it would be a way of earning a few bob in order to keep everything ticking over.

The meal that Shmel had ordered as we walked in came up and the waitress asked us if there was anything else we needed. Shmel waived her away politely as I sat in stony silence. He waffled on about his sad affairs, as he proceeded to tuck into his meal. I watched him as though in a vacuum, I could scarcely hear what he was saying, smell the food, nor did I have any recognisable sensation of self. All that kept running through my mind was the fact that…

My husband was a pimp, nothing but a sleazy, yiddisher PIMP.

I'm not quite sure when my normal feelings came back to me, but when they did he was still rattling on, trying to explain how he had arrived in this situation. Naturally it was the fault of everyone else and not his.

"Eat your food Shar." He said to me gently.

But I couldn't, I felt too sick even to pick up my knife and fork.

I can't remember what happened to my uneaten meal; I guess I must have sat there for some time before getting up in some kind of stupor and walking out. Shmel must have followed me out and drove me home. I really don't remember getting in or out of the car or whether he came into the house, or said goodbye, or what? My mind was a complete blank.

I lay awake that night trying to make sense of it all and to see if I could piece together all the missing parts of the jig-saw that I hadn't been able to find or sort out before.

He seldom stayed overnight and hardly ever talked in depth to me, and because he didn't involve me in any of his business plans or dealings, it meant that I never really knew what he was up to. We seldom, if ever discussed his work or any of his financial matters, as most of his business dealings were carried on when, from my point of view, he was on the missing list. Mind you, once I knew what was going on, the fact that we had money to burn and was living the high life with fabulous holidays, houses, top of the range cars, designer gear, etc. everything very quickly fell into place.

His general attitude had changed somewhat of late too. I always found him quite controlling at the best of times but in the last couple of years he had become even more so. He seldom, if ever asked me what *I* wanted to do or where *I* wanted to go. It was always a case of, pack your bags we're going to this place or that, therefore, apart from choosing the odd restaurant now and again that was about all the decisions I was allowed to make. He was a control freak and the more money he had the more power it gave him over others, in order to get and do exactly what he wanted.

Apart from my meal being ruined that evening, my sleep was disturbed also. I not only lay awake that night, but for many nights to come, trying to imagine what he might be doing. Such as, when he left me did he go back to his bed-sit or did he go straight to this sauna and massage parlour? Was he making any effort at all to be faithful to me or was he having other women on a regular basis? Was he *really* a pimp or was that just my imagination blowing things up out of all proportion? After all, the crime of pimping was rather unusual for a man of the Jewish faith.

During the coming weeks he continually tried to reassure me that he was only in the business for the money and that he had no interest whatsoever in the women or the men that frequented the place. I so much wanted to believe what he was saying that it hurt, but knowing his reputation of old, his words did nothing to comfort me or allay my fears.

Time and time again, over and over I would question myself as to what I should do? I was married to this man, I had taken holy vows in the sight of God so what should I do? Should I leave him and end it, divorce him? But nowhere could I find an answer to my queries.

When Shmel was off the scene for a while I would become very positive and decide that next time we meet I would ask for a divorce, but every 'next time' he came back I would end up feeling low, depressed or miserable and he would talk me round with his soothing voice and assurances. All I wanted was to believe in my husband and for us to be normal.

Eventually, I decided to try and live completely separate from his business dealings and I tried very hard not to get involved in anything. I resolved never to talk about his sauna and massage parlour and he made a point of never broaching the subject.

Taken to the Cleaners... Some weeks went by during which time, it emerged, that he had already taken over a second sauna in the East End of London. I only found this out one day when we were out for a ride in the car. Driving towards Hackney and the Shoreditch area Shmel suddenly announced that he needed to pop into his business premises in order to pick up some 'stuff'.

I didn't know what business premises he was referring to, but when we eventually stopped, it was outside a place that looked rather like an ordinary, run of the mill, small shop front, but instead of having the usual clear glass windows its panes of glass were darkened and smoky. He disappeared into the building, in order to check up and see that everything was alright and running smoothly. He must have been gone for about ten minutes or so, during which short time, alone in the car, I was forced to come to terms with the revelation of this second sauna. Upon his return he said that all was well and that he had picked up the 'stuff', which turned out to be money!

Once back on the road, he felt the need to explain that, just like any other shop, there was no way the management could leave money on the premises overnight as that would make it a target for thieves to break in and rob the place of all the takings. I now know of course, the only real difference being; that any theft from this type of property could not be reported to the police for fear that they might get suspicious and raid the place, which of course, *would never do.*

The drive to his premises to pick up his 'stuff' became a bit of a habit, I suppose he had taken a chance by doing it once and since I hadn't passed any comments, he became brazen and did it more frequently and as a matter of course. Around about the third or fourth week, when he stopped off to check up and collect his money he said that he would be an extra long time as he had to wait for a builder to come along to do some repair work on one of the massage rooms and he needed to speak to him.

The Betrayal... During these, now regular visits to the East End sauna, while I stayed seated in the car, the receptionist would come out to pick up a fresh delivery of clean towels from the boot of the car. These were special, thick towels that were cleaned at a good laundry who made sure they were returned beautifully white, soft and very fluffy. The sauna's receptionist was a pleasant young girl and when collecting the towels she would always make a point of speaking to me. She would often make some pleasant comment about my hair-do or clothes, she was indeed, very sweet. I like people in general and love to chat so we struck up a relatively friendly relationship always remembering of course, that she was one of my husband's employees and I was his wife. Nevertheless, this young girl was to be the final straw in the, already, shaky relationship I had with my husband. This would also prove to be the very last visit I made to this sauna, for while my dear rat of a husband was waiting for the builder to appear, this young lady came out to collect the towels as usual and we chatted for so long that it must have given her the confidence to speak out. But I most certainly wasn't prepared for the revelation she was about to make.

During our casual conversation I happened to speak of my husband and when I mentioned his name, the young girl suddenly looked at me most puzzled and said, "Tell me; why on earth did you marry this man?"

Being rather taken aback by her question, I said, rather defensively, "Well, why does anyone marry anyone? I love him of course."

The girl then sighed and looked at me with a sad, much older than her years, expression and lowering her voice said, "Look, I'm sorry if this is going to hurt your feelings but I think you ought to know something about him..." At that she hesitated...

"Well, go on; tell me." I urged...

The girl took a deep breath then continued saying, "The night before your husband was due to be married, he spent it here with a 'working' lady who also does the cleaning to earn a bit of extra money."

While I sat in stunned silence she went on to inform me that my husband also spent every Tuesday afternoon at the sauna and he would take a Latin prostitute to a vacant room where she would take care of every one of his sexual needs.

Today: Okay, well, I can hear you saying that I must have expected it and the fact that I wasn't totally naïve, meant I should have suspected, but remember, I was newly married and quite honestly, although Shmel's infidelities were always in my thoughts, I would push them to the back of my mind because I didn't want to believe this of my husband. Just ask yourself ladies, would you believe that your husband spent the final hours with a scrubber on the night before his wedding? Well, would you? No! I guess not. Well neither did I and that's the truth!

This damming disclosure about my husband was truly awful and I found it extremely demoralizing. I decided that after this I really couldn't be expected to tolerate such behaviour from my husband any longer so I became determined to ask him for a divorce. We had a major row, during which he denied all tell-tale rumours, saying it was all supposition on the part of a young woman who had nothing better to do than try and wreck other peoples' relationships.

We had been married just two months and I was already thinking about a divorce. I was absolutely gutted and felt completely let down, I would question my own motives; over and over again as to how and why I ever got involved with such a disgusting person in the first place. I had completely lost my way and didn't know what I was doing or where I was going. I continually questioned myself but these questions produced no logical answers, nor did they give me any indication of which course I should take.

He disappeared out of my life after this latest row and didn't make any attempt to contact me in order to talk things over or at least console me. I had become dependent on him and floundered when he wasn't around. I just needed to talk things through with him.

I didn't file for a divorce after all; instead, I just went quiet and withdrawn and tried to get on with my life despite him. The only contact he made with me was to text me now and again to say that he had put money in the bank for housekeeping and in one particular text message he said that he had put two weeks money in the bank, this time, as he was off to a bridge tournament in Bournemouth.

The Clever Dick... This latest, seemingly, innocent text message set alarm bells ringing for me, he must have felt very clever saying he was going to Bournemouth as opposed to Brighton. He knew I was very familiar with Brighton, owing to the fact that my mother had lived there for years and that it would be so easy for me to check up on him. Whenever my alarm bells rang I was almost always one hundred percent right about him and his 'goings on'. It was as if my guardian angel would alert me to his wrongdoings and this time it would prove to be no exception.

I was so incensed by the recent revelations that had unfolded and his behaviour of late that I decided to spend some of his own money having him investigated. With very little to go on I hired a private detective and asked him if he could locate my husband's true whereabouts. The detective was very professional, having done it so many times before, I assumed, and after requesting a brief outline of the situation he asked for my husband's full name and age, his car registration and physical description. He also asked me who I thought he might be with. Short of being sarcastic and saying something like 'any other woman bar me,' I resisted the temptation and instead told the detective that I had no idea who he was with, it was just that he was lying about his whereabouts and, being his wife and a new one at that, I was naturally intrigued. The detective bid me goodbye and said he would be in touch as soon as he had some information. I waited with bated breath and just three days later the P.D. telephoned me to say that my husband was in Malta and would be returning the following Tuesday at 2:30pm, into Heathrow Airport.

I must admit that there was no shock reaction from me, just incredible anger and I was left to wonder as to whether he was alone, with some old prostitute or perhaps it was a long standing girlfriend. I couldn't wait for the next Tuesday to come around!

On the instructions of the private detective I was to meet him at the airport wearing a blonde wig over my dark, auburn hair so that my husband wouldn't instantly recognise me and together, we would confront my husband when and if it was appropriate.

The detective and I met in the lounge at Heathrow by the Hertz Car Hire stand, and we then went and mingled with the waiting crowd near to the gate that said 'NOTHING TO DECLARE'.

And Who Are You?... We kept our eyes on the monitors and once Shmel's plane had landed we had to wait for some time while he collected his luggage. My heart was pounding and I kept looking over towards the detective for reassurance and each time I did, he would nod his head towards me then look away.

Sure enough the passengers from my husband's flight started to dribble through, and then suddenly, there he was in all his glory. There was my husband strolling along through the green channel with nothing to declare except... Oh, No! I couldn't believe it, it was his old 'bit' on the side, none other than the 'so called lady' who was with him in the Southend Casino on that fateful day in 1994. I truly thought it was going to be a big busty prostitute, or maybe an attractive, old flame. But it turned out to be a very old flame that was not only to show herself as being his bridge partner but his bed partner too.

I looked across at the detective and flashed my eyes over towards my husband. The detective frowned deeply and looked quite stunned at the sight of these two old codgers walking along pushing their baggage trolley. The detective made a swift movement over towards me and whispered in my ear, "Bloody hell, is that your old man?"

I nodded.

"Well, all I can say is that you must have had shit in your eyes, or you must have needed extra-power glasses, my love."

He really couldn't believe that the 'person' coming towards us was my husband.

I was to be further gob-smacked as, following up behind him was…. Wait for it! - None other than his ex-wife, Anne and her mother, Shmel's daughter, his youngest son and his girlfriend, a real, happy family entourage, all relaxed and seemingly happy after a great time in Malta. Well, as happy as they all appeared to be, I was about to change all that…

I waited my chance and when it came, without any hesitation, I stepped smartly forward in front of them and dragged off my blonde wig. My husband stopped dead in his tracks which brought his old lady friend to a sudden halt which in turn, created a knock-on-effect for some of the other passengers who were following up behind them.

There we stood, the three of us re-enacting the confrontation that was held at 'High Noon.' My husband looked straight up at me with surprise and shock and said, "WOW! What are you doing here?"

"More to the point," I replied, "What are *you* doing here?"

The old girl muscled in at this point and jutting her face towards me said, "Who are you?"

I turned fully towards her saying, "I'm his wife, who are you?"

She obviously hadn't recognised me, but then she may not have seen me properly before and in any case, if she had seen me in the past, she wouldn't have recognised me as I was unusually slim at the time and was wearing heavy make up to help with my disguise.

I noticed she moved a step away from Shmel as she introduced herself to me.

All this happened within a very short space of time, during which, Anne and the rest of the mob were still merrily making their way towards us.

Suddenly, coming to his senses, Shmel turned away and frantically tried to catch Anne's eye, in order to warn her of the imminent danger of a *real* shoot-out. But it was all too late and as our eyes locked, Anne's chin hit the floor. I watched the thoughts run across her forehead, similar to one of those electronic notice boards that you see at railway stations, with digital words saying. Good heavens! How on earth had she found out about this holiday? And, how did she know all the details? And, how…?

At that point I said no more and just looked away, having had just enough for one day. The private detective had taken photographs and a video film of Shmel and his lady-love while all this confronting had been taking place, so there was little left for me to do now but go home.

Shmel and his followers moved off quickly as I turned away towards the private detective. We looked satisfyingly at each other, although, I thought I noticed in his eyes, just the slightest hint of sympathy for me and the situation

I now found myself in. After all, it's all very gratifying to be proved right in one's assumptions and to have caught someone out who has been unfaithful, but at the end of the day I would have to go home and go to bed that night knowing that not only was my husband a pimp, living off the immoral earnings of prostitutes, but he was substituting me, his wife, for some elderly woman who had seen better days.

The detective put his cameras carefully into their cases and then into his briefcase and we moved away, I sullenly walked along beside him with the blonde wig now dangling from my hand. We made our way towards the airport exit area in silence; my mind was too full to talk. I tried to imagine what they were all saying to each other, wondering how I had come to be standing there just as they all walked off the plane. How would I have known about their holiday? Who could have told me and who would have given me the information? I bet their questioning conversations were buzzing. I had obviously not mentioned the presence of the P. D. who was standing some feet away from me when I confronted my husband. The fact that he was taking photographs probably didn't register to anyone at that time, as they were all so shocked to see me, plus, there were a good many people milling around that area anyway.

The detective and I slowly walked along with dozens of other people, down and through the exit areas that led to the parking lots. His car was on the first floor and by the time we had arrived at the car park I had recovered my composure to a great extent. Having already pushed the blonde wig into my bag I walked with my head held high. I am sure the detective must have admired my spirit as he smiled broadly at me and led me confidently over towards his car. He zapped the car from a short distance away and it sprung into life as we approached, and just as we were about to open the car doors, a huge passenger lift that was situated directly opposite the car opened up to reveal none other than my husband and his mob.

They all jostled with baggage-laden trolleys to get out of the sardine-packed lift as quickly as possible, while the detective and I stood poised, watching the action. Until that was, Shmel, Anne and his ex mother-in-law all spotted me in unison. Immediately, the action ceased and without any more ado, they all did a very quick turnaround and all tried to jostle and squeeze back into the lift from whence they had just emerged.

This very sudden change of heart was probably brought on because none of them were ever too sure what I might do in any given situation. Consequently, their flight responses must have kicked in instantly! But they were not fast enough, for they were trapped and without doubt, heard me shout across to them saying,

"*You've been had again, you RAT, for this is a private detective!*"

-:: *You've been Had!*::-

As the lift gates closed on the mortified family, taking them to, God knows where, the detective and I got into the car and he slowly made his way out of the parking area and onto the road that would take us home. The detective kindly said that he would drop me back at my house, so while we were on the way I rang my husband's mobile and when he answered, I shouted down the phone, "How could you? How could you treat me so?"

To which he replied, calmly, "You could have had all this."

"You're joking" I yelled back at him, "A holiday with your ex-wife, *no thank you.*"

I flicked the 'end-call' button and threw the mobile into my bag, desperately trying to fight back the tears. I tossed my hair back and turned and forced a smile for the detective. He returned a reassuring smile back, for he seemed to think that I would be alright.

He dropped me outside my house and said that he would be in touch soon and would send the photos and the video, along with his invoice. I thanked him very much and we shook hands. He got back into his car and drove away leaving behind a sad woman who had just lost yet another piece of her, already, broken heart.

Today: This latest episode may have seemed quite amusing to you and, looking back, the antics of this tacky event now seems hilarious to me. But at the time, it was far from funny. The mental torture I was going through was killing me. Yet despite all he was putting me through and all the pain he was inflicting on me, deep down I loved him and desperately tried to keep alive a glimmer of hope that in the fullness of time he would come to appreciate me enough to live with me properly. I often used to say to him that he needed a psychiatrist to help him sort out some of the serious issues that made him act the way he did, but perhaps he was past help, who knows? Without exception, though, he would always turn the tables on me and say it was indeed I who needed a psychiatrist, and looking back at it now, he was probably right.

Curiosity... Just three days after the embarrassment and upset I had endured at Heathrow Airport the private detective telephoned me with more information, this time, on Shmel's elderly girlfriend. He had managed to get hold of her mainline-home telephone number, her exact home address, the make and registration of the car she drove and the address of the shop where she worked and said that he would pass all this information on to me by letter.

I told him that the invoice for his work had been received that morning and that a cheque would be sent to him by return of post. Accompanying his cheque was a 'Thank You' card expressing my appreciation for all his services and all the vital information he had passed on to me. The very next morning I received a first class letter with all the relative information on 'Minnie' (The nick-name I gave her) and it appeared that she lived and worked within a short distance from where I lived.

With all this information in my hand I was prompted, just out of curiosity of course, to go and give this old bat the once over, so that very afternoon I drove down to the high street and found the shop where she worked, it was a jewellers. Through the window I could see her serving a customer and wondered how I could make myself known to her without creating too much of a scene.

I had no intention of disposing of my wedding ring as yet, but I suddenly hit on an idea which meant that I had to remove the ring from my finger then, holding the ring carefully in my hand I walked into the shop. Unfortunately, there were already a couple of other customers waiting to be served so I had to wait my turn hoping and praying that she would have to serve me, but there was another assistant attending to customers, so I had to take my chances. Standing defiantly in the centre of the shop she eventually looked up and made eye contact with me. I saw the look of horror on her face as she recognised me, but she quickly looked away and carried on serving. Gradually the waiting customers were served and when it came to my turn I was to be disappointed as she craftily took an extraordinarily long time dealing with the young lady before me, which meant that the other assistant leaned forward and asked if he could help.

Moving up to the counter, I asked, in a slightly louder than necessary voice if they would be interested in buying my wedding ring and in so doing, I tossed the ring on the glass counter sending it spinning like a two-pence coin. The assistant put his hand over the ring to stop it twirling then, picking it up carefully and handing it back to me said, "No, I am sorry madam, we do not deal with second hand items, but the jewellers across the road might, if you would like to try there."

I could see Minnie, watching me from under her eyelids; she seemed to be keeping a very low profile, just in case. But there was no need for her to worry, for after giving her one more look of contempt I left the premises.

I walked out into the fresh air and just strolled along the pavement looking in the shops, but my mind wasn't concentrating on what was on display. My curiosity had got the better of me and I just had to see for myself, exactly what kind of woman my husband was bedding.

Seeing her close up just proved to me exactly how odd my husband was. When men go off and have affairs one would presume that the majority of them find a younger, more attractive, prototype than that of their wife. Not Shmel though, quite the opposite in fact, from my point of view this elderly lady had absolutely nothing going for her whatsoever. Mind you, she must have had *something* that Shmel liked. Or was it the fact that she was something in a skirt and an easy lay. I never did work it out!

Periodically, when going into town, I would purposely drive by her apartment, and more often than not the rat's car would be parked at her side entrance. For a man who liked space and opulence, one would have thought that Minnie's residence was far from being in his league. Still there was no accounting for the taste of a rat was there.

Today: I never did sell my wedding ring that day after all; instead, it was sold in the year 2000 to a Camden pawn broker and I received the princely sum of seventy pounds. Not a quarter of what it cost but I didn't care, just getting rid of that one item alone was all it took to help me come to terms with my miserable situation and helped me look with a little more certainty towards the future.

The Check-Out... Being a relatively new bride without my husband, I took to going out as much as possible. I had many good friends, thank God, and I used them unashamedly in order to offload my weighty marital problems. It was about this time I was invited over to one of my girlfriend's apartment for a coffee. On arrival I was pleased to see her there with her husband, Brian.

They both knew about my problems as I had often gone to them for support and a shoulder to cry on, in fact, we were so close I sometimes felt that they were living my life with me. That evening I sat telling them all about the saunas and what the young receptionist had revealed to me. My friends were extremely shocked and dismayed to hear what happened on the eve of my wedding and they naturally sympathised with my anguish and depression.

Whilst talking, Brian tentatively asked me if I knew whether Shmel was sampling the goods, so to speak, before they reached the shop floor. I told him that I really had no idea and that I had tried, purposely, not to think of it. Anyway, all these revelations were still very new to me and I had scarcely had time to come to terms with them, let alone think up new reasons to worry. Although, after what I had found out recently, one would have assumed it was pretty obvious, he was!

Brian then asked me if I would like him to check out one of the saunas, just to see what was going on and what might be said. I told him to go ahead, for I needed to know the whole truth, no matter how upsetting and depraved.

He rang my husband's East End sauna using the number on a business card I had and by pure chance Shmel actually answered the call.

Brian flapped his hand at me quickly and pointed rapidly to the phone, mouthing, "It's him, it's him, Shmel."

Brian then said, "Good evening," and proceeded to ask all kinds of pertinent questions, in order to find out what kind of woman would be most appropriate for him to become acquainted with and who would be the most suitable for his requirements. Brian listened intently for a while and then eventually thanked my husband for his help and recommendation saying that he would be in touch soon. He slowly replaced the receiver and looked at me sadly. I was stunned when Brian told me that my husband had replied, that, on his *very own* recommendation he had sampled this new Croatian girl and that he could assure him that she was fantastic, in fact, he ventured to say she was, "La crème de la crème."

I just sat quiet and wondered how on earth I could possibly take much more.

Here We Go Again... My husband had been on the missing list for some weeks by now. In fact, the last time I had seen him was when he was at Heathrow Airport with his family on his way back from Malta.

It was mid July and I had been married four whole months, when one day he came a-knocking at my door. No matter how many times I told him that I couldn't stand the pain he caused me to suffer each time he cheated on me, he would end up, coyly saying how sorry he was and that he only went with other women because I would continually argue with him. All he wanted was a quiet life, or so he said. He tried to assure me that he would much rather have taken me to Malta instead of her, (Minnie), but because I quarrelled with him so much, he had the audacity to say that he was left with no other choice but to take, what he called, second best - lying swine.

I constantly told him that he would indeed have a quiet life if he stopped seeing other women and lived properly with me. Trying to reason with Shmel was like hitting one's head against a brick wall. Of course he would make promises, as they were so easy to do, but keeping those promises was something he was incapable of, for being reliable and having integrity was something Shmel knew little, if anything about. Again and again he would promise, pledge and swear that his philandering days were a thing of the past and he would wear me down until I gave into him and took him back.

Part of my problem was that I was still quite unwell and as a result of my diabetes, when I was under stress, my blood glucose level would shoot up and stay quite high and I have since learned that when one's blood glucose is high it tends to contribute to weight gain and this was exactly how I was being affected. Having become depressed and stressed, my weight would start to escalate, which made me even more depressed, and with no one to confide in or lean on, I would eventually fall back into Shmel's trap. (The Rat Trap).

It took quite a time for me to see a pattern develop with my state of health. It is now quite obvious that when Shmel was with me I would feel ill and generally unwell and would get depressed which made me prone to row and argue. This in turn would result in him storming off and into the arms of another woman. Consequently, once he had departed and I had recovered from the initial hurt, things would begin to perk up and I would feel a lot better and far more confident. I knew of course, that it must have been the traumas and stress that I was continually under, yet for some unknown reason I allowed this man to manipulate me and treat me in this awful manner. It was as if he was a drug that I had become addicted to and until I could set myself free from this craving, I would continue to be my own worst enemy. Each time this man was allowed back into my life my addiction was being fuelled. I was a rat-poison junky who couldn't work out how to break free.

Today: I cannot begin to assess how much all this affected my children while they were growing up. I tried to keep my problems to myself as much as possible but inevitably, because we have emotional and psychological ties, my disturbing traumas must have affected them no end. I have purposely not spoken too much about my children, but would like to take this opportunity to say, thank you, to them for having stood beside me at all times. I tried to care for them as much as I could and give them my love and attention whenever they needed it. I have never overlooked the fact that our unusual way of life couldn't have been easy for them, living with us in our unsettling, love-hate relationship. I appreciate the fact that it must have been very difficult, seeing me hurt so much, especially as I was their mother and bearing in mind that blood is thicker than water! I admire the fact that on most occasions they tried to remain neutral when their step-father and I were going through harrowing times. Thank God, I like to believe that it hasn't scarred them too much as they are both now enjoying normal, healthy relationships. If anything, it is possible that my weakness has helped to make them even stronger.

The Birthday Boob... It was now August and Shmel's sixtieth birthday was drawing near and as our relationship was well and truly back on again it was his suggestion that we have a family get-together to celebrate. We were more than happy with the company who catered for our wedding so we employed them again to organise his birthday bash.

I threw myself into organising the small party and with the help of a professional cake maker, for a joke, I asked her to make his birthday cake in the shape of a double bed in which there was a man and two busty women, one blonde and one brunette, lying in a sexual position. I thought it was a brilliant idea and that it would be very apt. The cake was delivered to the venue on the day and when I took a peek at it, I laughed and said I thought it was absolutely great. But unfortunately, my joke bit the dust as it didn't go down very well with Shmel. I could tell by his face that he wasn't amused by it, in fact if anything, he was quite annoyed. Nevertheless, the rest of the party was good and towards the end of the evening the birthday boy got up and made a speech, thanking everyone, blah, blah, blah, and when the speech ended and he was about to sit down I handed him a beautiful dress-ring.

In return and to my surprise, he announced to everyone that he was taking me on holiday the following day. I smiled with delight and everyone clapped and said hoorah! But quite honestly the holiday was a gift for him rather than me, but at least it looked good to the onlookers.

On Top Of the World… As soon as Shmel's birthday party had ended, and all the guests had departed he quickly run me home in the car so that I could pack my cases. The next day early, our journey began, not by air this time but by rail, an experience I hadn't had before.

Our tickets were marked for Switzerland, but we not only went to see the magnificent Swiss glaciers, our travels took us to other beautiful places such as St Moritz, Zermatt, Geneva and the very famous Matterhorn. Being August, we were out of the winter skiing season but it was still very breathtaking, even without the snow.

We stayed at several different hotels and chalets during our holiday. In one particular hotel we attended a Raclette evening, where a traditional dish of hard Swiss cheese that melts very easily is served on boiled potatoes and bread. It was absolutely delicious and the company was great and entertaining. We also attended an amazing candlelit dinner served by a beautiful lake. That was absolutely wonderful too.

St Moritz is where the rich and famous play their games, but as it was out of season, the place was very quiet and sedate. I spent a lot of my time looking around the designer boutiques and expensive jewellery outlets (eat your heart out Minnie) and there were times when I could have so easily mistaken the place for Knightsbridge in London. St Moritz, has hosted the winter Olympic Games twice and in 2003 it hosted the World Skiing Championships, all in all, it was a very exciting place to be.

Our wonderful holiday lasted seven long days, and I would have liked it to have gone on forever. Shmel and I were enjoying a particularly passionate and loving phase in our relationship and anyone seeing us together would never have believed the troubles and traumas that had dogged our volatile union. This, then, was the addictive drug that I had become accustomed to and found almost impossible to dispense with. I would often and still do, reminisce on the most wonderful of all holidays shared with Shmel, my provider, my lover, my husband.

1999

Chapter 12 – Soothing Times.

New York – New York... In early February of
the year 1999, Shmel decided to do something
special for my birthday. I loved him being around
at these special times. As a rule he would be very
well behaved and very generous, which in turn
would make me feel very much appreciated and
wanted.

It was coming up to my forty-seventh birthday
and being an Aquarian who loves travel and all
the good things in life. Shmel, without hesitation,
reserved two tickets for us both to go to New
York. It was to be a four day trip during which we were booked to take in
two amazing shows and have a helicopter ride in order to view the Statue of
Liberty up close. We managed to do a lot of shopping which involved Shmel
taking me to a street that was lined with jewellery shops and where he bought
me an emerald and diamond dress ring as he knew I loved emeralds, along
with a diamond, pavé set, oval, pendant necklace as a birthday present. We
also took in as much sight-seeing as possible, all interspersed with loads of deli
food. If you ever get the opportunity to go to New York, you must try their
beef on rye. I just couldn't believe the size of the sandwich that came up, it
was so huge that I swear it would have been enough for a least four hungry
British teenagers. Shmel and I did our best when we tucked into the feast,
but unfortunately, by the time we were both full and near to bursting there
was still almost three quarters of the sandwich left. What a shameful waste!
But then New Yorkers are well known for filling one's plate to the brim and
beyond.

I had successfully lost around half a stone before going away but after,
seemingly, eating for England, on my return home I was informed by my
bathroom scales that I had put on around ten pounds, admittedly I wasn't
one bit surprised, except now I had the ghastly and depressing task of trying
to lose it all again.

For some reason or the other, 1999 was a relatively good year for us and
our relationship. After my birthday trip to New York, things went along pretty
smoothly, well as smooth as possible, taking all things into consideration.

I made sure that I never lost sight of what my husband was, and I could never dismiss the distressing thoughts I had wondering whether my husband was seeing other women, or whether perhaps, his old girlfriend was still on standby just waiting for his return so that she could occupy my shoes again.

Unfortunately, Shmel and I seldom, if ever, woke up beside each other in the mornings, as he still insisted on returning, on most nights, to his London bed-sit.

Although this state of affairs troubled me, I was getting evermore used to this strange way of living. By the August of this year, Shmel was now another year older and he decided it was time for another holiday. He found that he could often get amazing deals on teletext and one day when he noticed a special deal was being offered on a holiday in Sharm el Sheikh, he jumped at the chance, as it wasn't only a place he had always fancied, but the heat of the desert was known to be very good for his distressing skin condition.

So it was Sharm el Sheikh, here we come.

We took a flight from Gatwick and landed at Sharm Airport. We were fortunate enough not to have flown with Egypt Air as we would have needed special visas, but for us, everything went smoothly.

Sharm airport was quite a small, run of the mill place and we felt that it was little short of amazing that they could accommodate all the tourists and visitors that passed through it every day. Sharm el Sheikh is quite well known for its deep sea diving and I got to know quite a few people that would take a holiday there at least twice a year to indulge in this wonderful, tranquil and exciting hobby.

Once we had cleared passport control we made our way to the taxi queue. Everyone appeared to speak English so we had no problems.

The place looked rather more primitive than I had expected but the indigenous people were very hospitable and obliging. The heat was overwhelming and very oppressive, but then, we *were* in the desert, after all.

It wasn't a very big town but it supported rows and rows of beautiful hotels and had a fabulous casino situated right in the centre. When looking around this exciting destination I reckoned that with all these great and comparatively new amenities it wouldn't be long before this delightful place was bound to become very much commercialised, although I sincerely hoped not.

My heartbeat quickened at the sight of the casino, I do so enjoy a little gamble or two and I thought I would have to spend at least some of my time there.

Smoothly Does It... A taxi pulled up and getting in we gave the driver the name of the hotel we had booked into. The journey was relatively short and I was quite taken aback when we stopped outside the hotel. It was the very imposing, Ritz Carlton. This building must have been the most amazing and most modern I had ever seen. The hotel was virtually surrounded by vast darkened glass windows. Inside the hotel was a huge reception desk in the most spacious and sumptuous lounge, come bar area, where at cocktail time a trio of singers would perform for the guests' enjoyment. Directly opposite the cocktail bar was a wide, spiral staircase that went up to the first floor where four restaurants were situated. One restaurant cooked and served Thai food, the other three served all buffet foods for breakfast, lunch and dinner. For the duration of the holiday we had a beautiful suite with a balcony that overlooked seven swimming pools that were spaciously laid out in the enormous grounds.

Most days were spent lazing around one or other of the pools, while at night, it was but a short journey away to a part of the town where we found a couple of streets that were lined with shops. One shop was full of beautiful and unusual souvenirs, in which I purchased some Arabic ornaments as gifts and I bought some special items to keep as reminders for myself.

Twice I paid a visit to the casino, but lady luck deserted me each time and I came away financially lighter than when I started out.

What I considered gave this hotel that little bit of extra opulence was the fact that any guest occupying a 'suite' had automatic access to a 'members only club' lounge where we could relax while enjoying cocktails, canapés and even breakfast if we so wished. To serve us, we were allotted our own personal waiter. While there we were surely made to feel like the King and Queen of Sheba.

To make this holiday complete Shmel treated me to an exhilarating body massage each day in the beauty room that was just situated beside the reception area, during which every part of my body (well, almost every part) was massaged with the most heavenly-perfumed, essential oils and was executed by the most handsome Egyptian hunk you could possibly imagine.

I can assure you I just didn't want to return home, believe me!

Father of the Groom... Shortly after we returned from our holiday in Sharm, Shmel and Anne were once again walking arm in arm down the aisle of the Synagogue in St John's Wood, No! Shmel had not had a brainstorm and decided to re-marry Anne it was to participate in the wedding of their eldest son, the very same son who tried to ruin his father's wedding.

It appeared that Shmel had spent weeks trying to negotiate with his son, hoping that he would agree for me to attend the wedding also. I didn't have a very good relationship with his children as you know, so I didn't think that an agreement would be reached although, I felt that I should be there seeing I was Shmel's wife and the young man's stepmother. But at the very last minute an agreement *was* reached and an invite was sent to my mother and myself.

Shmel lavished nothing but the best on his son and his bride. He pulled out all the stops and gave them everything. No amount of money was spared on this young couple. The wedding feast was to be held in one of London's plushest West End hotels. There were limos, top-class caterers and a fantastic band of musicians, in fact, you name it and he had it.

The ceremony was conducted with great reverence and was most sincere and enjoyable although, throughout the service my mind was filled with some amount of wonder as to where mum and I might be seated at the reception.

I must admit that when we did get back to the reception I was a little surprised when I saw that I had been placed at the end of the large top table. The same table in fact, where Shmel and Anne, being the bridegroom's parents, were seated, along with the brides parents, the happy couple and their grandparents, as is traditional.

I was actually sitting next to my mother-in-law, while my own mother had been seated some way down the room along with some of the less important family members and friends, people she didn't know at all.

Seated at the top table along with us was a guy of Middle Eastern appearance who sat smoking as many of the free, expensive cigars, as possible throughout the evening. He looked at me constantly, but I avoided eye contact with him like the plague. I assumed he didn't know I was Shmel's wife. He later came up to me smelling strongly of booze and asked me to dance. I declined the offer as I thought he was rather disgusting. I later learned to my amazement, that he was Anne's new boyfriend.

Shmel was busy mingling with the guests, making sure everyone had everything they needed. He was in his glory, strutting around, playing the part of the proud parent and doing the 'father' bit, while I was left feeling rather out of it all and having to amuse myself. The atmosphere was somewhat strained with us all under one roof and eventually it made me feel rather depressed. Shmel's mother was also feeling at a bit of a loss, as I was under the impression that she had never played an important part in the life of her grandchildren and from what I could see, they never appeared to show her much love or respect either. The fact that the children had lost touch with their grandparents to some extent, could have been caused by the breakdown of Shmel and Anne's marriage, for there is an awful lot of animosity created when a marriage fails and besides, Anne told me that she never really got on with her mother-in-law at the best of times.

After some fraught hours trying to keep up a false impression and having to refuse yet another request to dance by Anne's boozy boyfriend, I had had enough for the night, so I went and found my mother and when I suggested we went home she was only too pleased to depart. She was tired and weary and like me, wanted nothing else but to go.

We collected our belongings and I went looking for Shmel. Needless to say I found him captivating an audience of young women, as usual. I eventually managed to get him to one side and told him that as I was tired I wanted to go home. His reaction was as bland as usual; as he didn't seem to care that much what I did. I could stay or go whatever... It was all the same to him.

I never saw him that evening instead, I had to wait until the next day before I had the pleasure of my husbands company again. As per usual, within the week we argued about something or the other only to have him walk out on me, once more.

This Is Your Life... I didn't see Shmel again until a few weeks later when I was driving back from the West End after having had lunch with a girlfriend. While travelling back through Camden I spotted my husband driving towards me. I flashed my lights to attract his attention, and on seeing me he immediately indicated and pulled over into the curb. I also drove into the nearest space and parked the car. When I looked up Shmel was running across the road, as though he couldn't wait to speak to me.

I hadn't seen him for some weeks, but was delighted to meet him at this particular time, as I was wearing black leather trousers with a matching fur-trimmed coat and I was looking particularly good and felt happy after having had a wonderful time with a girlfriend.

Winding down the car window, he glanced in and his first words to me were, "WOW! You look great."

To which I replied, "Yes, I know."

It was thrilling that he should see me like this, as it would have been truly awful if he could have seen how I was feeling inside. Nevertheless, we started chatting and after a few minutes he proceeded to inform me that the TV programme called 'This is your life,' was going to feature the life story of his cousin, Sylvia and that he had been invited to the surprise show that was being presented by Michael Aspel.

Shmel's cousin, Sylvia Young is a lady who owns and runs a very well established theatrical school in London called 'Sylvia Young Theatre School'. She has taught many children who have later gone on to become well-known TV and stage-stars. I knew Sylvia reasonably well as Shmel used to have a family re-union, roughly every three months in order to catch up with all the latest news and gossip. I was always included (when we were on speaking terms of course) and really enjoyed these get-togethers. More often than not, we would all meet at a classy London hotel for brunch. Therefore, Shmel didn't hesitate to ask me if I would like to accompany him to see the program being made. I was invited to be a guest in the audience and agreed to go, not only because it would be a very interesting experience, but it was yet another opportunity that I didn't want to miss out on.

The day the program was to be filmed we all met up at the Teddington Film Studios in Northwest London. It was all very exciting and it wasn't long before the film crew started recording. After surprising Sylvia and bringing her onto the stage, the presenter then brought on her own daughter, Frances Ruffelle, who is Shmel's second cousin and a lady who had recently been featured in 'Hello' magazine. Frances was the original lead singer in 'Les Miserables', the very successful, long-running, stage musical by Sir Andrew Lloyd-Webber, when it first opened in the West End and who eventually went with the show to Broadway.

Among some of the other guests that had been invited on stage to be re-united with Sylvia Young, was Emma Bunting, better know perhaps as 'baby spice' of the Spice Girls pop group and Adam Woodyatt who plays Ian Beale in 'EastEnders', which is a top rated English 'soap opera,' who were both former students of the 'Sylvia Young Theatre School'. Also presented on stage were a couple of the members of an all-boys band called 'Five'.

When the programme had come to an end and the filming had finished, we were all ushered into a large room where a buffet had been laid on and where guests and stars mingled and chatted. Naturally, there were kisses and hugs all round, especially for Shmel's cousin Sylvia. During the buffet, I took the opportunity to ring home to my teenage daughter Shireen, who was a great fan of the pop group 'Five' at the time. She had posters of one of the young men belonging to the group pinned up all around her room whose name was, Scott Robinson and I knew she would be ecstatic to speak to him. She was just on her way to bed when she received my call, and when I handed the telephone to her favourite guy in the group, he was only too pleased to speak to her.

I had explained to him beforehand that I had a teenage daughter who was crazy about him and he willingly said that he would say a few words to her. I handed him my mobile and was delighted when he said, "Hello" and started to chat. I could hear my daughter screaming down the telephone with excitement. I knew that would put a very big smile on her face and I guess it must have given her lots to talk about at school the following day.

We had a great time there and I enjoyed myself very much, but eventually the evening drew to a close and we all started to make our way home. Shmel drove me back to my house and when we pulled up onto the driveway, I noticed a large, bulging bin liner lying on the bonnet of my car. Shmel and I looked at each other curiously; surely someone hadn't dumped a bag of rubbish on my car? We got out of Shmel's car and cautiously walked over to the bin bag. Upon opening it up, we saw that it was full of Shmel's belongings including clothes and photographs of him and his elderly girlfriend. Many years ago, I had dumped his belongings at his wife's house, and now it seemed, I was getting the same reprisal, for Minnie had thrown him out along with his clothes. She must have realised much to her annoyance, that after this special day out, he would be back with me again. Well, back for a while at least.

Today: The bizarre relationship we had, which involved him going back and forth between me and his other women went on throughout the whole time he was part of my life. It was a wonder he had any clothes left the way we carried on, as each time he left I would gather up all the clothes he had in my house and take them to the nearest charity shop, as did his other women no doubt. You would have thought he would have learned a lesson and kept his clothes where they rightfully belonged, which was in his poky London bed-sit.

2000.

Chapter 13 – Everything New.

Millennium Celebration... To celebrate the new millennium, Shmel decided to take me to San Francisco. He booked us two superior tickets with Virgin Atlantic. I hadn't been very well the week prior to the holiday, but I wasn't going to let a head-cold, no matter how bad, stop me from going.

We arrived at the airport and after checking in we made our way to the V.I.P. lounge where the upper-class passengers were treated to complimentary drinks and sandwiches. This was very satisfying and relaxing but when you are paying in excess of eleven thousand pounds for a couple of one-way tickets you would expect to sit in comfort and be waited on. I found this kind of service just takes the edge off being stressed out, especially if you aren't feeling too well, or like some passengers, feel anxious about flying. It also presents one with a golden opportunity to sit among some rich and famous people. That particular day there weren't many people in the lounge, but I was delighted to see Gary Rhodes the well-known, celebrity chef sitting near to a window. Priding myself on being a good cook and taking advantage of the situation I went over to him and asked him for some advice on the best way to cook Beef Wellington. He was polite and helpful and spent a few minutes giving me some hints and tips. After our very brief meeting I can honestly say that he is now one of my favourite TV chefs.

Eventually it was time to board the aeroplane and take our seats. Once settled, a pretty, young, blonde stewardess approached each passenger asking if they would be interested in having an Indian head massage during the flight and that she was taking bookings. Shmel was immediately up for that, so the young lady took his name and seat details.

Although it was a long-haul flight the journey seemed to go quickly. We were offered ample food and drink, watched a couple of good films and after having a couple of hours sleep; followed by a freshen-up we started our descent into the San Francisco Airport.

Unfortunately, poor old Shmel never did get his head massaged, as the service offered was so popular, especially amongst the male passengers that the pretty masseur didn't manage to get round to him.

We landed in good time and had to wait around for our luggage which seemed to take an age to appear, by which time I was feeling quite ill. The cold I had suffered the previous week seemed to have returned with a vengeance. My temperature had shot up and by the time we got to our awaiting car I was coughing very badly and even started to bring up blood-stained phlegm. I thought my condition might have been aggravated by the air-conditioning in the plane, a circumstance in which germs are known to circulate. But for whatever reason, I was so unwell that on the way to our hotel the cab driver suggested we stop off at a drugstore to get some medication. He pulled up outside the first convenient chemist he came across and as he got out, he advised us to lock all the doors as we were downtown in a no-go area and that it could be dangerous. I must admit to feeling rather nervous, especially as I was an avid fan of the TV series, 'The Streets of San Francisco'. Nevertheless, the driver left us sitting in the car and disappeared inside the store. A few minutes later he reappeared with some vitamin tablets called Echinacea.

I dosed myself up on the vitamin tablets but unfortunately remained ill, rapidly becoming worse. Consequently, once I reached our hotel I took straight to my bed and remained there all the next day. My body was aching so much that I told Shmel I needed a doctor, believing that anti-biotic medication might be the only thing that could help me. Later that day a doctor arrived, examined me, asked some relevant questions then prescribed some tablets. I didn't know what they were, but took them all the same. By the third day I was feeling slightly better so we managed to get out for the first time since our arrival. We made our way to the 'Fisherman's Wharf' which was a much-commercialised tourist spot and I indulged in a light fish lunch consisting mainly of prawns. With so many restaurants to choose from, we hit lucky as the food and service were excellent. After lunch, as much as we wanted to walk around the area and look in all the shops I just couldn't, as this feeling of weakness and tiredness still hung over me. I knew it must have been miserable for Shmel, but the sickness, although not of my making, was out of my control and after a short while we returned to our hotel and I went straight back to bed.

By now Shmel had had enough and thought it best if we returned to England. He contacted the Virgin Airline ticket office and asked if we could have the first available flight back to England. Usually, people go out fighting and hopefully come back in glory. Whereas, Shmel and I went out in glory and came back economy class, as the upper-class seats on the plane had all been taken. There was very little comfort on the flight home, but I didn't care as I slept most of the way and was only too pleased to be going home. Once back, I contacted my own doctor who came out immediately and gave me the correct medication and within four days I was feeling one hundred percent better, thank goodness.

All in all, the holiday was a complete disaster from start to finish and I felt bad about it for weeks thinking that it was through my illness, I had managed to ruin a holiday that could have been a wonderful experience for both of us – I couldn't help feeling that this disastrous holiday was entirely my fault.

The New Baby… It was February and my birthday was fast approaching, this was the time when Shmel suggested we go out for one of those special candlelit dinners. Whilst talking in the restaurant he casually asked me what type of car I liked or would like to drive if I had the choice. He knew I was very unhappy with the Saab and that I didn't like driving it very much. so I was more than delighted to launch into one of my dreams and tell him how much I would like to be the proud owner of a Mercedes CLK model.

I had always loved the Mercedes 190E that my mother had bought me many years before. It was a car I adored and was passionate about. Without hesitation, Shmel said that if I would like to go to the nearest Mercedes showroom and choose the model I liked, I could have it as a birthday present.

Bloody hell! I couldn't believe my ears and was over the moon. I remember jumping up from the table sending Shmel's knife and fork flying and leaning over, I gave him the biggest kiss you could imagine. I had to pinch myself to make sure I wasn't dreaming and kept saying, "Really, really, is that really true?"

I found myself early the next day at my nearest Mercedes showroom looking around at the latest models; It was so unusual for Shmel to ask my opinion or give me a choice that I thought it best to get in quick before he changed his mind.

I ordered the model and colour I wanted, but as the car had to be built to my own specifications it meant a wait of about three months before I could have it delivered to my door, but I can assure you it was worth every single minute of the wait. When the car was finally delivered it was like having a brand new baby, the only difference being, you don't have any choice with a human baby, you have to have what God gives you but here, I was getting everything I could have ever wanted – in a car, that is.

Pointless to say, of course, that the relationship I had with my husband had taken a turn for the worst towards the end of the waiting time, for while he was playing the dutiful husband, he must have been neglecting his other concubines and it wasn't long after acquiring my new car that he made damn sure to cause an argument which developed into a blazing row, resulting in me doing just what he wanted and that was to throw him out of the house. At that time I didn't care very much. I had my new car and was quite happy to bomb around, showing off in this beautiful machine. It wasn't until the novelty wore off that I started to miss my husband again, after all, a car is only a lump of metal with wheels and it cannot give you the love, warmth and the companionship of someone you love. I realised, of course, that he must have been staying with his elderly girlfriend, one who perhaps, he had been neglecting of late, but by now it was me who was feeling neglected.

A week or so later, I had a telephone call from Shmel, right out of the blue, asking me how things were and telling me that he was ill. I asked him where he was and he said Sharm el Sheikh, which didn't altogether surprise me as he loved the place so much. When asked who he was with he said he was with his youngest son. Well... I believed he was in Sharm, but I didn't believe he was with his son or at least, not *only* with his son for he was such a liar. Nevertheless, I asked him what was wrong and why he felt so ill. He said he thought he had caught the flu. I sympathised of course and we carried on with our conversation for a short while, then after wishing him well we signed off.

A few days later he contacted me again and said that he was in the Cromwell Hospital in London with double pneumonia. Now, not wanting you to consider me to be wicked, as I am not, but they always say that 'God pays debts without money', and I somehow think that he was being punished for making our marriage little more than a mockery and leaving me alone at times, when I was sick.

I believe now, that he contacted me because he was hoping and expecting me to look after him while he was ill, but after all, as he had spent so much time with his old girlfriend of late, I couldn't see why he should expect me to drop everything and give up my own time to care for him. He must have realised that I wasn't going to fall for his old trick of using me, after having abused my trust and our marriage and it appeared that he must have eventually gone back to the old girl for his care and recuperation.

I later learned that even Shmel's mother didn't bother to visit him; even though one of her favourite sayings was 'I love every hair on his head', but as he was rather short of hair, this could have been a sarcastic way of saying that she hadn't that much love for him after all. Who knows! If he had treated his mother in the same, thoughtless and disrespectful way as he treated me, it was no wonder she felt the way she did.

They say that, '*every dog has his day*', but in Shmel's case it was '*every rat gets his pay*'

Despite all, he eventually recovered from his illness. Let me assure you, that without doubt, he has the constitution of an ox.

2001

Chapter 14 – What's All This 'Ere?

The Chin-Chin Chinaman... Shmel very rarely spoke about the saunas or indeed, any business matters to me as he knew I was not really interested and kept out of it purposely. But during the latter part of the year 2000 he did mention that he was thinking of going into partnership with another person.

It emerged that Shmel wanted to completely revamp the sauna and massage parlour he owned in London and in order for him to embark upon this project and do all he wanted meant that he needed a considerable amount of money to be spent in order to cover the whole refurbishment.

I don't know how or why he chose the partner he did, but the man who became Shmel's new business partner was a Chinese gentleman. Shmel had lots of great ideas for the renovation of his sauna, he truly thought of his business as if it was a fully, recognised and legitimate company. When the sauna's revamp had been fully completed, which took around three months, it had a security guard on the door, a proper full-time cleaner, plus a taxi service that was always on hand. Shmel also planned and had built a lounge area where filtered water could be obtained by the hot and thirsty. He even had a fast food, take away service set up that was convenient for those who might become hungry for food as well as sex.

The revamp went ahead, and all seemed to go to plan. The job was completed in the designated time so Shmel was more than happy. His days were taken up by his newly decorated sauna and he would habitually go there around lunch time and stay for a couple of hours before taking himself off to the bridge-club for the rest of the afternoon.

For some time all seemed to go surprisingly well, until one Wednesday lunch time when I received a call from Shmel saying that he and his partner had argued. He didn't tell me what the argument was about and I refrained from asking, but it appeared that after a heated disagreement the Chinaman grabbed Shmel by the collar of his jacket, pushed him up against a wall and beat the hell out of him, which resulted in him losing a front tooth.

Shmel telephoned the police and lodged a complaint against him, and the partner was duly taken away and dumped in a cell overnight. Shmel pressed charges on the man and promptly bought him out of his partnership contract. The doomed partnership was yet another one to bite the dust. You would have thought that Shmel might have known this liaison would not last, as he couldn't make a go of any partnership that he ever entered into, not one. Although, once the Chinese gentleman had been bought out and had departed the business, Shmel managed to persuade an old acquaintance from the bridge club to plunge his money into the sauna instead. This latest backer had been introduced to a very dishy black girl some years earlier by Shmel and apparently, the relationship was still going strong.

As for taking his ex-partner to court over the punch-up, Shmel had second thoughts and eventually decided against it, as he became rather afraid that the Chinaman might be in league with the Triads… Ahhhh – So!

-:: *The Chinaman* ::-

Happy Birthday Shar... Three weeks after Shmel's brawl with the Chinaman, he felt he needed a good break so he booked a long week-end for us at a hotel in Madrid.

It was a typical Spanish hotel, nothing too fancy but clean and spotless. It was run by a local family who provided excellent Spanish food, but spoke very little English. The few days we spent there were taken up with sightseeing, drinking Café-con-leche and of course, shopping. It was a quiet time of the year and every shop we looked in was displaying 'rebajas' signs. I was delighted, as one can get many a good bargain in the Spanish sales, so I couldn't wait to start clothes hunting.

As we walked through one particular shopping precinct I stopped to look in a shop window that was displaying a stunning fur coat. The fact that there was a huge 'Sale' sign spread across the double-fronted window was all the more reason for me to take a closer look. I went in, only to find that it was full of very expensive garments all at bargain prices. Shmel followed me in of course and after browsing a little I asked to try on the coat that was displayed in the window, before, trying on a couple of other equally expensive jackets. After I had paraded up and down the showroom a couple of times wearing each of the outfits, Shmel suggested I try on the first fur again. I quickly said, "Yes darling."

I was thrilled to bits, as the coat was so enchanting. It was a three-quarter length, silver fox-fur and once on, Shmel said, "Have it, the coat looks beautiful on you."

I was very appreciative of Shmel's generosity and I was delighted to be able to walk out of the shop wearing the fur coat, feeling like a million dollars.

Still wearing my fabulous fur, we made our way to the Ritz Hotel where we had afternoon tea. While sitting in comfortable armchairs in the tea-room, I glanced over towards the main restaurant, where I noticed a very slim, elegant and attractive blonde woman who was making her way over to a table. Her face looked rather familiar, although for the moment I couldn't place her until I had a further, longer look and then realised it was none other than Melanie Griffith the Oscar nominated actress and partner of Antonio Banderas. I am not really star-struck so I didn't go over and ask her for her autograph, although I was sorely tempted. But I did discreetly point her out to Shmel and was quite amazed at the negative remarks he made about such a beautiful and elegant woman, considering the old, goofy, girlfriend he would run back to whenever he rowed with me. I think it would be safe to say that it was a case of, 'Eat your heart out chum! You should be so lucky'.

The long week-end in Madrid passed quickly and no sooner had we arrived, than it felt that we were back at the airport preparing to return home. I had enjoyed the break very much and I was very thrilled and delighted with my fur coat, but it wasn't to be the end of my good fortune, for while we were looking around the duty free shops, Shmel started to hover around the jewellery department looking at the watches. I made my way over to see what had caught his eye and there under the glass counter were beautiful, matching, his and her Cartier watches. He turned and looked at me with a mock, stern look, in order to remind me of the time, thirteen years ago when I smashed his beloved Cartier watch to pieces. His look made me feel distinctly embarrassed but I passed it off by asking the assistant if I could try the ladies watch on. I made a great effort to be positive by making lots of admiring remarks when trying the watch on. I could see that Shmel was tempted to buy the two watches but he hesitated, so after a few more encouraging remarks from me, he produced his platinum credit card and said, "Si, we shall have them."

I was thrilled and delighted; I couldn't help thinking, my God, what with the beautiful fur coat and now the watch… I wondered what on earth might be the next goody to come my way.

With our matching watches safely stowed away in their gift boxes and my fur coat wrapped casually around me Shmel and I wandered into the main departure lounge and found a seat. Sitting there he took hold of my hand and said lovingly, "I love you, happy birthday!"

It was by far and away the most enjoyable week-end we had spent together in an age. I had a beautiful coat, a beautiful watch and I felt for sure that my husband loved me deeply and truly and from this week-end, I thought that our relationship would be more secure and much more meaningful.

He's At It Again? … It didn't take long before any hope of a new life with Shmel would be dashed. Just when I thought maybe, just maybe, we did stand a chance together; he did his usual disappearing act. This time he was off to Seville with his old girlfriend 'Minnie'.

Because I seldom saw him during the week, I could only assume that he was hanging around the saunas, socialising in the bridge club or relaxing back at his London bed-sit. The first inkling I had that he was away, was when my bank statement fell on the doormat and I found that he had already deposited my housekeeping money. This was always a sure sign that I would not be seeing him for anything up to a week or two, or maybe even more if he decided to stay away and that was even more likely if we had rowed. But it truly wasn't like that this time, as we had been so happy and I had kept quiet. I stewed over his disappearance for a couple of days and then decided I couldn't stand it any longer, so I telephoned the jewellery shop where I knew Minnie worked and after apologising, I very politely asked if I could speak to *her*. But of course, the manager gave me the answer I was expecting, which was... He was very sorry, but unfortunately, the lady I wanted was not at work and that she would not be in all the week as she was away on holiday.

My heart sunk with disappointment and frustration, I felt truly dejected. If I asked myself once, I would ask myself many times over, why he still needed her when he had me, his wife. Even when I had been good and not found fault, or not questioned him and not bugged him for anything, he still had the need to go off with someone else. I was in a 'no win' situation. I was gutted and didn't deserve to be treated in such a way. I felt therefore, it was time for me to take some action. I telephoned Shmel's mobile, which he was sure to have on him always, because it was like his bible, he would carry it everywhere so that he could be easily contacted by any number of women and, so called, business partners.

I knew he was abroad as soon as I heard the ringing tone. When he picked up I said, "What the bloody hell are you doing abroad? Where are you and more importantly, who are you with?"

He said that he felt the need to get away for a while and that he was alone. I didn't believe him of course and what with feeling so upset and disturbed, I thought it only right and fair that he should be as equally upset and disturbed while on holiday. I subsequently rang him repeatedly, anything up to thirty to forty times a day, regardless of the cost of the calls.

I just didn't care...

The £500 Windup... While Shmel was away on this latest holiday a friend telephoned one evening and asked me round to have dinner with her and her husband. I didn't really want to go out and explained, saying, that I would not be very good company owing to my husband being off on holiday with some old girlfriend, leaving me hurt and upset. My lovely friend wouldn't listen to any excuses and said that it would do me good to accept the invitation, so after a little further, gentle persuasion I went. She created a delightful meal during which I managed to relax down, for I felt it was great just to be with people who were genuinely concerned about my welfare.

After dinner we sat around her comfortable lounge and over coffee I poured my heart out to both my friend and her husband, telling them how I had found out that Shmel was abroad, and how I knew he was with his old lady friend. After listening to the sorry tale, my friend's husband Steve suggested we play a trick on the rat. I did so enjoy the thought of putting one over on Shmel after all; I felt he deserved everything that could be thrown at him after leaving me for no reason.

Between us we decided to put the frighteners on Shmel by phoning him with some tall-story while I listened to it all on the bedroom extension. I had absolutely no idea what Steve was going to say or do, but as he was a bit of a cunning character, I guessed it would be good. Steve said that he would use the phone in the hall, while my friend and I listened on the extension and watched the action from the bedroom. We got ourselves set up and when we were all ready, Steve proceeded to ring Shmel's mobile number. When Shmel picked up and said, "Hello," Steve put on a very convincing Spanish accent (a bit like Manuel, the mad waiter in 'Faulty Towers') as he pretended to be the Spanish security man in the hotel where the rat had his bed-sit. In spoof, broken-English Steve said, *"Ah! 'allo, Mr Shmel, I got your mobile number from dee management, for I 'ave to tell you that your bed-seet has been broken into and your TV is on dee floor sticking 'alf way out of dee door.*

Shmel went into his usual panicky war dance at the other end of the phone, whilst we all burst our sides with silent laughter.

"What, what are you saying? I have been robbed or something?" Bellowed Shmel down the telephone, trying to gather his thoughts together we assumed, then...

"Err, look, could you do me a favour, I had five hundred pounds in a jar on the coffee table, perhaps you would go in and see if it's still there?"

"One-a momento, Mr Shmel I weel go and 'ave a look."

Steve put his hand over the mouthpiece of the telephone and pulled all manners of faces at us, as we stood there quietly cracking up. But after a few moments, Steve straightened up, dropped back into his Spanish waiter's shoes and said, *"Ah! No, all thee money 'as gone..... poffff, w'at you want me do?"*

Shmel, now resigned to the fact that he had lost all 'ees' money had little left to say other than, "Okay, thanks for informing me, I can't do anything as I am on holiday in Seville with my girlfriend so I will have to contact my son and send him over to check it out."

With that, Steve and I put both of the telephones down and after hearing how frantic the rat had been, and how comical Steve had sounded we all just burst into fits of hysterical laughter. We went over the conversation again and again, repeating what Steve had said in his spoof voice and enacting what Shmel had said, in fact, we laughed so much I ended up with tears streaming down my face. After such a laugh at poor old Shmel's expense we all had to have a quiet cup of relaxing coffee in order to calm down. We talked through our windup a few more times, before finally deciding that I would have to ring Shmel back and own up to the trick we had played on him. So after we had finished our coffees I tapped his number and when he dismally answered I said, "Hi, Shmel - *eet es meeee.*"

As soon as he heard the giggle in my voice he became very angry realising he had been well and truly had. There was nothing much he could say of course, other than threaten to put a stop on my housekeeping money for the following week.

The Last Laugh... I wasn't worried about his threat too much as he must have forgotten the fact that, because he was gallivanting off to Seville with his girlfriend he had already put two weeks money in the bank for me. He was also very annoyed because he said that he had already been in touch with his son and that he had sent him on a wild goose chase across town for nothing. I remarked, saying sarcastically, "Oh dear, what a shame!"

Needless to say, after that the conversation dried up. It only left Shmel to repeat, yet again, his favourite saying to me which was.

"You could have had all this!" (Meaning of course, if I knuckled down, stayed quiet, and kept my mouth shut about his transgressions I could have had everything I wanted, except of course, his loyalty).

A short time after returning from Seville he took his old girlfriend on yet *another* holiday this time, to Marbella. I really couldn't understand why he felt the need to keep taking her away. I thought perhaps, that he was so furious with me over my latest prank it might have been his way of getting back at me. When I found out about this latest holiday I became so frustrated and was so exasperated that throughout the week I bombarded him with mobile phone calls yet again. One evening when I called, he answered saying that he was dining out with friends. I knew that was true as I have excellent hearing and I could hear other people chatting in the background. I was pleased that I had interrupted his meal, but I was angry and threatened him with divorce. I suppose being amidst his cronies made him feel brave and confident and he became very rude and arrogant. I assume that he must have turned away from the mobile, for I heard him say to his friends, in a very cock-sure tone.

"Guess what? My wife wants a divorce!"

A burst of laughter rang out, blasting my ears. I hit the end-call button and plumped down in the chair crying with temper, humiliation and sorrow. I had had enough, and didn't want to listen to any more of his sarcastic comments. He had no calls from me thereafter.

I was soon to learn that the reason for this latest trip to Marbella was to buy an apartment or villa for his future retirement

Today: Two months went by without a word from him. He continued to put my housekeeping money in the bank and I went back to being the quiet wife living in the background. I was still hanging on hoping for

what, a miracle? I knew it was hopeless and foolish of me to think the way I did and grew to despise myself for it. But I had lost belief in my own ability to strike out alone, as he had drained me of my spirit and had shattered my confidence.

My Yang Self... It was mid July and who should come sniffing around the corner of my street door one afternoon? Why, none other than Shmel the Rat.

He came into the house and after the smallest of small talk he asked me if I would accompany him to Marbella for a short holiday. I so much wanted to say, no thanks, you schmuck, get stuffed, instead of which I said okay and that I would go. I had been left alone for so long, at that moment in time I was feeling terribly neglected and of course, knowing Shmel of old, I guessed that if I had said no, he would have promptly turned around on his heels and taken 'her'.

After giving me the details of the flight etc., and telling me what time he would pick me up, he left, saying that he would see me in a couple of days time. I am sure that when he left my house he must have driven off thinking... Good old Shar, there she is, always the same, always ready and willing to do whatever I asked, and of course, he would have been right. But, he was to be in for a bit of a shock as I intended to change my attitude towards him and instead of being the lovey, dovey, falling-over-myself-to-please-him wife as in the past; he was to see another side of me, a side he hadn't seen before.

Eastern philosophy teaches that within each and every one of us there is an amount of yin and an equal amount of yang, yin being the quiet, passive and dependent side of one's nature, whereas, yang is the confident, impulsive, independent side. And just for once, I wanted him to feel the yang side of my nature, just to see if a stronger, more confident element would make any difference to the way he treated me.

He picked me up as arranged and by the afternoon of the same day we were in the Spanish town of Marbella. The reason for inviting me on this trip was to show me the apartment that he was planning to buy. I tried very hard to be nonchalant and off-hand about it all, but deep down inside, I was quite looking forward to seeing the place, for no special reason, other than curiosity. We went along to view the apartment the following morning and I was quite surprised to find that it had no special qualities at all, in fact, it was quite ordinary. Not being one little bit impressed by the place, I was able to remain quite composed. It was obvious that he would have expected me to look excited and make some positive comments about the apartment, instead of which, I said that from the look of the place, it must have been chosen with the help of his elderly lady friend. I think my matter-of-fact statement must have taken him a bit off-guard as he openly admitted that to be the truth, realising of course, that there was no way he could really deny it. I said in a sharp voice, that there was no possibility of *me* ever living in this apartment, if that was what he was expecting, especial as another woman had chosen it.

I suppose my unemotional reaction and curt statement surprised Shmel so much that he immediately suggested we look around for something else, something a bit more appropriate.

While we were out in Marbella one of Shmel's friends, Peter, introduced us to a local, English estate agent who gave us the addresses of some properties we might like to look at with a view to buying. We travelled around for a couple of days looking at the suggested sites, but none of them were very impressive, until that was, we came upon an attractive town house that had once belonged to a nineteen-fifties and sixties pop star called Dickie Valentine, now this I liked straight away. After having had a good look around, although we thought the place was quite small, because the layout of the rooms had been so well designed we decided it would be an ideal place for us as a family, to spend a month or two in the summer and there would still be enough space to invite a few friends or family members over to stay, even when the children were with us. Shmel agreed to put a holding deposit on the property, but not before I had *insisted* on having my name put on the deeds as joint owner. He wasn't too keen on the idea at first, but realising I meant business he eventually agreed. Hands were shaken on the deal and the estate agent said he would see to the documentation and finalise the agreed deposit.

34 Double D… As we had now found a place to buy and had organised the finance, we decided to take the opportunity to have a couple of days relaxing before returning home. We telephoned Shmel's friend Peter, who had introduced us to the estate agent and told him that we had found a lovely town house that we both liked and had put a deposit on it. Peter was thrilled for us and said that as he was having a family get-together on the Sunday, he would be delighted if we went over to his place for lunch so as that we could tell him all about it. Peter was divorced and now lived in Marbella permanently with his new, young, Brazilian wife.

When we arrived on the Sunday I was quite surprised to find not only his English ex-wife at the house but his two grown up sons and a couple of their friends as well. Peter's villa was quite beautiful. It was set in a secluded part of the country, well hidden from the town and tourist areas. He greeted us warmly and after some initial chit-chat and introductions all round he showed us over his villa and grounds pointing out spectacular views of the area as we went. Once we had seen over his place, Peter said that we could make ourselves comfortable by the pool or anywhere in the garden and that his young wife would join us soon. Shmel and I found ourselves a couple of loungers while Peter went and made us each a long cool drink. We settled ourselves down and soaked up some welcome sunshine while the others lazed around the pool or swam. About thirty minutes later Peter's Brazilian wife suddenly made an appearance on the terrace, wearing a bikini bottom only. She was followed close behind by her younger sister who was wearing a very tight, flimsy dress, under which she wore no bra. It was obvious that the sister had silicone implants as she needed no visible support for her 34 Double D boobs that were extremely high and pert.

With Peter's wife and sister-in-law wearing little more than the briefest of outfits, I don't need to tell you where Shmel's eyes were. He was in his element; after all, he was a boob man, have no mistake.

I, on the other hand, was feeling so overdressed it was painful. I was wearing a long Versace, floral-print summer dress, which, under normal circumstances, would have been very appropriate, especially as we had been invited to Sunday lunch. Needless to say, Shmel made his way down to the pool at the first opportunity in order to get a closer look at the semi-naked women, leaving me sitting alone. I must say that Sunday lunch was indeed beautifully prepared and very tasty, especially the roast potatoes that were positively wicked.

The afternoon quickly flew by and at 5:30pm we said our goodbyes as we had to get back to our hotel so that we could pack for our journey home to England the following morning.

If Shmel ever *did* get to buy our town house in Marbella, I couldn't help but surmise that being as hedonistic as he was, this would definitely be the place he would spend most of his time…

My Frog Collection… On our return from Marbella, Shmel decided to stay with me for the night. As this was such a rare occurrence I asked him why and he told me that he had a surprise for me the following morning. He wouldn't tell me what the surprise was and I just couldn't imagine what he had up his sleeve, so I was quite excited by the time morning came.

Once we had eaten our breakfast Shmel suggested we go out for a drive. He would hardly ever tell me where we were going and it was the same again this particular morning, so I settled down and I soon found myself being taken on a leisurely drive into the West End of London. Our first stop was at a jewellery shop in Oxford Street. Shmel knew I had sold my wedding ring the year before so he suggested buying his and her rings again, as he had a desire for us to renew our wedding vows. It wasn't his intention to return to the Synagogue of course, but he said that he thought having twin rings and exchanging them again would bring good fortune to each of us.

I didn't take anywhere near as long to choose our new wedding rings as I did with the originals, and once our purchase was complete, without any kind of ceremony I slipped the platinum and diamond wedding ring onto my finger. Shmel looked very pleased that I had accepted the ring and after putting his own ring on, just for once, he actually apologised for having treated me so badly in the past. I accepted his apology but then pleaded with him unashamedly, not to cause me any more unnecessary pain and anguish.

We left the jewellery shop delighted with our purchase and wearing our new rings we casually went along towards Selfridges Department Store where we stopped and enjoyed a satisfying lunch, after which, he said that he had yet another surprise for me as we made our way along to a classy shopping mall called the Burlington Arcade.

I have a great collection of ornamental frogs, and Shmel had decided to add to my collection by buying me a family of three frogs fashioned out of silver and enamel. I was absolutely delighted with my gift as I felt that they would sit handsomely along with many of my other designer ornaments. I truly felt that this special gift was his way of expressing his true feelings towards me and his real regret at having caused me so much upset and heartache in the past. My special day ended when he took me to dine in a London Casino. He had been so loving and caring all day; I just didn't want the day to end. It had truly been one of the best and most special days in our relationship and I felt exceptionally hopeful that this was to be a major turning point in our lives.

Whilst on the subject of frogs, a couple of weeks after Shmel had bought my silver frog family, I saw a delightful bronze frog in an antique shop in Epping. Naturally, I couldn't resist him and when I went into the shop to buy it I got chatting to the owner and told him I was an avid frog collector. He told me that he knew of a lady who had a vast collection of ornamental frogs and that if I was interested he could give me her address. I wrote to the lady that very same evening and told her of my interest and I was delighted to receive a personal invitation to go and visit the only frog museum in this country. Apparently, the lady started out with one frog ornament in the nineteen seventies and eventually, found it necessary to move to a mansion in Wiltshire, which enabled her to display the one million pound collection of ornamental frogs that she had gathered from all over the world.

Although Shmel didn't like my fixation with frogs, he did accompany me on this special expedition to Wiltshire. I was delighted of course, and he was pleasantly surprised to see this extraordinary display of these amazing creatures from all corners of the globe and we happily spent quite a few hours looking around.

When we finally left, 'Frog Mansion' instead of driving straight home Shmel booked us into a wonderful five star hotel called 'The Vineyard' in Stockcross, which is owned by Sir Peter Michael. It was an experience I would not have liked to have missed as we had a luxury suite for the week-end with the use of a spa. The restaurant located within the hotel was exquisitely decorated and served an excellent range of nouveau cuisine food. We had a very memorable stay. In fact, whenever I look at my own collection of frogs, very happy thoughts flood my mind.

9.11... Shmel had already booked for us to go out to Marbella again to sign some documents that would finalise the deal on the town house and we thought that whilst there, we could arrange to meet up with some friends for dinner and show them around our new abode. We were very excited and looking forward to going – it was marred of course, by the dreadful catastrophe of 9:11, when the twin towers of the World Trade Centre in the USA was callously targeted by terrorists. We went away as arranged the week after the attack and although we had a wonderful time with our friends, showing them over our new place, I must admit that 9.11 was the major talking point of our conversation.

The Web-Cam Buzz... Shmel was always coming up with new ideas, suggestions and surprises to the extent where, he ceased to amaze me any more.

We would often go for leisurely drives at the week-ends. Sometimes stopping in or near Brick Lane in Whitechapel where we would buy freshly baked bagels and smoked salmon to eat during the evening while curled up on the sofa at home watching a good film or two. This was our quality time together, something I valued very much.

After purchasing our bagels and salmon one Sunday morning, Shmel drove home, taking a different route to normal. After a short while he stopped outside, what looked like a small factory, I asked him why we had stopped and he said that these were his new offices.

"Offices for what?" I asked dubiously.

He explained saying, he had gone into business partnership with yet *another* person, this time the business involved telephone chat-lines with live web-cam services... Mmm! Can you imagine?

I asked who his partner was and he said that it was his sister's son who was a genius on the computer. Shmel's sister had three children who were all very talented in one respect or another. His nephews and niece were also very polite and considerate, unlike his own children. Shmel made sure that his own youngsters were given work there, Anne was also a regular visitor to the place and I found out some time later that Shmel's elderly girlfriend had persuaded him to give her daughter a job there too. This being so, I stayed well and truly out of it all. In fact, I never once entered the building, and made sure to keep my distance.

The Money God… Money was Shmel's God, it was his idol, and when things were going well he was on top of the world, he was generous and would spend money on anything and everything he wanted. On the other hand, he would become very sullen and moody if things went wrong. As soon as I heard his voice I could tell whether profits were up or down or whether business was running smoothly or not.

The type of business that Shmel was involved in was very lucrative indeed and money usually flooded in like a tidal wave, enabling him to spend, spend, spend, rather like Viv, the infamous football pools winner who couldn't stop throwing her money away until it had all disappeared.

It was about this time, when business was doing very well, that Shmel decided he would like to order the very latest Lexus sports car. It wasn't actually on the market when Shmel ordered it, as it was still at the drawing board stage, but he wanted to make sure he was the first, or at least one of the first people in this country to own one. He ordered the new car and arranged to have the Lexus saloon that he had at present used in part exchange. Shmel took delivery of his new Lexus sports car in the early part of 2002 and he was indeed the first person in this country to own this fabulous, beauty of a car.

A couple of weeks after Shmel had ordered his new car he decided that we should take another trip to Marbella so that we could look around for some furniture for the new town house. We only spent four days there and had no time to relax at all; instead, we spent hours going from one furniture shop to another choosing whatever we wanted. Money was of no object naturally; it was just a matter of finding what was suitable for the place and what we both liked. After purchasing the items we wanted, we returned home immediately to England. For speed and convenience rather than comfort we took a low-cost flight home on Easy Jet.

It was quite late in the evening when we finally arrived home to my house and after carrying my luggage into the hall, Shmel said that he was off to his bed-sit and that he would return sometime during the next day to sort out his personal belongings. I was tired, so we said a quick goodbye and he jumped in the car and took off, after which, I had a bath and retired to bed as quickly as possible.

'Allo, 'Allo, 'Allo... I was absolutely dead to the world when suddenly I was awakened with a start by my bedside telephone. I glanced blearily at the clock; it was 5:30am. I jumped out of bed instantly, fearing perhaps, a problem with one of my family, but I was totally amazed when I heard Shmel's voice over the phone informing me that he was standing outside my front door accompanied by no fewer than, six, plain-clothed detectives.

Apparently, the police had been keeping a close watch on my husband over the last three months, scrutinising the comings and goings of his two illegal brothels - sorry - saunas. Consequently, the detectives were more than ready to raid *my* premises. I looked out of my window and in the early light of morning; I could see that my husband looked white and shaken from the shock of it all. It transpired that the detectives had been waiting for him to arrive back at his bed-sit and when he turned up he was stopped and cautioned.

He had been up all night answering questions, etc. during which he had been forced, or rather persuaded, to take the police to his safe deposit box in the West End where, once opened, all the contents, which included one-hundred-and-twenty-thousand pounds plus jewellery were confiscated along with his dignity.

Fortunately, I had nothing belonging to him in my house as each time we had quarrelled, I had taken all of his clothes and other possessions to the local charity shops. I told the police about my trips to these shops and thankfully they believed me. It must have appeared very obvious to the detectives that I was an innocent party in all this and totally uninvolved in his dealings, so fortunately I was in the clear. All that was needed of me was to hand over Shmel's passport, which was still in a separate compartment of my handbag. The police came in but they didn't search my house instead, they thanked me for my assistance and then escorted Shmel back to the police station where he was formally arrested and charged with living off immoral earnings.

Many hours later, Shmel arrived back on my doorstep. I let him in and he plumped down on the sofa exhausted, tired and very depressed in fact, he broke down and cried like a baby. He told me that after hours of interrogation he was released on bail, but his passport had been withheld. He was instructed to close the two saunas down and warned against re-opening them. He didn't seem to understand what all the fuss was about and couldn't quite make out what he had done wrong.

We found out later that not only had Shmel's saunas been under surveillance for months, the police had also been watching the offices, which resulted in Shmel's nephew being arrested. All the business bank accounts were frozen, which effectively closed down all the chat-lines and web-cam projects. The company suffered to such an extent, that the whole business plummeted rapidly, ending in closure, which put Shmel's nephew and all who worked there in dire straits. His nephew, who was married with two small children, found himself without a job and had nowhere to turn, although, unbeknown to my husband he had already started looking at the possibility of starting up a similar business of his own. Shmel was so infuriated when he found out what his nephew had been planning to do that he decided to take legal action against him which resulted in the nephew being declared bankrupt. I begged Shmel not to take his nephew to court, but he ignored my pleas and went ahead with it. I felt that Shmel had gone too far in the first instance, by involving his nephew in the business to the extent he had and I thought it vindictive of Shmel to turn on him when things went wrong. After all, with a young family to keep, I considered it was no less than common sense for the nephew to look out for himself.

My husband was furious with me for siding with his nephew, but I have a heart and I didn't think that he should have gone so far as to cause the bankruptcy of a young man who had a wife and two little children to provide for.

Today: I have to point out at this stage that my husband was eventually given back all of the jewellery that was taken at the police raid and upon application, his passport was returned also but unfortunately, it was destined that he would never be able to regain what small amount of dignity he might have possessed. Shmel had been left with nothing after having had everything. For some years, literally hundreds of thousands of pounds had passed through his hands. But as fate would have it, his wrongdoings had finally caught up with him and it was now payback time. My husband was out on bail and had been ordered not to re-open his saunas. But, here was a man who was arrogant and defiant to the point where his character was to dictate otherwise.

2002

Chapter 15 – The Future Looms.

Family Breakdown… A few weeks went by before Shmel's nephew was told that all charges were being dropped against him but unfortunately, he did not escape bankruptcy. Because this affair affected a good number of my husband's own family, it was inevitable that the fairly good relationship he had enjoyed in the past with them had now turned sour. Shmel's mother was heartbroken and desperately tried to smooth things over, but all hope of reuniting her children had gone, it seemed that a family who were once reasonably close were now destined to be miles apart.

Swanning Along… Although it seems rather inappropriate now, at the time we felt a great need to get away from it all… so one day Shmel announced that we were going away for the week-end. It turned out to be one of those special week-ends that will stay in my memory for a very long time.

Shmel picked me up, the way he usually did when we were going somewhere special and we set out. The journey took us through the beautiful countryside for miles upon miles only stopping off once and that was for lunch at a country pub.

After resuming our journey we eventually came upon a charming place, the sort of location I had only ever read about. It was that of The Swan Hotel in Lavenham, Suffolk. It was every bit as lovely as I had imagined a place like this could be. It was beautiful and magical, with a charisma all of its own. We pulled up outside the hotel which had been built in the 14th century, originally as a coach inn. It supported around fifty bedrooms each with an en-suite bathroom. The room we were allotted was absolutely superb, it had a very low ceiling that was heavily beamed, the room had a splendid four-poster bed with chintz drapes, and to let in the sunshine, it featured the original, leaded-light windows. Apparently, it was considered to be a great attraction and especially recommended for American tourists. The members of staff were particularly friendly and at a cost of a mere two-hundred and fifty pounds per night, inclusive of breakfast and dinner it was considered to be well worth the visit. After arriving we made our way to the lounge where a real log fire was glowing. Here we sat and enjoyed a wonderful cream tea which was absolutely delicious. After having our cream tea we decided to go for a long, lingering stroll which also helped us to relax after our long journey.

I so enjoyed walking around the cobbled streets near to the hotel, taking full advantage of the fresh, country air and where I could cast my mind back and visualise the days when the horse-drawn carriage was the norm.It was here at this hotel, that Claudia Schiffer (no relation by the way!) the German super-model had stayed the night before her wedding and had walked out of the hotel wearing her amazing wedding gown. These were all to be very wonderful memories for me which helped in some small way to alleviate the sadness and despair I had to contend with most of the time and even more so of late.

Falling Apart... During this uncertain time Shmel was telephoning the Marbella estate agent trying to explain why it was necessary for him to cancel the deal on the town house which was to have been our dream home, along with all the beautiful furniture we had so painstakingly ordered. It didn't seem to bother him at all telling the agent about being picked up and charged with living off immoral earnings...

"It is only a couple of whore houses after all." He told the agent, as if he personally, had done nothing wrong whatsoever!

The months ahead proved to be very gruelling for me to say the least. It all started off one morning with an anxious telephone call from Shmel asking me to go to the Homerton Hospital in the borough of Hackney, as his mother had fallen off a step inside a bus while on her way to the shops. I rushed over to the hospital and stayed with my mother-in-law for about eight or so hours while she laid battered and bruised on a trolley in the A and E department, before eventually being sent for an x-ray.

During the long wait while my mother-in-law was having her x-rays, Shmel arrived at the hospital. Obviously, we were both very concerned for this elderly lady, and albeit in pain, she tried hard to remain bright and chirpy. Because I was there with her I felt sure it gave her confidence, and when Shmel walked in, she became even happier and seemed far less afraid.

The results of her x-rays were distressing to say the least. It appeared that she had broken her right leg and her hip was fractured. She was admitted and sent to a ward where we were told that she would have to be prepared to undergo surgery.

Shmel was devastated. "How much more can go wrong?" He moaned. What with the court case looming, (a problem he had kept from his mother, as he didn't want to worry her any more than necessary) losing the town house

he had been so looking forward to owning and now his mother's accident…
Oi!

Unfortunately, at the time of my mother-in-law's accident Shmel's sister
was in Greece with a new boyfriend. It was the first holiday she had been on
since the sudden death of her husband some months earlier. Her late husband
was a delightful man, very kind and considerate, he was also very spiritual.
He was a qualified hypnotherapist and had given me a couple of sessions of
this soothing therapy, at a time when my weight problem was at its height
and I was at my wits end.

I was quite surprised to hear that my sister-in-law had taken up with
another man so soon after the death of her husband, after all, they had been
married for about thirty years. Shmel wasn't surprised, in fact, he was quite
pleased, as he thought his sister's husband was very boring, and had said so
on a number of occasions. I, on the other hand, thought he was a nice, quiet
and gentle man, very caring and interesting, but of course, if people were
not interested in sex, women or sleaze, Shmel automatically considered them
to be a frightful bore. Shmel managed to telephone his sister in Greece and
told her about their mother, but surprisingly, she made no immediate plans
to return home.

With Shmel up to his eyes in worry and his sister away on holiday, it
fell to me to attend his mother, which I did every day. I would travel to the
hospital, stay as long as possible and when I felt she was comfortable and had
everything she wanted, I would return home. We were told that his mother
would have to be in hospital for some time, and it was roughly two weeks
before his sister finally returned home from holiday and took over from me,
by then it was nearing my birthday.

The Big Five-0… The tension at home was pretty fraught as you can
well imagine. Shmel had the court case pending and he was extremely worried
about the enforced closure of the saunas. In fact he became so concerned
about his fast-drying up cash-flow, that against police directives he decided
to re-open his illegal establishments, albeit for just a short period of time in
order to tide him over. He undoubtedly felt that if he had kept the saunas
closed, there would have been no income for him at all and with the vast
amount of commitments he had…Well! It was proving a nightmare of colossal
proportions for him. Nevertheless, this didn't stop him from making plans
for my big five-0 birthday due in February, even though it was extremely bad
timing, what with his mother in hospital and all the other dreaded events
that were approaching.

He booked a week-end away in Edinburgh, going by first-class train and staying in a boutique hotel, where we had the pleasure of in-room dining. Naturally I told him to cancel the holiday, especially as his mother was in hospital, but he wouldn't hear of it and said that, as his sister was back in England and could take over from us, there was no reason why the week-end break should not go ahead.

We duly set off for our holiday in Edinburgh, Scotland. Throughout the journey I noticed that Shmel received numerous text messages. They were disturbing our journey and got on my nerves, so eventually I asked him who the messages were from. He replied saying that it was nothing and that they were from his son. I didn't believe him of course, I assumed the messages were from his old girlfriend, but then, rather than have anything spoil my birthday treat I decided to shut my eyes and ears and ignore them.

We arrived in Scotland and found it to be a really beautiful place. The hotel we had booked into was great. It was February and very cold, but fortunately, the sun shone most of the time, which allowed us to spend hours outdoors sightseeing or just walking.

Edinburgh is steeped in history and has some amazing architecture that has to be seen to be appreciated. During our stay Shmel was not his usual self and at times he appeared very distant and lost in thought, which of course I understood, owing to the circumstances surrounding him. I didn't give much thought to the text messages he had been receiving during our journey down but it did occur to me that his mood had changed since receiving them. I guessed his girlfriend was giving him plenty of grief.

The week-end went quite quickly and we soon found ourselves back on the train which would bring us home. We had not been travelling very long when Shmel's sister rang him with some bad news. It emerged that his mother had been moved from the Homerton Hospital to the North Middlesex. It transpired that she had started to hallucinate so badly that the doctors had decided to admit her to a geriatric ward. The reason for this problem, we were told, was that his mother's complicated operations meant that she had been under anaesthetic longer than had been hoped and that there was a possibility it could have triggered off some form of dementia.

Although it was quite late, as soon as we arrived back home in London we went immediately to the hospital, where we found Shmel's mother to have changed so much, that it was like looking at, and talking to, a completely different person to the one we had left behind. Nevertheless, we felt quite confident that with the right treatment and medication, his mother would gradually return to near normal, but for the time being, we felt alien to his mother's strange behaviour and we found it difficult to cope with. I felt very sad for this lady, as up until now she had been very independent. She had been upright and able to walk without aid. Even at the age of eighty-six, she had never looked her age and she had never missed the bus or train ride that took her to the senior citizens club once a week, where she would enjoy a game of cards with her friends and fellow club members. Regrettably, all that had stopped instantly following her unfortunate accident.

Chicken Soup... The week-end following our holiday in Scotland, as an added treat for my birthday, Shmel had arranged a special dinner-party in my honour to be held in a private room at a Southend Casino for around thirty people. He even arranged for a magician to come along to help keep us all amused and in the party spirit.

During the week prior to my birthday dinner-party my own mother and brother were due to come and stay with me. When they arrived I was delighted to see them and we spent lots of time catching up with all the family gossip. On the Saturday, Shmel hired a people-carrier that would enable us all to go to the Southend Casino, together. While we had the rented, six-seater we thought we would take the opportunity to go and visit my mother-in-law in hospital on the Saturday afternoon. For my family's lunch I had made a large batch of chicken soup with chicken wings, and as my mother-in-law loves home-made soup I filled a flask to the brim and wrapped up a few succulent chicken wings with some lovely fresh vegetables and took them into hospital with me. My own mother and daughter said how much they would like to visit her as well, so they accompanied Shmel and I in the car.

Sitting up in bed in the hospital the poor lady tucked in heartily, saying how wonderful my soup, chicken and vegetables were compared to hospital cuisine. Once she had finished her feast we took her into the day room so that we could all have a good chat. Her mind was wandering quite badly now and we all felt very sad for her. Nevertheless, we tried hard to cheer her up by chatting about family and general, every-day matters. Suddenly Shmel's mobile warbled, indicating that a text message had been received. As it happened, my dear husband had just gone around to the other side of his mother's armchair so that he could sit closer to her, and in so doing had left his mobile on a low table near to me. I picked it up and there displayed on the screen were the words... *Is it safe to text you?*

Shmel dashed over to me and grabbed the mobile phone out of my hand, but he was too late as I had already read the message.

"Who was that?" I said sharply.

"It was the builder," he said. "It's only the builder."

Shmel immediately telephoned the builder, who at the time, was working in one of the saunas and said quietly but gruffly, "What the hell are you doing texting me in the hospital. What do you want?"

The builder must have been so taken aback at Shmel's question that he roughly replied, loud enough for me to hear.

"What the fuck are you talking about mate?"

To which Shmel replied, rather jovially, "Okay John, see you on Monday."

His phone call to the builder and the short, ensuing conversation was an utter farce, a complete fabric of pretence. He must have thought I was blind, deaf and totally stupid ...

I was so furious with my rat of a husband that I completely forgot I was in a hospital day room. I jumped up and shouted out at the top of my voice, "You crafty, bastard, that wasn't the builder who text you that was your old girlfriend, the one who continually text you while we were away in Scotland!"

My mother and daughter looked on open-mouthed with shock at the suddenness of my unexpected outburst. I dragged my coat from the back of the chair and told them to get ready as we were going home. Our rapid departure from the hospital left Shmel alone to sort out his poor mother, plus it meant that he would have no means of transport?

On realising this, he pleaded with me not to go, asking me how on earth, would he be able to get home if I took the car.

"*Get your girlfriend to pick you up!*" I yelled back at him over my shoulder as I stormed out.

The Big Let-Down... My mum, daughter and I climbed into the people carrier and set off towards home. I was terribly upset and shaking with anger. How that rat could possible lie to me so blatantly and cheat on me the way he did I will never know. Tears filled my eyes as I drove along. I had given his mother so much care and attention while his sister had been sunning herself in Greece. I had put up with so much from Shmel and forgiven him so many times and wondered what I could possibly have done to deserve such humiliating treatment.

My mum and daughter stayed quiet while sitting in the car as I ranted on about my husband; I think they had been stunned into silence by my angry outburst. Eventually, we arrived home and once in the house I announced that my birthday had been totally ruined and that my celebration dinner was cancelled. I felt dreadful saying that my birthday dinner was off and knew that everybody would feel let down but there was no way possible that I could sit with my husband and enjoy my day when I knew for sure that he was still seeing another woman.

I managed to contact most of my friends to tell them of my decision, I apologised profusely and fortunately, the majority of them were not at all surprised as they were only too aware of the volatile relationship Shmel and I had. By the Saturday evening there was only one couple left to inform, but regrettably I could not get in-touch with them.

Shmel telephoned me on and off all Saturday evening, pleading with me to go ahead with the dinner party. He kept telling me not to be so stupid as to let everyone down, he told me to, 'just turn up'. But I had made my decision and anyway, it was too late now as I had already telephoned my friends to tell them of the cancellation.

The following morning, Sunday, which was supposed to be my big, important day, Shmel rang my door-bell early. I opened the door fully expecting him to launch into pleas for my co-operation, instead, I found him quietly standing there with his handyman from the sauna. I glared at him, waiting to hear what he had to say, but instead of saying what I thought he would, he just asked me if he could have the keys to the people-carrier and his precious Lexus that was still adorning my driveway from the day before. I snatched the keys from my hall table and literally threw them at him, telling him to get away from my house, as he had ruined my special birthday and made me look a fool in front of my family and friends.

Never Mind Eh! ... Shmel bent down and picked up the keys without another word and gave one set to his handyman for the hired car, keeping the Lexus set for himself. As I slammed the front door on them, I heard both cars start up together and within a few minutes they were both gone leaving me alone again, with my much looked-forward-to special birthday in ruins and only my mother to comfort me as usual. I spent my fiftieth birthday feeling sad, angry, hurt and indeed, very lonely.

On the other hand, my darling husband actually went ahead with my birthday celebration dinner without me, filling the seats with some of his own family, including Anne, plus other friends and cronies. Mind you, during the evening he did telephone me a couple of times asking me to come to the casino. He even enlisted the help of the magician, in a vain hope that he could cast a spell down the line in order to get me there. But I just couldn't face any of his crowd now, not after having disappointed my own relations and friends. Anyway, I didn't want to be with my husband that day. Shmel told me that the two friends I hadn't been able to contact did turn up and were very upset that the birthday girl wasn't there and that they left shortly after arriving. Trying to make me feel bad, of course, he informed me they were not very pleased, as they had driven a very long way in order to see me on my special day.

I did manage to contact my long standing friends later the following day to apologise and explain the situation. They were very sweet and considerate, thankfully, and they accepted my apology with sympathy and understanding. They told me that they had left the party on purpose soon after arriving as they didn't particularly like the company that Shmel had invited.

Croak and Benson... The day after my non-birthday celebration, my husband's cousin, the jeweller who worked in Hatton Garden, arrived at my home in order to deliver the gift that Shmel had commissioned purposely for my special birthday. It was a diamond and emerald, frog brooch. My heart sank when I opened the gift box, as the brooch was absolutely beautiful and being an avid frog enthusiast I just loved it. Quite honestly, nothing could compensate for my husband's total disregard for my feelings and emotions and I didn't know what to do. But eventually, with much sadness, and against my own principles I accepted the gift, thanking the cousin very much, saying what a superb job he had done. I decided that there was no way I was going to reject the skill of such a wonderful craftsman; I would not have had the heart to do so.

After lunch I said goodbye to my mother and brother who were now ready to start out on their journey back to Brighton. I apologised to them, yet again, for ruining their stay, but they understood fully and said that they didn't blame me for acting the way I did. I was very much comforted by their love and understanding and was extremely sorry to see them go.

An hour or so later a knock on my door meant that there was yet another gift from Shmel. Due to all the upset and confusion I had completely forgotten that he had bought me a Cocker Spaniel pup that was to be delivered that afternoon. He said he would buy me a dog as it would keep me company if he was sent to prison.

As soon as I saw this delightful animal I welcomed it with open arms, he was absolutely adorable. In 2002 he was just six weeks old and unlike my husband, was destined to be faithful to me.

After my disastrous fiftieth birthday, Shmel did his usual trick of going on the missing list, but despite his disappearance I continued to visit his poor mother regularly in the hospital. As a rule I would be there on my own, but there were times when I would meet up with Shmel's sister and go along with her.

Some weeks later during one of our visits, we were called into the doctor's office only to be informed, that my mother-in-law was definitely showing signs of early dementia, there was nothing else they could do for her consequently, she would have to be returned to the Homerton Hospital and be put into a psychiatric ward. My sister-in-law and I decided to go the following afternoon to see where she would be placed. I can recall most vividly, calling for Shmel's sister and discussing her mother's plight. We each expressed our deep concern for the lady's welfare and desperately tried to think of ways to resolve the problem during the drive to the Homerton. We arrived at the hospital and made our way to the psychiatric wing where the doctors had proposed Shmel's mother should go and while there, we had a brief chat to one of the staff and from the comments she made, regarding this particular section of the hospital, we both decided then and there, that this would *not* be the most suitable place for the sick old lady to end up. We both felt that she may have become quite confused but she was in no way bad enough to be sectioned under the mental health act. We retreated from the psychiatric ward as quickly as possible, jumped into the car and made our way back to the North Middlesex Hospital. Our idea being, that we would ask the doctors there, if they could possibly keep Shmel's mum until we had found a decent nursing home for her.

On returning to the North Middlesex Hospital, I happened to look at the notice board and saw that one of the doctors on duty that day had exactly the same name as my uncle who had been murdered many years before. We sought this particular doctor out and as luck would have it, after talking to him and telling him the story of my murdered uncle, he said that he indeed knew of the incident and they had, in fact, been cousins. Needless to say, the amazing coincidence of meeting this particular doctor meant that I was able to appeal to him to have my mother-in-law stay where she was for a few more days until we could sort something out for her, or until we had found somewhere for her to go long-term.

The Calling… Although Shmel's sister was there, I thought it only right and proper that Shmel should be informed and involved in his mother's future. I had not seen or heard from my husband for weeks, so I started to ring around his friends and acquaintances to see if I could get hold of him. Unfortunately, he was not answering his mobile telephone and nobody seemed to know where he was at all. Out of desperation I decided to contact his old girlfriend to see if she could tell me of his whereabouts. Luckily, she was in to take the call and when I briskly asked her if I could speak to my husband urgently, she told me that he was not with her he was in fact, in Mallorca.

"Mallorca!" I repeated.

"Yes, he has gone there to rest for a week before his court case begins."

"Has he gone there alone?" I enquired…

"No, apparently he has gone with his ex-wife Anne."

Well, I was so utterly shocked I was speechless; I just couldn't believe what this woman had just told me. Nevertheless, after a moment or two of silence, I found my voice again and said, "I hope he realises that I am doing all this running around, worrying about his mother when he should be here to help?"

To which his girlfriend retorted, "You're mad, there's absolutely no way I would dream of doing such a thing."

After having heard this uncaring and thoughtless statement I decided that there was nothing more to say, so I muttered goodbye and signed off.

Eventually, after many tries, I managed to get hold of Shmel on his mobile and I explained the situation to him, regarding his mother. Feeling sure he would be concerned, I was therefore, very surprised when he said, "He was sorry and all that, but he needed to rest before his trial and that he had every faith in me to do what was right by his mother." He signed off by saying that he would see me soon.

Realising that it was no good trying to reason with him, as it was blatantly obvious he cared for no one but himself, I just got on with what I had to do. After all, someone had to care for his poor old mother and it looked like it would have to be me. To make matters worse, a few days later Shmel's sister came by my house and pushed all the paperwork and her mother's pension book through my letterbox, with a note saying that she had decided she had had enough and was going back to Greece with her lover. When I saw all those papers lying on my doormat and after reading the note, I guessed that this was her way of telling me to 'get on with it.' And that is exactly what I did…

I decided to bring my mother-in-law back to live with me at my house. I made up a bed for her in the lounge and saw to it that she was made as comfortable as possible. I had no idea how long she would be staying with me, but as her own children were too selfish to do anything for her I knuckled down and did everything including cooking, dressing, and I even bathed her like a small child.

A whole week went by before my rat of a husband returned home just as if everything was fine and dandy. I never questioned him about the holiday;

I couldn't be bothered quite truthfully. I was very busy and the last thing I wanted to hear was a pack of lies. At this moment in time my top priority was to get his mother settled in a good nursing home where she would be comfortable and well cared for. Shmel had no choice but to come with me to sort out this problem. As it happened, we were to look at quite a few nursing homes before we eventually found one that we considered suitable for all her needs.

Doodies All Around... Meanwhile, life in my house was hectic to say the least, believe me! What with having to visit nursing homes and deal with my mother-in-law. Having my own family to care for and a puppy dog scampering around, all this plus Shmel, My God! I didn't know which way to turn. During those chaotic days we ceased to live, we just existed from day to day. So much so, that to help us bring some semblance of order back into our lives a friend of mine arranged for a dog handler to come in once a week to help and give advice on training Benson my little dog.

The dog handler who was recommended by one of my friends was an ex-policeman who certainly knew his job. I was so pleased with his credentials that I booked and paid for him to come along five Sunday mornings in succession.

The first Sunday was fine and he spent quite a bit of time explaining the best methods by which to train my dog to use the garden in which to go to the toilet. He also gave me general hints and tips on obedience training and general care.

The second Sunday was a total disaster as mum-in-law was still with us and Shmel had been giving me a hard time by telling me that my darling puppy would have to go, as despite my constant effort at training him all the week he was still doing his doodies all over the kitchen floor instead of out in the garden. By the time the dog-trainer arrived at my house that Sunday morning my feelings were at fever pitch. We went out into the kitchen and when I tried to speak, I became so emotional, that as a result both my teenage children, as well as myself burst into tears. The dog-trainer looked at us all in amazement; he was rather lost for words to say the least, as he looked around at us all standing there weeping buckets. And when he asked me what was wrong, I had to tell him, between sobs, that the dog would have to go and did he know anyone who wanted my lovely, darling puppy.

The trainer bent down and ruffled Benson's gorgeous head and while running his hand over the puppy's back he tried to reassure me by saying that it wouldn't take too long to train the dog and he was sure that if I could hold out a little bit longer everything would be fine. He went on to say that dogs will often go to the toilet anywhere in the house until it had become accustomed to the habit of pooing where it was supposed to.

Just as we were beginning to dry our eyes as new hope dawned, my husband made a sudden appearance by bursting into the kitchen with his mother in tow, saying very abruptly. "Hurry up, I need to wash and cut my mother's hair and I want to get into the kitchen."

We all looked around in surprise at my husband's sudden, rude entrance and his abrupt manner.

Embarrassed, yet again, I led the way as the dog-handler and my children filed out of the kitchen towards the front door, leaving my husband, who had been a hairdresser in his younger days, to faff around with his mother. I knew instantly that we were not going to be able to do anything about the puppy today after all. It only left me to apologise to the handler profusely, for having had a wasted journey. The handler looked at me sympathetically and on leaving; he turned to me and said in a low voice, "If you take my advice, it's not Benson you need to get rid of, it's your old man!"

I apologised to him once more for my husband's bad-mannered behaviour, and as I was extremely uncomfortable about it all, I told him "Thank you, but not to bother to come back to my doody-house again."

In the week that followed the only bright spot to appear on my horizon was that we found a suitable nursing home for Shmel's mum and she was settled in after just a few days. Naturally, I was left to deal with the doctors, social workers and all the other arrangements that ensued when she went into care, as my husband didn't have a clue about anything. Once all the business with his mother had been done and finalised, his sister decided to return home from holiday and she was allotted the job of clearing out the old lady's apartment. Personal stuff and items that Shmel's mother had accumulated over a span of around fifty years all had to go, be sold or distributed around the family.

Today: I must say that my sister-in-law did show some amount of appreciation for all the work I did for her mother as she kindly gave me two beautiful crystal vases that she estimated to be about sixty years old. They had been gifts given on the occasion of her mother's wedding. Incidentally, to this day, they still sit adorning my table in the lounge and will always be cared for and treasured.

The Future Looms… With my mother-in-law settled, everything seemed to return to normal, well, as normal as could be expected. My puppy soon got the message and quickly learned when and where he should do his doodies so of course, we never did get rid of him thank goodness and he very quickly became, and still is, an integral part of our extended family.

Shmel was unbearably miserable, although I fully understood, as his court case was looming ever closer and it was looking evermore inevitable that he would receive a custodial sentence. Even the delivery of his long awaited Lexus Sports car failed to cheer him up, indeed, he took an instant dislike to this fifty-one thousand pounds, stunning machine, so much so, that I ended up using it more than he did. It wasn't too long before he decided to swap it for another Lexus Saloon. In the mean time, I tried to savour every single, pleasurable moment driving a car that I couldn't imagine would ever be my good fortune to drive again, in fact, to be quite honest, the future looked pretty bleak, not only for Shmel, but for the both of us...

Shmel spent days going back and forth to the solicitors who were preparing his case. I thought it best to stay in the background and let him get on with it, as there was little, if anything, I could do to help him, besides which, I found it very difficult to handle his black moods. There was one short period, prior to the trial when all that could be done had been completed and he no longer had appointments with the solicitors, so he decided to take off again and go back to Mallorca. He defiantly told me he wanted to cram in as many holidays as possible, because for one he had the court-case coming up and for another, since the closure of the saunas, he guessed he would never again, have at his disposal, the vast amounts of money he had become accustomed to. He did ask me to accompany him on his holiday to Mallorca but because of other family commitments I could not go. I wasn't too worried though, as I knew he would be able to fall back onto his old girlfriend who was always willing and able and guess what? She certainly was willing, able and she did go with him.

It transpired that he booked into the same Mallorca hotel as the one he had been to with Anne just a short while before. Apparently, the hotel offered a good all-round service for the price. But I didn't care, I was past caring, I thought I would bide my time and see what happened. After all, I wouldn't have wanted to have been in his shoes, having to face a court-case in the very near future and an inescapable gaol sentence.

Wisdom of Old... The Christmas of 2002 had just passed and in effect, I spent it on my own with just my children, their partners and my ever-faithful mother. I spent quite a bit of time over the Christmas period visiting my mother-in-law in the nursing home, as I guessed that she would have had very few visitors to brighten up her days. On one occasion, while sitting and chatting, she asked me where Shmel was as he hadn't been in to see her for a while. I explained his absence away, by saying that he was abroad on business and that I was sure he would get in to see her as soon as possible.

She looked at me with a perceptive eye and at that point she took hold of my hand, drew me near to her and whispered, "Why don't you get a divorce from him and try to find yourself someone who will love and respect you. You deserve someone better."

I was stunned by her words, for although she had been diagnosed with dementia, this proved to me that she was still able to think clearly enough to assess my situation. She knew her son very well and she knew what he was capable of. She must have been fully aware of the treatment he had continually dished out to me during our long relationship and marriage and so understood how hurt and humiliated I must have been feeling for most of the time.

Over recent months I had grown to admire this lady very much, for knowing one has a sewer rat for a son must have been devastating to say the least and unfortunately, in her failing years, she was not to be spared the shame of knowing that her son was more than a rat, for in fact she had known of the saunas and the sleazy business he had been involved in for a long time. But at least she was spared from finding out that her son had to stand trial for being a pimp and for living off the immoral earnings of prostitutes.

2003

Chapter 16 – Shmel The Rat.

Uncertainty... It was the first week of the New Year 2003 and I just couldn't help but contemplate with dread what the year ahead would bring forth. I didn't feel positive about anything, least of all my marriage to Shmel the rat. I couldn't plan anything, all I could do was to wait and wonder?

Shmel was back on the telephone as usual and I was back, listening to what he had to say. Forgive me if I sound very foolish, but I really believed that when the chips were down and his back was against the wall he needed to be with me. He rang me constantly asking me to go back with him and 'give it one more try'. I really didn't deserve to have this pressure put upon me now, especially after all I had been through with him and yet, I couldn't help but believe it was really me he wanted. Whether it was guilt or nerves I will never know but one day he rang me, pleading for us to try again, saying that he really and truly wanted me and no one else. I felt numb; I honestly didn't know what to do. After sixteen years of hell with this man, sixteen years of mental abuse, I was at my wits end. I was confused and shattered, I felt betrayed and exhausted, my emotions were completely messed up and I was drained of all logic. This man was an unremitting control freak and he had influenced me to the point where I had lost all sense of reason and self-worth.

I cannot say why, and I have no excuses to offer for giving in to him yet again, for no sooner had I relented, he was back controlling me once more. He said that he had booked a holiday in Mallorca and we were going with his friend and his partner. My heart was broken; I was depressed and angry with myself for having given in to him. After all, he made all the decisions; he never asked me where I wanted to go, or what I wanted to do. He manipulated me like a wooden puppet on a string, knowing that I would follow like a dog on a lead. Which I did!

The couple we went to Mallorca with was one of Shmel's closest friends, a friendship that went back to their schooldays.

Shmel's friend, believe it or not was the same man who, back in 1996 I had seen with an "actress" come girlfriend who together, habitually dined on smoked salmon and other goodies every Thursday afternoon before fucking the rest of the day away. It really felt odd and quite strange looking at this man who I knew had been knocking off a woman for years in Shmel's bed-sit, or the knocking-shop as I preferred to call it. But I had also found out that his delightful partner of umpteen years had once been one of Shmel's old acquaintances and, as he hadn't fancied her to that extent, had decided to pass her over to his friend.

How did I know all this and most of the other stories I have related? You may well ask. Well, to tell you the truth it was my dear husband who would often delight in telling me about the misdemeanours of others, as well as his own, on occasions. Shmel's friend had no idea that I knew about his charming partner or that I knew of his own philandering. He never, for a moment suspected that I had seen him with his bit-on-the-side in the past, so he acted quite the friendly gentleman and naturally, I never let on.

Looking Better... The hotel Shmel had booked us all into was the same one that he had recently brought Anne and his old girlfriend, Minnie to. Because of this, I tended to feel quite self-conscious, wondering what the staff and the concierge must have thought about him, or me, for that matter. Fortunately, we were only going to be there for five days and most of the time our thoughts were taken up by discussing and surmising about the forthcoming court case. There was so much to do, so much preparation, we constantly wondered and worried about our future financial position and how we would survive the duration of the prison sentence that he was bound to be given. There was so much to worry about, so much to talk over. Eventually, we found that we had talked ourselves and our problems out to the extent, where, apart from going over old ground, yet again, there was little left for us to discuss or comment on.

One morning, just to get away from it all, Shmel and I decided to go for a leisurely stroll, we thought we might walk into the small town. But as we walked around the corner from our hotel we came upon a charming and very classy boutique. I couldn't help but stop and admire the beautiful clothes, perfumes and cosmetics on display. We wandered in as a matter of course and while I was browsing through the gowns and outfits, the two attractive, middle-aged, German sisters who owned the boutique, came over and asked, in perfect English, if they could help. They were delightful and only too happy to assist me with anything I wanted to try on. While looking around I happened to notice a beautiful brown raincoat that was being displayed on one of the mannequins. Upon my request, one of the ladies went and got it for me. She helped me to put it on and attentively smoothed down the cloth of the garment. It fitted me perfectly. I walked over to the long mirror and turned this way and that to view the coat properly and as I did, the lady happened to make a comment, saying, "It looks better on you."

I frowned at her a little, not quite understanding what she meant, but vaguely thought that despite her apparent, perfect English, this time she must have chosen the wrong words to use. Nevertheless, I was very happy with the raincoat and Shmel was smiling his approval.

"We'll take it." He said.

As one of the ladies carefully folded the coat and placed it in a smart carrier, the other lady prepared the invoice. While doing so, Shmel asked the lady, in a very friendly way, if he could have a discount, to which the lady smiled and said that, "She was so sorry, but unfortunately, she could not give a discount, but if the lady wanted to, she could choose some item of cosmetic or a bottle of perfume instead."

I was quite happy with that and so was Shmel, so I chose a bottle of 'Arpège', which happens to be one of my favourite perfumes. So, not only did I come out of the boutique with a beautiful, stylish raincoat, I had a bottle of my favourite perfume too, I was really pleased and thought that I had done very well for myself indeed.

Angry Words… The time was quickly slipping away, so we decided to make the most of our last couple of days in Mallorca. On the fourth evening we went to one of the islands most exclusive restaurants called Samantha's. They served excellent and tasty European food, and they boasted a famous clientele. To prove it, I had actually been allotted the very same seat that Michael Douglas had occupied the evening before. Imagining myself, sitting on Michael Douglas knee, (in the spiritual sense of course) certainly brought a smile to my lips.

The smile soon disappeared from my face though, for during our second course a conversation we were all having slowly developed into an argument between Shmel and me. The two friends gradually went quiet as we tossed angry words back and forth, to such an extent that the lady sitting with us put down her knife and fork and retreated to the bar. A couple of minutes later Shmel got up and followed her over to the bar leaving his friend and I alone.

I started off the argument by mentioning one or two of Shmel's transgressions. There was no way I could forget the things he had done to me in the past and the pain he had caused me. I just couldn't pretend to my husband's friends that we had enjoyed a healthy marriage, for we hadn't. No way! I thought that if I could air a few matters that had been bugging me, while in a restaurant with friends, I would be able to clear the air, somewhat quietly, but it all went pear-shaped and we ended up spoiling, what should have been a wonderful meal and a pleasant evening. However, we all eventually calmed down, especially when I had resigned myself to the fact that I wasn't going to get any support from either of Shmel's friends and when all went quiet, my husband and the lady returned to the table and we resumed our meal.

Today: I was foolish ever to think, for one moment, that I would get support from my husband's friends. After all, if a man can cheat regularly on his partner for years with another woman, there is no way he is going to think of Shmel as being unusual. There was also the fact that the lady herself had been one of Shmel's old conquests who had been used and passed on.

Forgive Me Gifts… On the final day of our holiday we all went to a leather and suede outlet. I just adored looking around at the beautiful outfits and admiring all the different styles. I had no intention of buying anything of course and I certainly didn't expect Shmel to spend any more money. Nevertheless, while looking around, he called me back to one of the display stands, beckoning me to look at a beautiful blue suede coat with a matching fox-fur trim, while at the same time, pointing out yet another, beautifully-fashioned, black leather, swing-coat that also had a fur trim. He encouraged me to try each of them on, not that I needed much encouragement. We both agreed that they were nothing short of fantastic, especially as each of the garments fitted me perfectly. I reluctantly took the second coat off and just as I was about to replace it on the stand Shmel looked at me and said that he would buy them both for me as a token of his love. He said that he really loved me and was so sorry for all the hurt he had caused me. He asked me to forgive him and to accept both of the coats in order to make up for the miserable fiftieth birthday I had spent the year before. He kissed me and held me close.

What could I say?

Las Vegas - The Final Stop… During the return flight from Mallorca, Shmel sprang yet another surprise on me, by producing from his inside pocket two tickets to Las Vegas for yet another, week-long holiday. He had booked us into the Treasure Island Hotel, the one we had visited before, so we knew it to be good.

It was already half way through January and when I noted down the date of our intended departure to Las Vegas, it worked out that I would have only two days at home to prepare for this second trip. He was most definitely packing in as many holidays as possible before his court-case in February. I began to think that he envisaged getting a prison stretch that would extend for the duration of his life.

No sooner was I home from Spain, it seemed, when we were off again to Las Vegas. I knew the weather would be spring-like in January as opposed to the searing heat that desert countries are noted for and we were told on arrival that only the week before they had experienced snow.

We had a complimentary suite that had been arranged by Shmel's son. Apparently, he had been to Vegas a short while before and had befriended one of the hotel managers while playing poker. It was more than likely that he had offered the man a good rub down by a stunning, leggy blonde at the London massage parlour in return for a good suite at the hotel for his father. And from Shmel's knowledge of men in general, the hotel manager was hardly likely to refuse such a tempting offer?

The hotel suite we were given was very large, comfortable and very beautifully decorated. As it was coming up to my fifty-first birthday Shmel had arranged, prior to our arrival, an ice-cold bottle of sparking water, a bowl of exotic fruit and a sumptuous box of creamy chocolates to be set up in the room. Not forgetting the single red rose arranged lovingly on my bed pillow, all rather romantic, don't you think?

Shmel hired a gazebo and we had our own private waiter who attended to our every need. The weather wasn't quite warm enough for me to use the swimming pool, but we lounged the week away under the gazebo, eating fruit, drinking chilled drinks, we even had our own television on a side table.

Although, my husband seldom, if ever sought my advice on his business dealings, from time to time he would run things by me, rather like talking to himself. Obviously, he would not take on board or act on any comments or suggestions I made, but occasionally he did like to talk his thoughts out-loud.

Shmel was always thinking up new ideas which he hoped, would make him a bob or two. He was always scheming and considering fresh ways to make easy money. The trouble was, unless people are very intelligent or extremely skilful, the older one becomes the more difficult it is to push these schemes through to a successful completion. Despite this, for many months he had been toying with the idea of opening up a fish restaurant. He somehow must have guessed that eventually the saunas would be closed down for good and he felt he needed something mighty soft and easy to fall back onto. A fish bar he thought would be just perfect. During the past three months he had been involved in many meetings with an extremely wealthy man who had been in the video business for years. This man had recently sold his video organization for a huge sum of money to a very large, well-known company, consequently, the man had money to spare and was looking for a new interest.

Shmel had thought up the idea of the fish restaurant after having spent many enjoyable hours with me, and no doubt many others, in Leigh-on-Sea, Essex, at the famous 'Sheds' where one could enjoy fresh prawns, cockles and whelks, all washed down with a delicious cup of tea.

While in Las Vegas Shmel received and made many business calls to his new partner in London in order to discuss and make decisions on the location, name and décor of the intended new venture. It did seem to be a pity that, with all the worry and time spent talking about the business, my husband, whose idea it was in the beginning, would not be able to put any money into the restaurant, instead, he would only be able to control a five percent stake owned by someone else. Mind you, being able to concentrate on the new business helped to put Shmel in a reasonably good mood. With his thoughts otherwise engaged, we were able to put the rapidly approaching trial to the back of our minds, even if it were only for a short time.

During our stay, the manager of the hotel was able to get us tickets to see some of the wonderful shows that were being featured there. The first show we saw starred Gladys Knight and only one of the famous Pips, who, incidentally, was her brother. She is one of my favourite artists and I thought this was an amazing show. Another show was the fantastic "O" Cirque du Soleil. I am not a fan of the circus as a rule, but I must say that this was an outstanding show and the displays, costing in excess of three million dollars were tremendous. The "O" stood for 'Water', which meant that the whole show was performed on water. I was told that this particular circus tours the world. I don't know if all the shows have a water theme, but whether it is performed on water or not I would highly recommend people to go and see it, if they ever have the opportunity. The final show we went to see featured Danny Gans, who has a vast repertoire of over two-hundred impersonations, he and his sell-out show was just spectacular. While we were there we took the opportunity to have a boat ride across a lake to view the Hoover Dam, and I also visited the Guggenheim Museum in the Venetian Hotel in order to see millions of pounds-worth of paintings that were on display.

One of the most extraordinary visits we made was to the Bellagio Hotel where they boast of a six-million-dollar waterfall that pulsates to the rhythm of Sarah Brightman's beautiful singing voice. To think that her remarkable voice can be heard above all the noise of a bustling town whilst driving down the 'strip' is nothing short of amazing.

During the evenings we would go downstairs to the hotel's casino and sit around the roulette tables trying to win ourselves some dollars. Unfortunately, it was not to be, and by the end of the stay I could only conclude that we had well and truly paid for our luxury, 'complimentary' suite.

The week sped by and the time had come for us to go home and face reality. I would have to wake up from my fairy-tale dream to face, what?

Today: Little was I to know at the time, that this trip to Las Vegas would prove to be my last holiday as Shmel's wife. Thinking back, it was just like history repeating itself, for just as he had said goodbye to his longstanding Austrian woman in Switzerland and said a final farewell to Anne in Hong Kong, so Las Vegas would prove to be my very own last port of call.

Judgement Day… It was February 7th 2003, 9am, Southwark Crown Court.

The dreaded day had arrived at last. The day upon which Shmel's fate would be decided. We had been told by our brief in the morning that the sitting judge for the day was the least harsh in sentencing. Shmel took this as a good sign and hoped that he would get away with a suspended sentence and a fine, or something equally acceptable. But we were to be disappointed!

When I entered the court, I must admit that it was with some amount of trepidation. It was filled with friends, some of Shmel's family, a number of his standby girlfriends and reporters. The Crown Prosecution Service sat in their designated seats and I sat in one of the seats at the front of the courtroom. My husband was sitting in a caged dock looking like a scared animal. He looked pale, subdued and seemed very anxious. I kept glancing over towards him expecting to see his skin complaint kick into action, as it was inclined to do, on occasions, when he was nervous.

Shmel had been advised to plead guilty to all the charges, so the case was put before the judge clearly and simply. There wasn't very much to say or go on about, as everything was more or less, cut and dried. Shmel did request that he be given the opportunity to speak personally to the judge before sentencing was considered and he had taken the time to write a letter that he intended to read out. Shmel's Solicitor read his letter and told him that he couldn't possible put a letter like that to the judge, and *should* he be allowed to read it out in the court room, the judge would almost certainly laugh his head off, send him to gaol and throw away the key for good, so unfortunately, my husband had to sit-tight, cross his fingers and hope for the best.

I truly believe that my husband was under the impression that he owned and ran a clean, honest and legitimate business. He could see no harm, whatsoever, in what he had been doing over the years and I know for a fact, that he truly thought of himself as supplying a valuable and necessary service, not only to the men who frequented his establishments but to the women who worked there. As you will see from the unread letter, he thought that by appealing to the judge's sense of reason and understanding, rather than give him a gaol sentence, he would instead, shake him by the hand and give him a medal.

The Letter to the Judge...

It started off...Your Honour. – Shmel then went on to express how grateful he was to the judge for giving him the opportunity to read out his letter, and to assure him that he had always upheld, and had great respect for the justice system. He naturally agreed that people who flouted the law needed to be penalised. So he couldn't quite make out why he had been arrested, he didn't really know what offence the court thought HE might have been responsible for.

Shmel wanted to refer back a couple of decades hoping that the judge would be more understanding of the precarious position he now found himself in. He explained that after a few fruitless efforts to issue a journal around the beginning of the 1980s, he decided to open an entertainments business. So successful was this venture that within four years he had opened up another half dozen shops. During this time, and to coincide with his successful businesses, he launched an associated entertainment journal that was as equally successful, so a couple of years on he sold it for over a million pounds. Towards the end of the 1980s he now had a healthy string of entertainment businesses so he decided to trade them for a cut in a well-known corporation which regrettably, collapsed shortly after. Following this disastrous episode, he said that he kicked around for a few years before starting up yet another entertainment journal, this time with a partner who subsequently kicked him out after having had a disagreement.

A few years on, whilst sitting in a London coffee bar, Shmel met a man who had been a boyhood acquaintance, way back, when he lived in East London. After chatting and catching up on former times the old friend told Shmel that he possessed a 'Steam Bath' in London, but because he was experiencing some personal problems he was thinking of giving it up and was looking for a buyer. Shmel said that he might be interested, so he went to look at the place which he said was a complete dump, or in other words, a shithouse!

Shmel admitted that he was rather dubious, of the 'goings on' there but the friend reassured him by saying that there were similar businesses in the surrounding area and literally thousands in the UK. The friend said that he had been in the business over twenty years and everything had been okay, and if Shmel decided to buy it, some of the regular staff would stay on. He told Shmel that the major guidelines to follow when running a place such as his were that he should be careful not to have any adolescent girls or unlawful narcotics in-house.

Shmel said that he eventually acquired the place with money he loaned off some people he knew and started trading. Most days the business was used by the working-girls, and at the weekend it was used by members of the gay community. Shmel said that over the following months he became increasingly disappointed with the lack of customers to the business so he looked for an associate and eventually found an oriental gentleman who seemed happy to put money into the business. It was hoped that the new partner would encourage oriental people to visit, however, just prior to putting his signature on the agreement, Shmel realised that some of the girls who were being taken on had not been legally registered in this country, so he decided to pull out of the venture. The new partner was so furious that he stormed into the building a day or so later and attacked Shmel, knocking him out. He then assaulted the lady receptionist behind the desk. The man was duly taken off by the police and put into gaol but was soon released. Some time later Shmel said that he was accused by his intended partner for breaking their agreement and it only ended when Shmel agreed to pay him a considerable sum of money.

Shmel said that he had borrowed many thousands of pounds to refurbish the place completely, a lot of which, he still had to pay back to the lenders, and any cash that the working women gave him had been used in such a way, that it gave them a healthy and safe environment in which to work. He said that he had never taken any money from the women who worked in the establishment for his own gain, and what money he did make on the door, from the customers who came into his firm was ploughed back into the business, leaving him with very little to call his own...

Ahhh...

....

Shmel, I suppose, was hopefully thinking that if he could read his letter out to the judge it would enable him to understand better what he and his business was about. But as he had not been allowed to put his points across, all he could do was wait and see what would happen.

All eyes were on the judge as he prepared to sum up the case and pass sentence. It appeared that the judge was not overly impressed with Shmel's record and told the court that he considered him more of a menace to society than a service provider. The judge had no qualms in accepting Shmel's plea of guilty to all the charges and then he concluded by sentencing him to eight months imprisonment, although, the amount of time served would take into account his good behaviour. On top of his custodial sentence he was fined, one-hundred and seventy-nine thousand pounds and of course, the complete closure of the saunas for good.

My husband's skin erupted into scaly patches as he was led away to start his prison sentence. Shmel was absolutely gutted and thought the judge was far from lenient. Once my husband had been taken down from the dock, his solicitor walked across and handed me some documents and a walnut. The small brown nut was accompanied by a short, scribbled note that said.

'See, your walnut didn't help me after all!'

What a Nut... There's a bit of a secret surrounding the walnut... I have to tell you that I have been a great believer in the ancient Chinese art of Feng Shui for many years now, and just before going on one of our trips to Las Vegas I saw an advert for some 'lucky walnuts' from a Feng Shui Company that is owned and run by a very well-known feng shui consultant, so I decided to order a pack of these walnuts. The pack consisted of five specially grown nuts that have been hand carved with the images of ancient Chinese sages and Buddha's. The images are very small and exquisitely engraved and to the untrained or unsuspecting eye the images are barely distinguishable from the natural contours of the common walnut. They are said to be very lucky in as much as, if held in the hand when completing an oral exam, going for an interview or indeed, doing anything where luck is needed, they should be able to help. When I bought these special walnuts I showed them to Shmel and explained what they professed to do. He laughed and told me how incredibly stupid I must have been to believe in such utter rubbish, just as he had always laughed and ridiculed me over my collection of frogs. I told him, that regardless of his contempt at my beliefs, I felt that they had indeed helped my son when he had held one of the walnuts during the theory exam for his driving test, as he passed with flying colours. Shmel of course, scoffed at my perception and pooh-poohed the idea out of hand.

However, when Shmel was preparing himself to go to court the day before his trial, he had the audacity to ask me if he could take one of my special walnuts with him in the hope that it would bring him good luck. I was so incensed at his suggestion, especially after all the disrespect he had dished out to me regarding my beliefs that I thought I would give him an extra hard nut to crack, so that evening while he was busily preparing himself for the next day, I popped along to the local mini-market and bought a pack of ordinary walnuts and gave him one of those to hold.

The Gaol Bird... When the judge announced his sentence Shmel looked very shocked, his face went very red and his skin appeared to be going dry, patchy and sore before my eyes, it was indeed his old familiar complaint that would prove to be the only true friend to accompany him into prison.

With my husband's trial over, the court was dismissed and there was nothing left for me to do but return home. Although I was fully aware and expected that he would receive a prison sentence it was a great shock when it was announced. I shed many tears during the drive home although, I wasn't sure at that stage whether the tears were for him or for me.

Shmel managed to telephone me that evening and he cried like a young child as he related the awful four-hour journey he was forced to endure, stuck in the back of the small, confined space of a prison van. The good news, if any, was that he had been assured that it wouldn't be too long before he was relocated away from the high security prison, into an open prison in Sussex. He said that he had managed to bribe one of the screws with a tube of his special skin cream, as the officer suffered with the very same problem as he. Apparently, the screw had tried out the cream and found that it eased his skin problem almost immediately and, as he was so delighted he promised to 'see what he could do'. Knowing Shmel, he probably offered to introduce him to a good time girl as well, and let's face it, there are very few men who can refuse an offer like that, are there? Or so Shmel would often inform me.

The following week I saw a small piece in a popular daily newspaper, on page 13, saying:

Brothel Keeper Jailed... (From the original newspaper cutting)

Brothel keeper jailed.

A man who made a fortune running two brothels was find £179,000 and jailed at Southwark Crown Court last Friday

The man aged 65 pocketed over £1.2 million in two years by running the two brothels in Camden and Shoreditch behind the façade of apparently legitimate saunas. In sentencing him, Judge Paul Dodgson told him: "You did this purely to make money and make money you did. I am quite satisfied that the only sentence is one of custody".

The man, who lived in Regents Park, was fined £179,000 and jailed for eight months.

....

-:: *The Gaol Bird* ::-

The RAT... It wasn't long, just a week or so, before Shmel was moved to the open prison where he was able to enjoy more freedom. He would telephone me every day and every night saying how much he loved me and how he was longing to see me. The very first visit I paid to him in gaol was awful, I can remember holding him close and crying, as regret and sadness gripped me when I saw his plight. Mind you, once I had become accustomed to the place, it didn't seem anywhere near as bad as some of the other, more notorious prisons, we are always hearing about.

To begin with, the journey was quite pleasant with the institution being at the end of a very long country lane. The parking area was large. The waiting area itself was not overly large but would be filled with wives, girlfriends, relatives and children. Altogether, I would say they were a real mixed bunch of people. On the inside, the visiting area was ample, airy and bright with comfortable chairs for people to sit in along with tables for the prisoners and their visitors to sit at while they chatted and had drinks and food. There was a small shuttered area where we could obtain coffee and tea, plus a vending machine containing cold drinks.

Naturally there were always half a dozen or so prison officers milling around and there was also an area where we had to hand in all our personal belongings and anything we had brought in to give to the inmates. But no matter how nice the place appeared to the outsider I was always grateful knowing that I could walk out of the place, get in my car and go home, unlike Shmel and his cell-mates.

Every two weeks he sent his visitation slips to me and I would take him in anything he requested, even though money was suddenly, very tight.

I would often think of all the money that Shmel had frittered away on holidays, apartments and other unnecessary items and now, when I needed it most, I had none. I had a lot of commitments and my husband had at least ten times more. He would sometimes cry at what he had lost. The council had been quick to close down his saunas for good. All of our credit cards had been destroyed and the cars we loved were repossessed by the finance companies just a few months after the trial.

During one of my visits, when he was feeling particularly low, he made a point of warning me that upon his discharge he would have no money, no job and no resources upon which to build a new life. He said that our future life together would be very hard and difficult. He sounded so desperate and at that, he took hold of both of my hands and said. "Shar', things can only get worse for us." This statement, I hasten to say, proved to be one of the rare truths to come from his mouth.

But, he did promise that once he had been released from prison he would never cheat on me again and that his womanising days would be a thing of the past. He assured me that I would suffer no more pain or heartache through his infidelities. And, although I knew he was a notorious liar, just this once I really did believe the desperate words he uttered. I was under no misapprehensions about our fate and I did realise that our life would be hard, for many years, before there would be any hope of it ever getting better. Nevertheless, I was fully prepared to do everything possible to keep our marriage going. After all, he had little else to look forward to, for after having had, literally, thousands upon thousands of pounds to squander and everything a man could wish for, he now had nothing. In fact, everything he ever treasured had disappeared along with his freedom.

Further Revelations... On one of my prison visits Shmel advised me to ring Anne saying that it would be a very good idea and an excellent opportunity for me to make friends with her again; he seemed to think I would need all the help and support I could muster, so I did as he asked as soon as I arrived home that evening. I rang Anne and invited her over to dinner the next day. As you might expect, from the moment she arrived at my house our whole conversation centred on Shmel and his predicament. We went over it again and again and could only end up by saying that in his kind of business it was almost inevitable that he would have to serve time for being in such a sleazy occupation and we both wondered and were amazed at how he had managed to get away with it for so long.

After dinner we launched into talking about recent events and caught up on other happenings over years past. We spoke of the holidays we had enjoyed recently and I told her about the last two holidays we had in Las Vegas and Spain. When I mentioned the holiday in Spain, she quickly remarked, saying that he had taken her there also, (something I already knew about, as it was with Anne that he was 'resting' when I was trying to contact him with regards to his mother's welfare the previous year). Although, something I wasn't aware of came to light, when I happened to tell her about, and showed her the raincoat Shmel had bought me in Mallorca, directly Anne saw it she cried out with amazement, "Oh, my goodness, I have exactly the same coat as that and so does his elderly girlfriend."

Well! That explained the misconstrued comments the German Lady made, when she said that the coat looked better on me. It would also account for my rat of a husband asking for a discount, after all, most people expect to buy two - get one half-price - these days... Don't they?

It never failed to amaze me, but just when I was becoming susceptible to feeling sorry for Shmel or warming towards him, for some reason or the other, something would happen or come to light that would make me hate or despise him again. I had always felt a great pang of guilt whenever I thought of the fake lucky walnut I had given him. Just for once, I had purposely betrayed his trust, the one and only time I ever did. I would often wonder what would have happened if I had given him the genuine lucky walnut to hold, but after Anne's revelation I ceased to feel sorry for him and thought that he had deserved to go down, for if nothing else, cheating on me so many times.

After this meeting with Anne I knew that we could never really be friends again as she gradually became very bossy, trying to organise just who would or wouldn't go to visit Shmel and acting as though she was still his wife. I wasn't going to put up with her giving me orders and I told Shmel this directly he telephoned me that evening to ask me how we had got on. He wasn't very pleased with my remarks, in fact, he seemed quite angry, but I assumed that it was because I hadn't fitted in with the plans he had cooked up, again!

I continued to visit him and on one such visit, on his request, I took along a couple of his friends. It was good for me to have someone else there and he was delighted, as one of the friends was the gentleman with whom he wanted to do business with once he had served his time. The two of them sat discussing the fish restaurant most of the time, as Shmel was eager to catch up on all the latest happenings. It seemed that the restaurant was coming along so well that they even talked about an opening ceremony that would be performed as soon as Shmel was released. In fact, the opening of an up-market fish restaurant in the East End of London was featured in the 'OK' magazine and had a picture depicting the restaurant with a group of guests, which included one of Shmel's relations.

Amazingly enough, about six weeks after Shmel had been incarcerated, I was absolutely staggered when I had a telephone call from him telling me that he had been given a date for his release. I couldn't believe that he was being let out of prison so soon and after such a short time too. He told me that he had something very serious to tell me. I held my breath as I had no notion as to what he was going to say.

It emerged that the authorities had decided to release him after having made a decision to electronically tag him and impose a curfew which would operate between the hours of 9:00am and 7:00pm.

His release was assisted by the fact that he had a safe environment to return to and that he had a wife who knew everything... Oh yeah?

So there was Shmel on the telephone trying to update me on all the things I was supposed to know already. The big 'serious thing to tell me', turned out to be the fact that he had a North London apartment that he had been renting for a year at least, and that he had paid three months rent in advance just prior to having been sent down. I was totally amazed at the news of this secret apartment, but he had to tell me about it because he had managed to secure his release by informing the board of governors that it was at this apartment he wanted to live with his wife. He warned me, that if I were questioned I would tell them the same. Therefore, I had no other option but to agree.

Once he knew for sure he was coming out of gaol he was all over me like flies around a heap of steaming shit, and a day or so after my last visit to him a love letter dropped onto my doormat saying –

The Love Letter...

Thursday morning   *Inmate No: OO-----*
Hi sugar-pie,

It was good seeing you yesterday, you looked fabulous, really terrific, in fact, one of the guys here had the cheek to ask me who the stunning, sexy woman was talking to me. I quickly told him to get lost... I so enjoyed talking to you, and I know you will understand when I say that I feel much happier for it – you just wait until I get home I'll get you on the floor and give you a good fucking directly I get in and then make you walk around without any clothes on.

It is very dull here inside so I am writing this letter sitting here on my bed where I think about you most of the time. I can't get over how good you looked yesterday, I keep wondering if you have had a face-lift without letting on.

I was informed this morning that I may soon get the opportunity to see a consultant about my 'problem', although they think I may be released before the appointment comes up... I am keeping my fingers crossed!

Guess what? My cell-mate has threatened to commit suicide because he can't bear listening to the racket I make all night long – he reckons that the easiest way to end his torment would be to throttle himself with a pair of my unsavoury underwear – knowing my undies, I don't suppose it would take very long to do the trick.

I can't wait to get out of here, even though things will be very difficult for us for a while, at least.

The guy's here have asked me to write an article for the prison mag' about the videos and films they are going to show, I must admit that I am somewhat anxious in case the real villains don't appreciate my comments... they might decide to use a razor on me.

I know it's going to be tough, but I am going to try to slim down a bit before I come out and I am also going to borrow a pair of scissors so that I can give my hair and beard a bit of a trim, I look such a mess. Mind you, a bit of barbering will definitely keep me busy and out of mischief for a while, what do you think?

Once I have finished writing this letter I am going to relax and have a good long look through the daily rag, just to catch up on all the 'goings on' and have a good drool over the dishy females.

Can't think of anything more to say honey – I hope you write and come to see me again quickly.

I can't wait to get out of this place so that I can fuck you the way I did before I got shut away in here, and if my luck is in, don't be surprised, for I will certainly want to do it again.

lots of love darling

x   *from*   x

x   *Shmel*   x

x   *honey-lover* x

x   *Sugar daddy*   x

Snoochy   x

. . . .

Unfortunately, his love letter did little to cheer me up for by now; my health had plummeted again owing to the stress I had been under for months. By then I had already told Shmel that I hadn't been feeling very well, so as soon as he was given the date of his release, he rang me to say that, he didn't want me to bother to visit him any more. Appreciating the fact that I wasn't well and to save me the journey, he said he would rather me rest and be well for when he came out.

I thought he might be feeling guilty for not telling me about his secret apartment, but to be quite honest I was glad to be let off, as I really hated going to the prison. I didn't get his final visiting slip that week, so I took the opportunity to relax with my family and Benson my beloved dog.

During the week the authorities had contacted me regarding the apartment in North London, asking me if I knew the address, and was I living there, etc. I was only too happy to go along with it all, as I was pleased to know that Shmel was thinking of me and was concerned enough about my health to save me the trouble of driving miles in order to see him. I was also comforted by the fact that he had sworn his wayward days were a thing of the past and that he wasn't going to have anything more to do with his old girlfriends. Bless him.

Today: By now you will not be in the least surprised when I tell you that rather than have me go out of my way to see him on his last visiting day in prison, I eventually found out that he had sent my final visiting slip to his elderly girlfriend instead. She must have been absolutely delighted to have been given the opportunity to see him and have the pleasure of his company once again. It does appear that despite his solemn promise to giving up his other women in order to be faithful to me; he was only too pleased to take advantage of my ill health to wander from the path again.

Free As A Lark... To save me the long journey to the prison on the day of his release, Shmel telephoned me to say that he had arranged for his son to pick him up and take him home. He suggested that I should stay in my house and only go to his apartment to meet him once he was free. I didn't mind doing that as I thought it would give me some time in which to shop for food, cook dinner for us and then of course, I would have to find the new apartment, since I hadn't been there before.

I rushed around that morning doing all that was necessary, and at 4:30pm, he telephoned me at my house saying that he was home. He then gave me the address of the apartment in North London and the directions on how to get there. I followed his instructions and arrived at the apartment around 6:00pm. When I drew up outside the door, he was already at the entrance to greet me. We embraced warmly as I was so pleased to see him and I was delighted that he had his freedom back again. He invited me into the apartment and when I walked in I was amazed to see how splendid it was. I thought it was delightful. The layout of the place was open-plan with a nice sized entrance hall, lounge and kitchen that had patio-doors leading onto a small back garden. Here, I saw two sun loungers set out either side of a table with a smart umbrella.

We walked back into the hall, from where he showed me into the first of two double bedrooms. I looked into the smaller of the bedrooms and it was noticeably filled with black plastic bags, in fact, because the bulging bin-liners were everywhere, I asked him what they were and he said that they belonged to Anne. He explained that her apartment was in the process of being sold and that she was moving, and as she had nowhere to put her stuff he had kindly offered her some space. Thinking about it now, it wouldn't surprise me one bit, if Anne had her own set of keys to Shmel's apartment and I suspect, Minnie had that pleasure as well...

I asked him where Anne was moving to, and it was just as well I had sat down on the end of the bed, as I was flabbergasted to be told that she was just waiting for the documents to be signed before moving into the bed-sit immediately next door to the one Shmel had occupied in a London hotel for many years - would you believe! My senses were reeling, not knowing quite what to do or say. Shaking my head and sighing deeply, I got up and moved towards the other, larger bedroom. This was a really delightful room that had all the tell-tale signs of a woman's touch. I walked on and into the en-suite bathroom that was fitted with his and her sinks, which was littered with women's toiletries. I had no idea who they belonged to, I could only hazard a guess. What could I say, what could I do? He had been in possession of this apartment for over a year and his flat-mate had obviously become very securely established, behind my back.

The Final Insult... The next couple of weeks were one of adjustment for all of us. Shmel had to get used to his new found freedom even if there were restrictions on his comings and goings, nevertheless, he was out of prison and able to live as normal a life as possible. During the day he was relatively free to do as he pleased so I would sometimes go over to his place in North London to try and keep it running as smoothly as possible, regardless of the fact that it was full of Anne's stuff, and sometimes he would come over to my house for a meal or a quiet afternoon.

On about the third or fourth Sunday after his release I invited him over to dinner at my house saying that I would roast a lovely joint of lamb with steamed artichokes as an accompaniment, this was one of his favourite home-cooked meals and, at the time, he seemed only too pleased to accept. I busied myself that morning giving the house an extra sparkle and getting everything prepared for one of the special meals that I so enjoyed cooking. When he arrived I was pleased to see him and we sat chatting in the lounge for a while as I went back and forth to the kitchen putting the final touches to the meal. During our conversation he said that we needed to be quite realistic about our future, as there was no money coming in and the likelihood of him getting anything like we had been accustomed to in the past was very bleak, nigh impossible. He said that staying married with no money would be difficult to say the least. I replied assuring him that money was not the most important thing to me and that it didn't really matter, as many thousands of couples live quite happily with far, far less than we had so I couldn't foresee too much of a problem. I told him that I was quite willing to try everything possible to keep things ticking over and that we would have to get on with our lives and try to make the best of it. He didn't seem too happy about my remarks but as I had to dish up the meal I left him sitting on the settee to mull over what I had said...

When all was ready I took the meal through into the dining room and put our two plates on the table and Shmel and I took our seats. It was a beautiful dinner and to enhance the flavour I pointed to a dish of dressing saying, "I have made one of my special healthy, French vinaigrette dressings to pour over the fresh salad."

Well, that was it! – At my words, Shmel flew into a rage telling me that he didn't want my fucking, healthy dressing and that I could stick it, together with my dinner. At that, he jumped up from the table and tossed the dinner plate on the floor then, taking hold of the dish of dressing he threw it at me. I sat there totally shocked, I didn't know how to react and by the time I had gathered myself together he had walked out of the house slamming the door behind him. I just couldn't make out what had happened, or what I had done to cause such a sudden burst of outrage? The delicious meal that I had lovingly prepared had been completely ruined and it all ended up in the waste bin.

Sitting for hours that evening and then lying awake most of the night thinking about what had happened, I couldn't help but conclude that my husband must have been feeling so frustrated, so demoralised believing that his life was in ruins, with no future to look forward to, no work, no money, nothing, except of course, me. He must have snapped, after all I decided, anyone would in his situation, so I vowed then and there to do everything possible to boost his moral in a bid to help him cope.

The next day I telephoned him to say that I fully understood the way he must be feeling, but together we could make it work and suggested that I should come over to his apartment in the afternoon and cook a meal to make up for the one that had been ruined the day before.

I shopped for food that morning and when I arrived at his apartment in the afternoon we sat and talked for an age, reflecting on what had happened the day before, trying to smooth things out and calm everything down. Eventually, around 5:30pm I went to the kitchen area and started to prepare the food I had bought for the evening meal. While waiting for the food to cook I thought about preparing the table for dinner, so after gathering up some cutlery I walked back to the dining area. Just then the telephone rang. Shmel picked up the phone and after listening for a moment he turned his back on me and said in a low, suggestive voice… "Can't speak now, I have people here."

He replaced the receiver, sat down and looked at me deviously.

I asked him who that was on the phone and he replied saying it was, "Nobody, only Anne."

I knew damn well it wasn't her, instinctively, so I reached out my hand towards the telephone.

Shmel jumped up immediately and said heatedly, "Don't you dare pick up the phone."

Well, that was it, without any more ado, I grabbed the phone and hit 1471 and then pressed 3 and said "Hello."

The voice that came back at me was that of the seventy-year-old girlfriend who said, "Didn't Shmel tell you we were back together?"

Tell Me Why… Those fatal words said by Shmel's girlfriend proved to be the final blow to any hopes I ever harboured of saving my marriage. It hadn't occurred to me the day before that by rowing with me over nothing more important than a bowl of vinaigrette was the same tell-tale warning sign that meant he wanted to be free to go off with one of his other women. Without saying a word, I slowly replaced the receiver, picked up my bag and walked passed my husband. He had in fact only treated me in exactly the same way as on our first date which was to cheat on me, to lie to me and dishonour me. I therefore felt there was nothing left for me to do that day but open his front door and walk out into the sunshine, from which time, I have never looked back.

2004: At our very last meeting Anne told me that the main difference between us was the fact that she didn't love her husband any longer, whereas, I still loved him and wanted to be with him, but... I am now divorced from Shmel and looking forward to a bright new future. I have slimmed down and my health has improved a great deal. It hasn't been easy for me coping on my own, with no one to turn to and hardly any money coming in. I have also had to change my mobile number as this man has text me in excess of thirty-six times in the last few months. And I know for a fact that on occasions, he drives past my house, just to see if I am around. Nevertheless... I can now truthfully say that the ties are broken for ever and I am no longer addicted to him, although, from time to time I cannot help but ask myself—

Je ne sais pas, pourquoi?

About the Author

In November 2004 Sharman was delighted to be invited as a guest on the
'Trisha' TV show talking about her weight loss.
Sharman also won a bronze prize for 'Super Slimmer Awards' featured in the
'Woman's Own' magazine January 2005. Part of her prize was a fabulous
make-over followed by a photo-shoot, which meant her picture being printed
on the front cover as well as on page 23, dressed in a stunning evening gown.
A few weeks later Sharman was thrilled to win a cash prize for losing over
42lbs on the Cathi Graham Plan and is now a testimonial for Cathi's
Canadian-based company. Sharman has also modelled for a catalogue called
Box 2.

After submitting and having the outline of her true life story featured on a
double-page spread in the January 05 magazine 'Take a Break', a very
positive feedback ensued which prompted her to write her extraordinary story.
Here you can see Sharman signing contracts with her publishers
AuthorHouse, for the printing and distribution of her book.
After yet another double page spread of her story being published in the
'Chat' magazine (November 05) and in The People newspaper Sharman has
finally overcome the traumas of her disastrous marriage to a womaniser and
pimp and looks forward to a happier and more rewarding life following the
launch of her true-life-story…

- :: Shmel the Rat ::-

2005

Printed in the United Kingdom
by Lightning Source UK Ltd.
108151UKS00002B/61-96